MW00466609

THIS IS TUCSON
GUIDEBOOK TO THE OLD PUEBLO

Peggy Hamilton Lockard

THIRD EDITION

Photographs by the Author
Maps and Cover by W. Kirby Lockard

PEPPER PUBLISHING
A Division of Arran Enterprises, Ltd.

Library of Congress Cataloging-in-Publication Data

Lockard, Peggy Hamilton
    Bibliography: p.
    Includes index.

    1. Tucson (Ariz.)—Description—Guide-books.

I. Title.

F819.T93L62   1988   917.91'77   87-60321

ISBN 0-914468-23-5

Third Edition

ISBN 0-914468-23-5

Published by PEPPER PUBLISHING
           433 North Tucson Boulevard
           Tucson, AZ 85716-4744

PRINTED IN THE UNITED STATES OF AMERICA

FOR KIRBY
Whose Idea it Was

CONTENTS

THE AUTHOR

Peggy Hamilton Lockard lives in Tucson and has watched the city grow from the small town she moved to in 1958, when the city rolled up its streets at 10pm (and some of those streets, like Wilmot Road, were unpaved in those days), to the bustling cultural metropolis Tucson represents now.

Before becoming a photographer, author and publisher Peggy was a model, legal secretary and real estate broker. Her commitment to the city of Tucson is strong and she can usually be found deeply involved in community issues.

Her community service to the city of Tucson includes having been a member and vice-chair of the Tucson Planning and Zoning Commission (during the time when the commission implemented Tucson's Historic Zoning Ordinance), a seven-year member of the Tucson Board of Adjustment, where she served as chair for four of those years, and a member of the Sign Code Revision Committee. She is presently a member of both the Citizen Sign Code Committee and the City Sign Code Advisory and Appeals Board.

Peggy has lived in nine states and traveled in forty-five of the fifty states, including Alaska and Hawaii. She has also traveled in Egypt, Canada, Great Britain and Continental Europe and extensively in Mexico. With this background she has written *This is Tucson* to introduce you to her favority city, the Old Pueblo.

MAPS

The maps have been customized to communicate specific information about particular areas of Tucson, and much of the information included in conventional maps has been deleted. This kind of selective graphic editing makes the maps useless for locating a particular street or address, but it should help you find the many interesting places our community has to offer.

All city maps include free-form ovals delineating specific valley areas, to which each subject in the text is referred. Half of these ovals relate to the natural environment: the Santa Cruz, Rillito and Pantano Rivers; the Catalina Foothills, Rincon and Tucson Mountains. The other half relate to the built environment: El Presidio (downtown), South 4th Avenue, University (UA), El Con (former resort hotel), San Xavier and the Airport.

ACKNOWLEDGMENTS

Continuing on-going thanks to all of those who have answered questions, read copy and made suggestions for improvements in *This is Tucson*.

Special thanks to Robert Vint for his excellent diagram and guide to Mission San Xavier del Bac and the mission's new historic museum, and to Beth Hodges for her assistance and tour of the Environmental Research Laboratory. Plans from Jack DeBartolo for the Convention Center and from John Mascarella and the UA for Centennial Hall were invaluable in preparation of new maps and seating plans.

Thanks to Susan Beebe for assistance in updating the maps (keeping up with Tucson's rapidly changing road system is a real challenge) and again mil gracias to Kirby Lockard for delineating those changes.

And it couldn't have been done without the talented assistance of Carrie Gauthier, Chris Evans and Chris Sternberg.

NOTES ON THE THIRD EDITION

In a continuing effort to assure that *This is Tucson* is helpful to both our visitors and newcomers. I have made major changes in the format of the third edition. One chapter is dedicated to our numerous museums and our outstanding outdoor life is presented in a different manner than previous editions.

I have included prices for the first time, however you must consider that over time these will change. They do give you a basis to go on from 1988 costs, however. For those calling out of Arizona, our phone area code is 602.

The city continues to grow, but not always in the best direction. The future is bright with a proposed downtown Arts District, but we must do something about providing alternative modes of transportation.

Changes, right up to printing, continue to frustrate my efforts to be accurate. Accept my apologies if something has changed and please call ahead to save yourself a possibly inconvenient trip.

Seasonal events are listed according to the calendar year. Look up the time of the year you are interested in and you will find the events available during that period.

All locations are keyed to free-form ovals on the maps. (See pages XII-XIII.) Half of these ovals relate to the natural environment: the Santa Cruz, Rillito and Pantano Rivers; the Catalina Foothills, Rincon and Tucson Mountains. The other half relate to the built environment: El Presidio (downtown), South 4th Avenue, University (UA), El Con (former resort hotel), Mission San Xavier and the Airport.

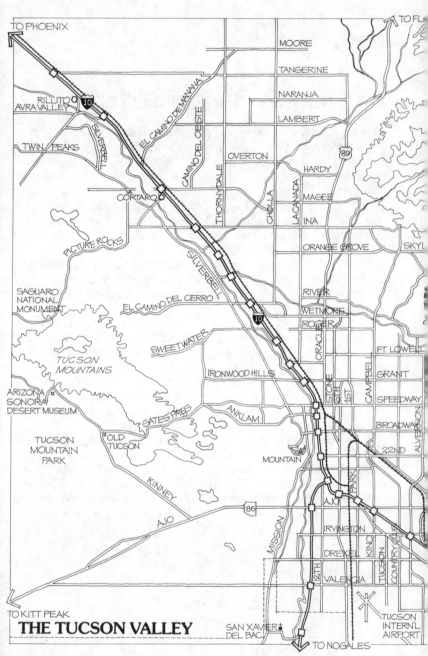

THE TUCSON VALLEY

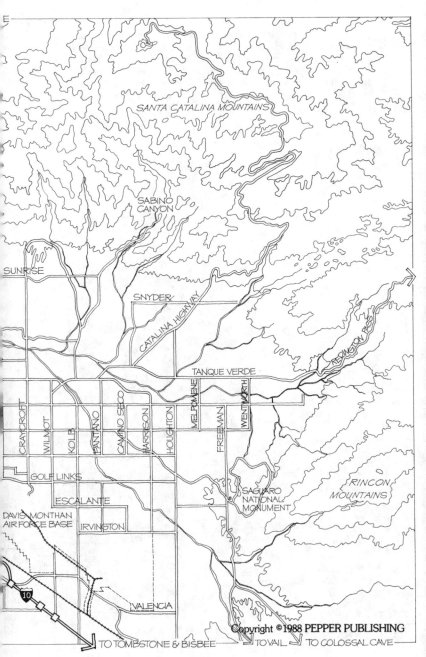

SANTA CATALINA MOUNTAINS

SABINO CANYON

SUNRISE

SNYDER

CATALINA HIGHWAY

REDINGTON PASS

TANQUE VERDE

CRAYCROFT
WILMOT
KOLB
PANTANO
CAMINO SECO
HARRISON
HOUGHTON
MELPOMENE
FREEMAN
WENTWORTH

GOLF LINKS

RINCON MOUNTAINS

ESCALANTE

SAGUARO NATIONAL MONUMENT

DAVIS-MONTHAN AIR FORCE BASE

IRVINGTON

10

VALENCIA

TO TOMBSTONE & BISBEE — TO VAIL — TO COLOSSAL CAVE —

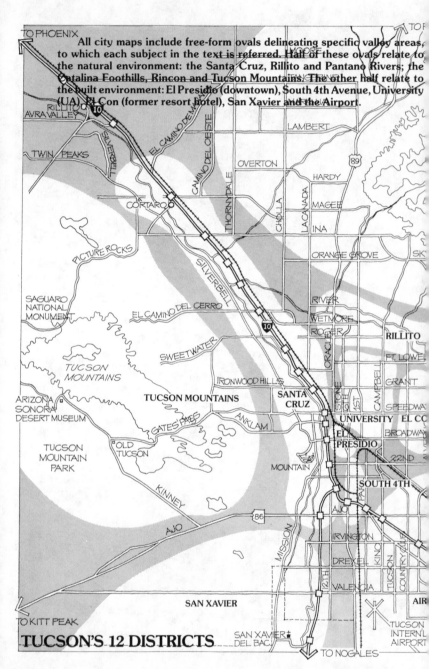

All city maps include free-form ovals delineating specific valley areas, to which each subject in the text is referred. Half of these ovals relate to the natural environment: the Santa Cruz, Rillito and Pantano Rivers; the Catalina Foothills, Rincon and Tucson Mountains. The other half relate to the built environment: El Presidio (downtown), South 4th Avenue, University (UA) El Con (former resort hotel), San Xavier and the Airport.

TUCSON'S 12 DISTRICTS

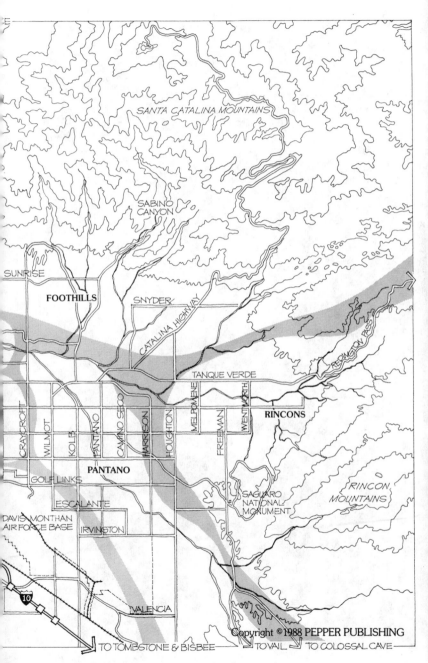

Copyright © 1988 PEPPER PUBLISHING

Mission San Xavier del Bac

The people are the city.

Shakespeare

BIENVENIDOS A TUCSON

Welcome to Tucson. The Old Pueblo's appeal stems not only from its scenery and outstanding weather, but also from the friendly, warm attitude of its citizenry and the wealth of historical and cultural background we Tucsonans revel in.

Tucson's unique desert location, surrounded by majestic mountain ranges, presents a picturesque environment matched by few other cities. A scenic hour's drive to the north, the **Santa Catalinas** provide a cool summer retreat from the desert heat, with flora, fauna and climatic conditions similar to that of the Canadian rockies. In wintertime the same drive takes you through a snow-covered wonderland to Mount Lemmon Ski Valley.

The outstanding feature of the **Rincon Mountains** to the east (other than as the perfect backdrop to Saguaro Monument—East) is the lack of roads. Over seventy trails through the 58,000 acres allow access to rugged hiking and a bounty of desert and mountain animals. The Rincons also unveil stunning sunrises to early-rising Tucsonans.

The **Santa Ritas** to the south include Mt. Wrightson, the highest peak (9,453 feet) near Tucson, and an extraordinary wildlife refuge with deer, fox, bobcats, mountain lions, coyotes and black bear and over 200 species of birds, including twelve varieties of hummingbirds.

1

The grandeur of the **Tucson Mountains** completes this necklace of pinnacles around Tucson. Although much lower in elevation than the other ranges, these mountains, with their craggy, volcanic peaks and sparse vegetation, provide a dramatic accent to some of the most spectacular sunsets in the world.

Summer provides our most magnificent sunsets. After a summer rain, enjoy the brilliant colors of the sinking sun as the jagged peaks of the Tucson Mountains are silhouetted against the sky. Marvel at silver-lined clouds, glowing in shades of purple, lavender, blue and pink to mauve, grey and white, towering above the translucence of reflected sunlight against the Catalinas. Wonder at the ephemeral rainbow stretching east to the Rincons. Now you can say you've seen a sunset.

Luxuriate in our light. Not only at sunset, but from morning's dawn and throughout the day. Such spectacular luminosity is unavailable in other climes. Painters and photographers travel to Italy to capture Italian light in their creations. You'll find Tucson artists feel the same about the splendor of our light.

Amidst this natural splendor is the incomparable history of a city over which five flags have flown and whose origins include settlements by the Hohokam Indians in the first century A.D. As a growing high-tech center, two of the most renowned astronomical sites in the world look down from mountain peaks upon Spanish missions built in the 18th and 19th centuries.

Our cultural events include a professional symphony and theatre company, numerous amateur theatre groups, several dance companies, many musical organizations and over twenty museums. And for those searching for the wild west it lives on at guest ranches, numerous "western" sites, and in the longest non-mechanized parade in the world.

Tucson's proximity to the Mexican border greatly affects the tempo and character of our city. Until 1854 there was no border and Tucson was the northern perimeter of Mexico. This Hispanic inheritance contributes to our relaxed, casual southwestern living. However, as part of the unexpected burgeoning of the sunbelt area and the resulting increase of 2,000 residents per month, we are acquiring a sophistication unknown thirty years ago.

Our unique cultural heritage emanates from the Indians, Spaniards, Mexicans and late-arriving Anglos. In the cherishing and enjoyment of our cultural similarities and diversities, and our incomparable histories, we unite frequently to celebrate divers festivals, ceremonies, fiestas, fairs, galas and boondockers, and we offer a friendly welcome to you to join us.

My historical information was garnered from many references (some of which are listed in SOME OTHER GOOD BOOKS). As the facts and authenticity of history are frequently determined by the prejudices of the author, and as southwestern authors have not been known to allow facts to obstruct their story-telling (the precedent for such embellishment having been established early by Fray Marcos de Niza and his hallucinations about the Seven Cities of Cibola), I cannot guarantee the authenticity of all incorporated herein.

Restaurants and shopping are included, as are several bed and breakfasts, but other than the mention of a few other unique lodging places, hotels, motels or guest ranches are not. We have exceptional lodging facilities, including world class resorts, but to include them would require another book. I assume you have found your "place in the sun" and now wish to explore the Old Pueblo.

I have made every effort to be accurate. However, ownerships change, as do business days, hours, prices and telephone numbers. Phone beforehand if you are going some distance. *This is Tucson* is updated frequently and if you have suggestions or additions, please contact Peggy Lockard at Pepper Publishing.

Using the booklet, *Access, Tucson & Green Valley,* published by the Architectural Barriers Action League, Inc., the International Symbol of Access has been included. As some museums, galleries, restaurants, etc., have only minimal access, I recommend that disabled visitors obtain a copy of that pamphlet from the Easter Seal Society, 5740 East 22nd Street, Tucson, AZ 85711, 745-5222.

INTERNATIONAL SYMBOL OF ACCESS

 This symbol tells people who have physical handicaps that a building or public facility can be entered or easily used by them.

NOTE: All city maps include free-form ovals delineating specific valley areas, to which subjects in the text are referred. Half of these ovals relate to the natural environment: the Santa Cruz, Rillito and Pantano Rivers; the Catalina Foothills, Rincon and Tucson Mountains. The other half relate to the built environment: El Presidio (downtown), South 4th Avenue, University (UA), El Con (former resort hotel), San Xavier and the Airport.

Use these reference points to assist you in locating the sight you wish to visit.

Petroglyph—Sabino Canyon

A VERY OLD PLACE

With bells ringing and tall ships sailing, the United States celebrated its bicentennial in 1976, but the Old Pueblo—Tucson—celebrated its bicentennial a year earlier in 1975.

Tucson and Arizona are very old. The discovery of spear points in the bones of a mammoth found near Naco, Arizona indicates humans lived in Arizona over 11,000 years ago. Pit houses throughout the Tucson valley and petroglyphs carved in profusion on rocks surrounding the valley show that native Americans resided here long before the white man arrived.

HISTORY OF TUCSON

Tucson's first citizens, the Hohokam (a Pima Indian word meaning "those who have vanished"), lived in those pit houses and farmed the Tucson valley during the first century, A.D.

Other Indian tribes followed the Hohokam, settling along the river and farming the lands near Chuk-son. Pima Indians originally settled at the foot of volcanic Sentinel Peak, which we now call "A" Mountain. This "black mountain" is referred to by Indians in their naming of the village. The name was a contraction of two Indians words, "chuk" (dark mountain) and "son" (foot of). Ultimately, Chuk-son became Tucson.

The Spaniards arrived in the 1500s and in 1699 a lieutenant of the Royal Spanish Army provided the first written reference to the region.

In 1768, Father Francisco Garcés, O.F.M. designated the permanent Indian village at the foot of Sentinel Peak as "San Agustín del Tucson" and in 1775 Colonel Don Hugo O'Conor of the Royal Spanish Army selected and laid out the site for the Presidio de San Agustín del Tucson. The soldiers and their families survived on the plain for over six months in brush and adobe huts, before construction of any fortifications.

Captain Don Pedro de Allande y Saavedra, arrived in 1777 and began construction of a log palisade to enclose the buildings of the presidio. Due to the lack of funds from Spain, the captain funded these fortifications from his own pocket.

The Spanish flag flew over the village of Tucson until Mexico gained her independence from Spain in 1821. The sixty-five settlers in the area found little change necessary other than the lowering of one flag and the raising of another.

The Gadsen Purchase brought Tucson into the United States in June of 1854. It wasn't until March, 1856, however, that the U.S. First Dragoons rode into the presidio to raise Old Glory to the top of the plaza flagpole.

During the 1850s, Anglos began arriving in force in Tucson, marrying the daughters and sons of old Mexican settlers and forming the foundations of Tucson's cultural background. These inseparable Mexican and Anglo relationships are reflected today in Tucson's culture, dress, cuisine, languages and lifestyles.

The Butterfield Overland Route went through Tucson in 1858 and in 1860 the Tucson census went over the 600 mark. During the 1860s, street fights were a daily occurence and Tucson's reputation as being ungovernable and lawless resulted in every man being armed to the teeth.

With the outbreak of the Civil War, the U.S. frontier forces were called east, leaving the settlers all but defenseless against the raiding Apache. Tucsonans were only too happy to accept the Confederate defense of their small community when, on February 26, 1862, Captain Sherod Hunter and his 200 mounted Texans raised the Confederate flag as the fourth banner over Tucson. Shortly, however, 2,000 Californians, under the command of Union Colonel James H. Carleton, moved on to Tucson from Yuma. After an April battle at Picacho Peak, north of Tucson, Captain Hunter withdrew his Texans and headed east, and on May 20, 1862, Colonel Joseph R. West took possession of Tucson for the Union.

Lincoln signed the document giving Arizona territorial status on February 24, 1863 and Prescott was chosen as the first territorial capital. In 1867 that capital was moved to Tucson, where it remained for a decade.

When the first train arrived on the Southern Pacific tracks on March 20, 1880, Tucson had grown to more than 7,000 persons. The train was followed in 1881 by the first telephone exchange and in 1882 by the first street lights, in gas.

The Thirteenth Territorial Legislature, in 1885, agreed to appropriate $25,000 for the establishment of a university in Tucson, but attached a string: the town had to provide forty acres of land for a campus. In 1886 one of the regents convinced a pair of professional gamblers and a saloon keeper to donate land they held for the university—thus the Arizona Territorial University had its rather inauspicious beginning.

By 1906 electric streetcars traveled the three-mile loop from downtown to the university; in 1931 they were replaced with gas powered buses; and in 1988 hope abides that sometime again we will have public transportation between downtown and the UA. (Tucsonans are a persistent lot.)

President Taft signed the proclamation admitting Arizona as the 48th state on February 14, 1912, at 8:55am. Ringing bells and shrieking whistles announced to Tucson's population of 13,125 that Arizona was now the "baby state," which it remained until the entry of Alaska and Hawaii into the Union. Even then not known for its far-sightedness, debate in Congress regarding Arizona's statehood included the charge that Arizona was "worthless."

Tucson remained a slowly growing city for the next thirty years or so, with a population in 1920 of only 20,292. The Old Pueblo's arid climate drew many here for their health, but the real growth boom was the result of Davis Monthan Air Force Base being designated as an Army Air Corps Base just before the Second World War. As a base for training pilots to fly B-17 bombers, the many servicemen stationed here discovered what an extraordinary place Tucson was and they and their families returned to visit and live here, creating, in 1950, a population of 55,454 in the city and 118,034 in the metropolitan area.

Tourism mushroomed, and high-tech industry, discerning the advantages of Tucson's clear air, climate and growing population, started moving into town. These two industries, coupled with the more recent migratory move to the sunbelt areas, has combined to make Tucson one of the fastest growing cities in the United States.

We have lived under the five flags of Spain, Mexico, the Confederacy the United States and Arizona. We are a conglomeration of races, cultures, backgrounds, politics and ideas, creating one of America's privileged cities in what is one of the world's most ideal climates.

Stevens House—El Presidio

THE PAST IS STILL WITH US

Proud of their past, Europeans have always made an effort to preserve it, but we in the United States, claiming we must clear the way for the present and the future, blithely tear down "old" buildings with no concern for their historical or cultural significance.

Since 1961, concerned citizens and the Tucson/Pima County Historical Commission have been working to preserve the city's landmark historic buildings. The commission's efforts and those of other interested Tucsonans have resulted in the establishment of six districts listed in the National Register of Historic Places: four of these neighborhoods are downtown or near the university: El Presidio, Barrio Historico, Armory Park, and West University and the fifth, El Encanto Estates, is just west of El Con Shopping Mall; the sixth is toward the foothills in the Fort Lowell Park area, part of which is also a County Historic District. All of these neighborhoods, except El Encanto, are also established Tucson Historic Districts. These districts are by no means the only historic areas in Tucson, but they are the only ones protected by national or city historic status. It is believed that the seventh neighborhood to be given historic status will be Pie Allen.

Many homes for sale around town are advertised as "territorial" designs; supposedly referring to a style popular during Tucson's territorial status from 1863-1912. In reality, these flat-roofed homes, with parapet walls, are more similar to Tucson's earliest homes (most of which are found in El Presidio and the Barrio) and should be called Sonoran style. These earlier homes, built of mud adobe walls often two feet thick, were flat-roofed, single-story homes with dirt floors, small, glassless windows, and high ceilings of saguaro ribs packed with mud. Built right to the street, gardens were located in a patio to the rear or center of the home.

The Territorial style arrived around 1880 (along with the train), with pitched roofs, wood-trimmed windows and doors and front yards. By 1890, rail travel was well established and Victoriana had arrived. Many excellent examples of this era, with decorative brick and gingerbread construction, are found in the Armory Park and West University Historic Districts and Pie Allen Neighborhood. In El Presidio, several of the earlier Sonoran style homes are found with Victorian trim added to the still-used mud adobe bricks.

The walking tour takes you through El Presidio, Barrio Historico and the Tucson Convention Center. A driving tour directs you through El Presidio, Barrio Historico, Armory Park, West University and Pie Allen neighborhoods, El Encanto Estates and Fort Lowell Historic District.

WALKING THROUGH THE PAST

EL PRESIDIO

El Presidio is bounded approximately by Alameda and 6th Streets and Church and Granada Avenues. The accompanying map includes several public parking areas from where you may begin your tour, however, the walk begins at El Presidio Park, site of an underground parking garage. Enter the parking garage from Alameda, going either east or west. An elevator will bring you to the park level.

El Presidio Park (1), the southern half of the original presidio, was known in the late eighteenth century as the Plaza de Las Armas. In this, the largest plaza within the presidio, soldiers drilled and practiced military formations and residents gathered for fiestas, circuses and public events. Tucsonans continue the tradition, gathering here for **Tucson Meet Yourself,** occasional theatre and other public gatherings. (*See also* SEASONAL EVENTS.)

The restful, tree-shaded refuge, with bubbling fountains, sculptures, office workers, and occasionally a strolling troubador, is the nucleus of Tucson's government center. To the east is the Pima County Courthouse, which you will stroll through later on your tour. Pima County office buildings are to the south and City Hall is on the west. Slightly west and south is the Federal Building.

In El Presidio Park, are fountains and sculptures by: Charles Clement, Jack Hastings, Don Haskins, Nancy Macneil and Phil Bellomo. Further descriptions of these works are in PUBLIC ART.

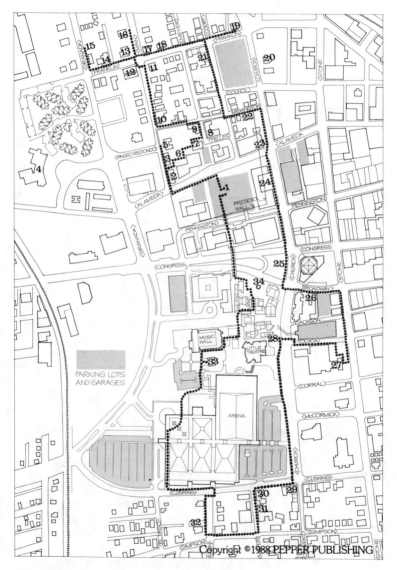

HISTORIC WALKING TOUR

Walk toward the northwest corner of City Hall grounds. A memorial to Father Eusebio Francisco Kino (1645-1711) stands here. Father Kino, a Jesuit missionary, explorer and scientist, contributed greatly to the development of the Sonoran area of Mexico and Arizona. (*See also* MISSION SAN XAVIER DEL BAC.)

The only entry to the walled presidio of San Agustín del Tucson was located at the intersection of Alameda and Main Avenue. Original street names were Calle de la Guardia and Calle Real (Street of the Guard and Royal Street).

The original presidio was approximately 750 feet square encompassing ten acres of grounds. Adobe walls, three feet wide at the base and twelve feet high, enclosed barracks, the military chapel of San Agustín, a well, cemetery, granary, stables, three plazas and a number of windowless dwellings. Construction, begun in 1775, was completed in 1783, a date which was probably hastened by two Apache attacks, one in November, 1779 and one on May Day of 1782.

Bolted at night and during times of danger by great iron bolts, a massive mesquite door, located about where Alameda Street now intersects Main, was the single gate into the presidio. A soldier stood guard on a platform above it, while across the valley, an Indian guard stood watch for Apache from atop Sentinel Peak ("A" Mountain).

Facing north and east, the block in front of you, encircled by Alameda, Main, Washington and Meyer, is the Tucson Museum of Art Complex, which comprises the northern portion of the original presidio, the Plaza Militar. All of the historic buidings on this block are listed on the National Register of Historic Places. (*See also* TUCSON MUSEUM OF ART.)

The **Edward Nye Fish House (2)**, on the northeast corner of Alameda and Main, is a typical, though more elegant, Sonoran row house. Built in 1868, its adobe walls are over two and one-half feet thick and the ceilings, originally built of packing boxes from E.N. Fish & Co., are fifteen feet high allowing hot air to rise and keeping the living area cool. President and Mrs. Rutherford B. Hayes enjoyed the hospitality of the Fish family in 1880, possibly not realizing the elegant Brussels carpets were laid over dirt floors which first had been tamped down and then covered by burlap or paper.

Mr. Fish, operator of one of the largest general mercantile businesses in the territory and owner of the city's first steam powered flour mill, married Maria Wakefield, the first Anglo woman to be married in Tucson.

Fish and Stevens Homes, Circa 1880 Courtesy Arizona Historical Society

Maria, a school teacher from Stockton, California, accepted the job of teaching in the first public school in Tucson. Traveling with another female teacher, they arrived at the frontier town of Tucson in November, 1873. They traveled by train to San Francisco, steamer to San Diego and overland by stage (through Apache country) to Tucson. They opened school two days later, becoming the first two female school teachers in Tucson.

As a prominent educator, Maria played a leading role in the establishment of the territorial university and her daughter was the first woman to graduate from the university.

Until September, 1988, the Fish House was the location of the Tucson Museum of Art Library. At this writing, I am not sure who will be leasing the space. The director of TMA stated that the museum hopes to retain access to the historic Fish Room, furnished in the style of the 1870s. If access is retained, you may be able to enter and view the family trunk and photograph album.

The **Stevens House (3),** next door at 150 North Main, is also of Sonoran style architecture, though again much more elegant than those in the Barrio. Its first section was built in 1856 by Hiram Sanford Stevens, a successful businessman and a good friend of Edward Fish.

Mr. Stevens, also in the mercantile business, held many political positions, including county treasurer and county supervisor, and served as a territorial delegate to the United States Congress.

Hiram married Petra Santa Cruz, the granddaughter of his Mexican washer woman. Petra moved from a life of privation, washing clothes in a small Mexican home, to the elegance associated with her husband and his assocates in a home that played a large part in Tucson society. Assisted by servants, she frequently entertained Washington officials and other dignataries in the house on Main Street. Her happiest moments, however, were feeding and caring for the numerous birds who made their home in her back yard.

In the spring of 1893, following a drought and the death of most of the cattle at his ranch near Fort Crittenden in southern Arizona, the financially-ruined Hiram shot the few remaining cattle, returned to town to shoot his wife and then fatally shot himself. The bullet bounced off the Spanish comb she wore in her hair, only grazing Petra's scalp; she recovered and lived in her home until 1916, when she moved to California.

During reconstruction in 1980, archeologists excavating sections of the oldest portions of the house, found the original earthen floor ten inches below the existing floor; at twenty inches below the surface, a hard-packed adobe caliche was found. This might be a portion of a prehistoric Indian pit house or part of the footing of the Spanish presidio. Due to possible damage to the home, additional excavation was not undertaken.

Janos, one of Tucson's most elegant restaurants, now occupies the restored Stevens home. (*See also* TOMORROW WE DIET.)

As you walk north past the Stevens House, look west on Paseo Redondo to an area once known as "Snob Hollow," a prime location for exclusive residences. The **Levi Manning House (4),** one of Tucson's most elegant mansions can be seen in the distance. Designed by Henry Trost and built in 1907, it is listed on the National Register of Historic Places. Manning arrived in Tucson in 1884, and was a mine owner, newspaper reporter, merchant, builder and mayor of Tucson from 1905 - 1907.

Completely renovated by THE NBBJ GROUP/GRESHAM LARSON in 1984, the mansion's facade and color scheme has been restored to its original appearance, however, the interior has been adapted for business use. During renovation, workers uncovered the original Mexican floor tile laid in 1907. Further research discovered a firm in Nogales, Sonora still had the same pattern of floor tile available, 77 years later!

The **J. Knox Corbett House (5),** restored to its original Snob Hollow elegance is at 257 North Main Street. J. Knox arrived in Tucson from South Carolina in 1880. He began his career selling newspapers, clerking at his brother's grocery store and working in the local post office. A wise investor in stage lines and ranches, he also became very successful in the lumber business he founded in 1892. He served as mayor of Tucson from 1914-17 and began the city manager form of government under which Tucson operates today.

J. Knox married Lizzie Hughes, eldest daughter of Atanacia Santa Cruz and Sam Hughes. Lizzie's mother, Atanacia, was the sister of Petra Santa Cruz Stevens.

The Corbett house, built in 1907, was designed by David Holmes, a prominent Tucson architect of the time. Originally from St. Louis, he arrived in Tucson in 1893 and held a position as professor of the newlyformed Arizona Territorial University.

After the 1880 arrival of the railroad and Tucson's boomtown status, house construction abounded. The influx of new building materials and architectural ideas from both the East and California contributed to the new Tucson architecture. The Corbett house, of white stuccoed brick, is California mission style, very popular in the early 1900s, with the mission design influence evidenced by its clay tile roof and arched front porch.

Retrace your steps past the Stevens house and walk through the archway connecting it and the Fish home and you will be in the **Plaza of the Pioneers (6)** dedicated in November of 1982, and honoring Tucson's pioneer citizens, some of whom lived in the homes you will view. Plaques in the northwest edge of the courtyard display the names of these honored pioneers.

The Tucson/Pima County Historical Commission, on December 11, 1976, buried a Bicentennial Time Capsule under the large black rock (which is from Sentinel Peak or "A" Mountain) also found in this part of the plaza. The capsule contains documents from city and county governments and local organizations and is to be opened on August 20, 2025, the occasion of Tucson's 250th anniversary.

The **Tucson Museum of Art** stands on the southeast side of the plaza. (*See also* LA CIUDAD DE LOS MUSEOS.)

La Casa Cordova (7), (The Cordova House), situated on the east side of the plaza, is named for its last resident, Maria Navarette Cordova. Through the gate you'll see a typical Tucson patio of the 1880s. Residents cooked in the patio, using well water for cooking and cleaning only and purchasing drinking water from the city of Tucson.

Patio—La Casa Cordova

Built in three stages, the western section is the oldest. Records are not complete, but it is believed this section was built in 1848 by Mrs. Cordova's great uncle, Manuel Carrillo, making the building one of the oldest surviving buildings in Tucson. Gabino and Carmen Ortega added on to the house in 1879. The Junior League of Tucson has restored the home as a Mexican Heritage Museum with furnishings depicting the era in which each section was built.

La Casa Cordova is as an excellent example of the original adobe buildings constructed during Tucson's early growth. With little wood available, builders used the natural elements of dirt and cactus.

Introduced by the Spaniards, adobes are mud bricks, made of clay, sand and a binder of straw or wood shavings. This mixture is shoveled into wooden forms and left to dry in the sun for two or three weeks. An excellent insulator from heat, adobe facilitated the cooling of homes without electricity. Dirt also became the floor foundation, merely sprinkled with water, tamped and swept daily. Ceilings of vigas (pine beams) and saguaro ribs, with over a foot of dirt packed on top of the ribs for protection from the elements, completed the structure. Note the canales (drains) in the upper walls, allowing the rain water to drain off the flat roof onto the ground below.

The oldest building (on the west) was used for storage of farm implements and dried foods. Ollas (large Indian pottery jars) and crates hung from the ceiling held various foods. The next doorway, to the east, opens into a typical 1850 family room. Furnished sparsely, with mostly Indian and religious items, you will note there were very few imports in those days. The family still cooked and slept outside.

Changing exhibits are displayed in the newer portion of the house. The bedroom, furnished in 1880s style, incorporates the Anglo influence of glass, plastered walls and paneled doors. In those early years, a manta, or cloth covering to catch falling dirt, would have hung from the mud-packed ceiling.

As you leave La Casa Cordova, walk through the parking area on the north toward Meyer Avenue on the east. Across the street is **Old Town Artisans (8),** an adobe restoration where you may purchase handmade gifts from local artisans, Southwest Indian tribes and cultures around the world. A typical Mexican patio provides shade and the **Courtyard Cafe** is open several hours a day. You might wish to wander through here now, or finish your tour here. (*See also* IMPROVING THE ECONOMY.)

On the southwest corner of Meyer and Washington (101 West Washington), stands the **Leonardo Romero House (9),** now used as a Ceramic Studio by the Tucson Museum of Art. Built in the 1860s, the home has undergone many renovations and changes: as a private home, a restaurant, rental apartments and a gasoline and service station, with cars driving through the building at the corner. Visual evidence on the east wall shows where the passage was bricked in; the large opening on the north facade was the other end of the auto passage. Brick replaces several of the original adobe walls and a gabled roof covers the flat mud roof on the Washington Street side.

Walk west on Washington to the northeast corner of the street (233 North Main), where you find the **Sam Hughes House (10)**. Presently a series of garden apartments, it is difficult to see the residences due to the heavy growth of shrubbery.

Born in Wales, Sam immigrated to Pennsylvania with his family in 1837, and then, seeking gold, moved to California in 1850. After a mining accident injury, he moved to Tucson for his health, arriving by wagon pack train in 1858 and becoming the sixth Anglo to live here.

Mr. Hughes helped organize both the first bank and the first public school. He was one of the incorporators of the city as a municipality and served seven years as alderman. One of Tucson's most popular residential neighborhoods and a local grade school are named after Sam Hughes.

As a business partner of Hiram Stevens, Mr. Hughes became acquainted with Petra Stevens' younger sister, Atanacia Santa Cruz. Sam and Atanacia were married at Mission San Xavier Del Bac in 1862 when she was twelve years old and he was thirty-two. They purchased a small adobe building on the corner of Main and Washington and enlarged it as needed to accommodate their fifteen children and celebrated their fiftieth wedding anniversary there.

The **Julius Kruttschnitt Home (11)**, 297 Main Street, is thought to have been built in the 1880s. Originally a flat-roof adobe with a surrounding veranda, the high ceilinged rooms opened into a 12-foot wide zaguan (center hall) which led to a rear garden. Eventually a gabled roof was added, with a widow's walk. With its combination of adobe walls, gabled roof and Victorian trim, this home is truly an American territorial.

Kruttschnitt acquired the home in 1912. He was a Yale graduate and his wife was the daughter of a San Francisco real estate developer. They were one of the numerous well-educated and established couples who came to the city after the turn of the century.

Jerry and Patti Toci, with help from numerous students from the UA College of Architecture, have painstakingly restored the home to its Territorial grandeur. Complementing the architecture, their magnificent furniture collection includes period antiques and collectibles. Patti's charming creation of a Victorian courtyard with its elegant Mexican stone fountain, replaces what was once an asphalt parking lot. A little inflationary note: The original adobe cost $1,200 and improvements in 1899 amounted to $1,500; the Tocis, to date, have invested around $350,000!

Patti is most proud of the inclusion of their home in a delightful 1987 book, *The Desert Southwest*. Commentary and excellent photos introduce you to their and three other Tucson homes. If you appreciate southwestern architecture, this is one book you'll wish to add to your library.

If you wish to relive a part of Tucson's territorial heritage, the Tocis enjoy being "innkeepers" and share their Tucson heritage as a Bed and Breakfast. **El Presidio Bed and Breakfast Inn** offers three suites of rooms, all with kitchenettes, private baths and entrances into the tranquil courtyard. You'll also be served a full country breakfast. Call 623-6151 for information.

Beautifully restored by THE NBBJ GROUP/GRESHAM LARSON, the **Steinfeld Mansion (12),** across the street at 300 North Main, presently houses offices. An excellent example of an affluent Tucson residence at the turn of the century, the brick stucco Spanish mission-style home, originally known as the Owls Club, was designed for several bachelors in 1899 by architect Henry Trost. Cost of the 8,000 square-foot-home in 1899 was $10,000. Restoration in 1979 was $625,000!

Albert Steinfeld and his wife, Bettina, purchased the home in 1904 and established a new standard of elegance for the city. The richly-decorated interior included parquet floors, tile-framed fireplaces and the finest of Oriental carpets. Chinese teakwood antiques and massive mahogany pieces made the home the "showplace of Tucson." Mrs. Steinfeld installed the first bathtub with running water in her home and other affluent Tucsonans quickly followed her example. Soon "at home" bathing was commonplace, marking the quick demise of Tucson's public bathhouses.

The Steinfeld's son, Harold, participated in naming one of Tucson's least attractive streets. He and Barney Oldfield, America's most famous early automobile racer, raced up and down the street when it was merely a dirt track going nowhere. The street? Speedway, of course.

Walk around Franklin to the rear entrance and peek in the back patio area. A lovely two-story wooden porch, with double bannisters overlooking a small garden area, creates an Americanized Mexican patio. The area served as a setting for many social get-togethers and for the marriage of one of the Steinfeld daughters.

Across the street, at 340 North Main, stands the **Hereford House (13),** designed by Trost & Trost, Architects and built in 1903. Note both the Sullivanesque ornamentation and the prairie architecture influence of Frank Lloyd Wright. Frank H. Hereford, a prominent lawyer and socialite, lived here with his wife and four children. A few years after completion, several additions to the home were designed by David Holmes, architect for the Corbett home.

In 1971, Attorney Bob Stubbs, perceiving images of his childhood home in Ohio, purchased the Hereford House. Since then, he and his wife Mary Ann, and several of his associates, have spent countless hours and thousands of dollars renovating what Bob calls his "toy." This labor of love has restored one of Tucson's majestic old homes to its previous elegance.

Turned into apartments in 1937, a great deal of work entailed removing the extra kitchens and stripping, sanding and refinishing the elegant wood floors. Luckily, the magnificent oak used throughout the home in ceiling beams, moldings, etc. (a wedding gift from Mrs. Hereford's father in Minnesota), had not been painted and its dark, elegant beauty can still be enjoyed.

Note the resplendent leaded glazed doors and windows. Some are originals and some are replacements obtained by Mr. Stubbs. The interior decorating, done by Mrs. Stubbs, includes specially made furniture and Oriental rugs similar to those originally found in the home.

The original radiators heat the house, although the present heating process employs the use of a swimming pool heater and pumps that pump the heated steam into the radiators; a much less costly solution than the cost of a new steam plant.

Tours are possible, but reservations are required. Please call Kathy Dehn at 623-5466. She is proud of the building and if she has the time, she will be happy to show you through.

A short walk west to 325 West Franklin brings you to the **Samuel Latta Kingan House (14).** Originally built in 1900, the home was remodeled sometime after 1901 by Holmes and Holmes, Architects, for Judge Samuel and Mary Kingan. A great deal of renovation and remodeling, including the restoration of the carriage house on the rear of the property, has been accomplished by attorneys and owners, S. Leonard Scheff and Alexander Sears.

A few steps north around the corner of Franklin onto Granada will bring you to the **Alene Dunlap Smith Sculpture Garden,** designed and created by Barbara Grygutis. (*See also* PUBLIC ART.) The garden blends contemporary ceramic sculpture with stone work crafted of volcanic rock quarried from "A" Mountain. Alene was beloved by many and is remembered, among other projects, for her perseverance in winning historic status for El Presidio.

Alene Dunlap Smith Sculpture Garden

Across the street at 405 West Franklin is the **Rockwell House (16).** This beautiful gabled Queen Anne home, built in 1908, was designed by David Holmes, who was commissioned by Eliza Ward Rockwell to recreate her home in Wisconsin. The oak flooring, paneling and bricks were shipped to Tucson from the East for the 4500 square foot home. Mrs. Rockwell lived here until her death in 1930. The home remained a residence until 1930 when it became offices.

In 1986 attorney Lawrence M. Hecker and his partners, who had purchased the home some time before, found a need to increase their space. A two-story, 2,500 square foot addition, designed by architect Bill Mueller and built by Charles DeConcini has been constructed immediately adjacent to the old building. In an excellent demonstration of detail and construction, the addition looks as though it too has been there for over 80 years. The offices are furnished with numerous antiques collected through the years by the attorneys.

Walk back towards Main and turn north past the Hereford House to what was the second **Owls Club (17),** at 378 North Main. Levi Howell Manning commissioned, and Henry Trost designed, this home for several of Tucson's most eligible bachelors.

The two-story mansion, with its parquet floors and pipe organ-decorated stairway, was the height of magnificence at the turn of the century. The main floor included a huge dining room, sun porch and lounge which opened into each other, allowing space for the masked balls and soirees given by the high-living young men. The motto carved on the mahogany mantel over the fireplace stated, "Let us live while we live;" an apt motto for Tucson's young men about town who selected European furniture to fill the home's fourteen rooms!

Purchased in 1985 by Collier-Craft Development Company, the building was a crumbling mass from years of neglect, with none of its previous beauty evident. To restore the decorative facade, the company hired craftsman and artist, Robb Boucher of Bisbee. After much research in Arizona and Texas, Boucher found an 8x10 glass plate negative featuring the fine detail of the front facade in the El Paso Public Library. Making a slide of the negative he used it to map the ornamental detail. The elegance of Boucher's work, the architecture of Garth Collier & Associates and the funding of Collier-Craft has added another gem to Tucson's historic life.

The **Rosalia Verdugo House (18),** is across the street on the northeast corner of Main and Franklin. Originally built in 1877, in the Sonoran tradition the Anglo gabled roof was added later. Note, on the Main Street side, that the traditional canales for draining water off of the flat roof have been left in place.

Wright-Zellweger Residence

The **McCleary House (19),** is directly east of the Verdugo House at 241 West Franklin. MacTroy McCleary and his wife, Carmen Valenzuela owned the home in 1880. With its Anglo porch, and Victorian details added to what was originally a flat-roofed adobe built right up to the sidewalk (a Mexican design still widely used in Mexico today), it is an excellent example of the blend of Mexican-Anglo heritage evident throughout Tucson's older neighborhoods.

When you reach the corner of Meyer and Franklin, be sure to look north on Meyer and note the picturesque row of traditional adobe buildings here.

At 127 West Franklin Street stands the **Hoff House (20).** Built in the 1870s, the outside has been preserved much as it was originally with its pink stucco exterior. The inside has been converted into sleekly modern offices for Richard Grand, Attorney.

Looking across Church Street to the east, you will see the **Wright-Zellweger Residence (21),** a classic in Victorian architecture. Originally built in 1889-1900 by Charles W. Wright, Mr. Wright died within the year and the home was purchased by John H. Zellweger. It remained in that family until its purchase in 1977, by Mrs. Margaret Carmichael.

After seeing a photograph of the home's original elegance, Mrs. Carmichael undertook to restore it. The restoration included removing the plaster that coated the entire structure to find redwood siding in near-perfect condition.

The interior has hardwood floors of one and one-half inch quarter-sawed oak, while the chandeliers are of solid brass with vaseline glass globes made in Germany. Over 396 8"x8" glass window panes adorn the building.

Walk back to Court Street and head south. The second building is **El Charro (22),** situated between two renovated adobes, both typifying the character of Mexican architecture. El Charro, a longstanding member of the Tucson community, was originally located in La Placita, near the kiosko, where Mexican food was served for over forty years.

The old home now housing El Charro was built of the dark volcanic stone from Sentinel Peak and was erected in 1900 by a stonemason, Jules le Flein, as his family home. Mr. le Flein (who changed his name to Julias Flin) was brought to Tucson from France to carve the stone facade and rose window for the first Catedral de San Agustín when it was remodeled in the 1880s. (*See also* ARIZONA HISTORICAL SOCIETY AND TOMORROW WE DIET.)

As you walk south on Court, glance through the gate between 297 and 299 Court. The charming garden patio, typical of old Mexican patios, was (and still is) a distinct part of Mexican architecture. Homes are built adjacent to the sidewalk or street frontage with deep walls and few windows overlooking the street, but inside is found an attractive, cool retreat.

Continue south on Court where you will note several attractively renovated buildings or new buildings architecturally designed to fit in with the old neighborhood. One of these is located at 135 West Council, a building designed by three Lockard architects for my son-in-law, attorney Phillip Larriva, who assisted in the writing of the fishing portion of *This is Tucson*. Phil says numerous clients please him by commenting on how well the remodeling was done on their "old building." Continue south on Court to Washington Street and turn east toward Church Avenue.

On the south side of the street, just before the corner, is the spot marking an **Indian Pit House (23),** and the northeast corner of the old **Presidio Wall.**

During demolition of a building, and subsequent construction of a parking lot in 1954, archeologists from the UA were called to dig in this area. Portions of the presidio wall of San Agustín del Tucson had been discovered earlier, eighteen inches below ground level, but eighteen inches below that level was the most exciting discovery, the remnants of a *pit house,* an Indian hut dug into the ground. Bits of broken pottery and the shape of the pit house lead the archeologists to determine the house had been inhabited between A.D. 700 and 900, and then abandoned and burned. Although no household utensils were located, dating was possible through accumulated trash.

Excited by the discovery, interested Tucsonans made an unsuccessful attempt to raise money to purchase the site. Photographic records were made, a bottle containing newspaper clippings describing the excavation was placed on the pit house floor, and the exposed area and ruins were covered with paper, three feet of dirt and the blacktop of a parking lot.

Walk south on Church to Alameda and a place known as **Governor's Corner (24),** having once been the location of an adobe home of the Eleventh Governor of the Territory, Louis C. Hughes. The corner, as it appeared in 1893, is part of a series of paintings by Sheridan Oman presented in the Valley National Bank located on this corner. Visitors are welcome during business hours to view these paintings.

Continue south on Church Avenue, cross Alameda and on the west is the **Pima County Courthouse (25).** Designed by Tucson architect Roy W. Place and built in 1928, this eclectic third Pima County Courthouse combines Spanish Colonial, southwestern and Moorish architecture in its columns, tiled dome and fountain, while arches reminiscent of the Renaissance open into a central patio. You may recognize the east facade as the location where Barbra Streisand and Kris Kristofferson were married in the movie, *A Star is Born,* and many scenes from the television series *Petrocelli* were filmed here. (Tucson was known as San Remo in that series.)

Tucson, as the seat of Pima County, built its first courthouse in 1868, with specifications stating that there be a rock foundation and "walls of adobe made of good dirt." That first courthouse served triple duty, being used also for church services and as a theatre for traveling performers. (A local pundit has commented that the courthouse is still being used for traveling performers!) A second courthouse, built in 1881, was more in keeping with the architecture of that era. The two-story Italianate-style brick building had gable attics and a tower with a cupola surmounting the center.

A brass plate, located on the floor between the assessor's office and the treasurer's office, marks the southeast corner of the **presidio**

wall, while a portion of that wall is enclosed in a glass case on the second floor of the courthouse. If you wish to see it, go to the south wing of the second floor, past the Sheriff's Civil Division and turn left. The wall portion is down the hall, just before the Justice Courts.

Continue south on Church past the Pima County Superior Courts Building and you will note a small park between Congress and Broadway, **Parque Veinte de Agosto (26),** or the Twentieth of August Park, the official birth date of Tucson. A letter written by Father Fray Francisco Garcés, dated August 20, 1775, stated that was the day the new presidio was established.

A plaque marks the site of the first church near the Tucson presidio, Catedral de San Agustín. Construction began in 1860, with towers added in 1881, finally "making it look like a real church." In 1883, Jules le Flein was brought here from France to do the stonework on the church. The stone facade he carved can now be seen as the facade of the Arizona Historical Society at 949 East 2nd Street. (*See also* ARIZONA HISTORICAL SOCIETY.)

In 1981, the Republic of Mexico, in "Friendship to the State of Arizona," gave the statue of General Francisco Villa, better known in history books as "Pancho" Villa.

Five flag poles stand in the park, which, if they are flying, will carry the five banners that have flown over the Old Pueblo: the Royal Crest of Spain, 1775-1821; the flag of the Republic of Mexico, 1821-1854 (except for a few hours in 1846 when the Mormon Battalion raised the Stars and Stripes over the community); the flag of the United States since 1854, following the Gadsen Purchase; the Confederate flag, flown during a short period in 1862; and the flag of the State of Arizona.

Turn east on Broadway and on the south side of the street is **El Adobe Mexican Restaurant (27),** also known as Old Adobe Patio. (*See also* TOMORROW WE DIET.) The building, a state historic landmark listed in the National Register of Historic Places, is the property of the Arizona Historical Society, which leases space for the restaurant and several specialty shops.

The Old Adobe is also known as the **Charles O. Brown House.** Mr. Brown was famous as owner of the Congress Hall Saloon on the corner of Congress and Meyer. The saloon, a meeting hall for civic and political organizations, became the most popular gaming place in Tucson and members of the Territorial Legislature gathered there.

In 1868, Brown purchased an adobe home on Jackson Street, thought to have been constructed in 1858, making it one of the oldest structures in Tucson. Over the years he made several additions on

Camp Street (Broadway) and in 1877 he connected the two buildings, creating a large home with a lovely central patio and garden. No expense was spared and the Brown home epitomized the elegance of its era with two-foot thick adobe walls, lathed and plastered inside, iron mantels, bathrooms, handsome gas fixtures, and a tin roof over the original dirt roof. The Broadway facade and its Victorian wood trim was added during this period; however, the basic design remained Sonoran.

The boards holding the dirt roof in the 1876 addition (now the dining room) were from crates containing glassware, mirrors and other furnishings shipped to Tucson from England, going around the horn to San Francisco and then being freighted to Tucson by mule team. The Brown home, like the Steinfeld Mansion, claims the distinction of being the first private home to have had a bathtub installed. Your guess is as good as anyone's as to which was really first.

The patio is an enchanting place to spend a quiet hour or two on a warm summer (or any other) day. Fig, pomegranate, orange and palm trees provide filtered shade and the serenading of birds accompanied by cathedral chimes imparts a brief impression of the serenity of an earlier, quieter lifetime.

Walk east to the corner of Broadway and Stone, turn south and go to **St. Augustine Cathedral (28).** Originally constructed in 1896, the church went through an extensive remodeling in the late 1920s when the Spanish Colonial Revival style was popular, and again in 1967 when it was enlarged to accommodate the large number of parishioners. The 1920 renovation included the addition of stained glass windows and the sandstone facade, which is modeled after the Cathedral of Querétaro, Mexico. A bronze statue of St. Augustine stands above the entry, along with the saguaro, yucca, and horned toads of Arizona's desert.

Reminiscent of ancient European churches, the high interior includes tall, thin windows. A 1900 painting of the Lady of Guadalupe, donated by a church in Mexico City, hangs on one wall.

Return north a half block to Ochoa Street. The **Metropolitan Tucson Convention & Visitors Bureau** is east one block at 130 South Scott Street. They are housed in a 1928 building originally built for medical offices of the Thomas-Davis Clinic. Everyone there is very helpful and are available to answer numerous questions on Tucson.

After visiting the MTCVB, return to Ochoa and head west toward the **Tucson Convention Center** and **La Placita Village.** Across Church Avenue is the Samaniego House and a post office if you're in need of stamps. (NOTE: It is best to walk to the corner at Broadway and cross with the light. The Ochoa intersection has no marked crosswalk.) The **Samaniego House (29),** a typical townhouse of the 1800s, has been refurbished as a bar and restaurant. Built in the 1840s and purchased in the late 1880s by Mariano G. Samaniego, a rancher, political leader and stageline owner, the traditional adobe walls and saguaro rib ceilings are all intact, with very few changes having been made in the structure.

If, at this juncture, you are running out of steam and wish to cut short your tour, walk between the **Leo Rich Theatre** on your left and the Samaniego House on your right to arrive in the middle of the **Tucson Convention Center,** with the **Music Hall** directly ahead of you. (See map on page 44.) You can then walk down the stairs on the south side of the Music Hall and reach the **Freemont House Museum/Arizona Historical Society (34).** (You will miss several of the stops in the Barrio Historico, sites 30-33.)

If you wish to remain on the tour, continue south on Church Avenue and note the **Tucson Convention Center Arena** on your right. (See also A CULTURED COMMUNITY.) Continue past the Arena, cross Cushing Street and you will be on the north boundary of another historic district, **Barrio Historico.**

BARRIO HISTORICO (Historic Neighborhood)

Also known as Barrio Viejo (Old Neighborhood) and Barrio Libre (Free Neighborhood), or just the Barrio. Bounded by Stone and the railroad west of Main, and Cushing (14th Street) and 18th Streets, this part of town was independent of the rest of the area in the wild days of the 1800s and took little cognizance of the law, hence the "free" term. Over 150 old adobes endure here, probably the best collection in the old west; although a study of the area by UA architecture students in 1972 stated that there were few historically-significant places: "Its importance is in the collective whole or spirit that the barrio expresses in its demonstration of the traditional elements and modes of Mexican-American life." Some adobes await rehabilitation and renovation, while others unimposing, crumble into dust.

After crossing Cushing Street, turn west to the **Montijo House (30),** located at 116 Cushing Street. Owned by a prominent Mexican ranching family, it was remodeled into an elegant Victorian home. The Anglo porch, added in 1974, is reminiscent of the original.

The **Cushing Street Bar (31),** on the corner of Cushing Street and Meyer, typifies the delightful rehabilitations in this area. Built over 100 years ago, it is furnished in 1880s style and photographs of the site and the old neighborhood are displayed inside.

America West Primitive and Modern art Gallery (32), at 363 South Meyer, just south of the Cushing Street Bar, exemplifies further Barrio architecture. Originally the townhome of rancher Francisco Carrillo, the original mesquite and pine beams, saguaro-rib ceilings and wooden door lintels have been well-preserved in the restoration. The patio includes a collection of Mexican millstones, while the gallery sells antiques, tapestries and primitive art collected around the world.

Immediately next door, at 373 South Meyer, is the office of **U.S. Representative Morris K. Udall,** D-Arizona. Restored several years ago by the Kelly Rollings family, maps show the building was in existence in the 1880s.

Stroll around several blocks of the neighborhood and you will find classic examples of both the new and the old, with a superior collection of buildings along Convent between Cushing and 17th Streets. Lacking front yards and abutting the sidewalks, the dwellings, decorated with soft pastel colors, remind one of scoops of ice cream sherbet. Colorful art displays symbolize both the Mexican and Indian cultures and heritage and vivid paintings enhance the walls of some of the structures. (*See also* PUBLIC ART.)

To continue your tour, walk south on Meyer to Simpson, turn west on Simpson, cross the street and turn north on Main Avenue. Just ahead on your left remains the shrine that stopped a freeway, **El Tiradito** (the Castaway), or **The Wishing Shrine (33).**

The countless tales told of the sinner who died and was buried where he fell conceivably equal the number of adobes in the barrio. The official version, accepted by the city council in 1927 when the site was donated to the city by the owner, Teofilo Otero, is as follows:

> A young sheepherder who lived with his wife and father-in-law on a ranch north of town became infatuated with his mother-in-law, who lived in town. One day he took the opportunity to visit her and was surprised in his adulterous liaison by his father-in-law. In an ensuing struggle, the father-in-law killed the young man and fled to Mexico, while the sheepherder was buried unceremoniously where he had fallen.

The Arizona Daily Star of March 15, 1931 states the most authentic of the 1886 legends was that of a gambler becoming enamored with the wife of another man. Shot by the enraged husband, he staggered away to die on the spot now containing the shrine.

And so the legends endure. Almost all involve a love triangle and the death of the man sinfully involved; residents lit candles for his soul. Gradually prayers were said and candles were lit for others and the belief grew that if the candle stayed lit all night, the prayer would come true.

The architect for the shrine, Eleazar D. Herraras, designed it to be practical and to keep maintenance to a minimum. In 1940 the shrine became a local monument, the only such shrine known to exist in the U.S. dedicated to the soul of a sinner buried in unconsecrated ground.

An additional demonstration of the power of the shrine occurred in 1971. A proposed freeway would divide three historic inner-city neighborhoods: Armory Park, the Barrio Historico and El Hoyo. Characteristic of the bureaucracy, plans could not be altered and it appeared probable that the bureaucratic powers were too great to save the old neighborhoods.

Refusing to accept this decision, Barrio residents initiated an intense campaign. Ultimately, in 1971, El Tiradito was nominated to the National Register of Historic Places, thus protecting it and the neighborhoods from destruction by the federally-funded freeway. The consequences of this decision resulted in a moritorium on all inner-city freeway projects throughout the state. (In 1978, the entire Barrio Historico was listed in the National Register.)

Leaving El Tiradito, cross the street and walk north on Main (which becomes Granada). On the east side of the street stands the **Fremont House Museum/Arizona Historical Society (34).** Named after Governor John C. Fremont, the Fifth Territorial Governor, it is believed he resided here in 1881. (Although some say he never lived here, but rented the house for his daughter.)

Members of the Sosa family, whose ancestor was a junior officer with the Spanish troops who first garrisoned the Tucson Presidio, constructed the house around 1850. Another Tucson family, the Carillos, also resided in the home for many years.

FREMONT HOUSE MUSEUM/
ARIZONA HISTORICAL SOCIETY
151 South Granada Avenue
622-0956

Admission free
Open year-round
Wed—Sat   10am—4pm
Closed   Sun Mon Tue

Built of adobe, the original roof was of mud packed over vegas and saguaro ribs, and the dirt floor was tamped and sprinkled daily. The central entry area is known as a zaguan. Originally open front to back, the zaguan provided direct access from the road in the front of the house to the corral in the back, while also providing a breezeway which helped cool the house. With a gate across the front, settlers being chased by renegade Apache could ride into the safety of the building and quickly close the gate.

The several rooms include a study, parlor, music room, dining room and bedrooms. The antique furnishings represent periods from the early nineteenth century to the 1920s, with emphasis on Victorian antiques, including crystal punch bowls and candelabras, a Mathushek square grand piano, circa 1860, a genealogy quilt, a lap harp and an 1890 Swiss music box.

Most of the ceilings show off exposed saguaro or ocotillo ribs, which in the 1880s would have had mud tamped over them. One ceiling includes a manta, or cotton cloth, used to keep bugs and dirt from falling through onto the residents.

Although luxuriously furnished, there was no kitchen as we know it; the women cooked in the patio in an open fireplace. Frequently, summer sleeping also took place in the patio as a respite from the Tucson heat.

A special children's program with games, puppets, pinatas, animals from the Desert Museum and demonstrations by various groups opens the Christmas holidays on the first Saturday in December. Festive decorations include trees and Victorian ornaments, a lighted fireplace and refreshments of cider and cookies.

Rodeo days celebration in February/March include an exhibit on the Vaqueros (cowboys) of the 1890s. On the 4th of July, luminarias illuminate the house and it is open in the evening hours to watch the fireworks display on "A" mountain.

Guided historic walking tours (for which you need reservations) are available Saturdays at 10am, November through March and slide shows on various topics of Arizona history are presented during the day on Saturdays, October—April. (*See also* IF YOU NEED A GUIDE.)

In conjunction with Pima Community College, an eight-week lecture series begins every January on "Caring for Your Family Treasures." Museum experts present sessions on the preservation of photographs, furniture, textiles and Indian artifacts. Registration is through Pima College.

Rental of the museum is possible for weddings, receptions and parties at a very nominal fee. Call for further information.

As you emerge from the Fremont House, the building on your right is the **Tucson Convention Center Music Hall.** Walk up the stairs

31

on the south side of the building and you will be in the middle of the **Tucson Convention Center** complex, a tranquil, landscaped sanctuary with sculptures, fountains (not always working), community facilities and a connection to La Placita Village. The **Leo Rich Theatre** is to the east and the **Arena** is the large building on the south.

Tucson's Convention Center complex resulted from the Urban Renewal projects so popular during the 1960s. This area, originally comprising a large portion of the oldest part of town, was selected as the site of Tucson's Urban Renewal project. The only buildings remaining from bygone days are the Samaniego House, The Fremont House Museum/Arizona Historical Society, and the old El Charro building and stables on the north portion of La Placita. (*See also* A CULTURED COMMUNITY and PUBLIC ART.)

As you walk north, you'll pass several shops and offices, including the Arizona Theatre Company box office. Known as **La Placita Village,** this complex of offices, retail shops and restaurants was designed in the mode of a Mexican village by Architecture One Ltd. in 1972.

Head north-northeast to a sunken plaza where stands a **Kiosko (34),** moved from its original site near city hall. As part of the Mexican heritage of the territorial capital, this area was known as the Plaza de la Mesilla. When the church of San Agustín was built nearby, the designation changed to La Placita de San Agustín and it is now known as La Placita. The buildings to the south of the plaza date to the 1870s and included stables, apartments, bordellos and the original El Charro Restaurant.

Return to El Presidio Park by crossing the brick footbridge (named for Fray Francisco Garcés) to the west of the kiosko. Garcés, an explorer and first Franciscan missionary to the Pima village at the foot of Sentinel Peak, was a principal founder of Tucson, dividing his time between Tucson and Tubac. He and Captain Juan Bautista de Anza, commander at Tubac, were totally responsible for opening the land route between Arizona and California.

While walking across the bridge, look to your west to see "A" Mountain, the volcanic peak originally known as Sentinel Peak. The "A" is whitewashed every fall by University of Arizona freshmen.

After crossing the bridge, walk between the Pima County Buildings and you will find yourself in El Presidio Park and the end of your tour.

Anticipating the arrival of the railroad in Tucson in March of 1880, the mayor dispatched telegrams to dignataries far and wide, including the Pope in Rome, asking for his benediction. It is quite probable the message never left the telegraph office, but the clerks there, determined to have a little fun, had a telegram delivered to Mayor Leatherwood reading:

"His holiness the Pope acknowledges with appreciation receipt of your telegram informing him that the ancient city of Tucson at last has been connected with the outside world and sends his benediction but for his own satisfaction would ask, where in hell is Tucson?"

Tucson: Portrait of a Desert Pueblo by John Bret Harte

DRIVING THROUGH THE PAST

As Tucson's historic zones extend a great distance, you may not have the desire or time to spend on the walking tour, therefore, the following driving tours are suggested.

EL PRESIDIO

Bounded on the north by 6th Street, on the south by Alameda Avenue, on the east by Church Avenue, and on the west by Granada Avenue, El Presidio includes some of the oldest adobe structures built in the middle 1850s to some of our most elegant mansions, built in the very early 1900s. The area also includes the boundaries of the old Spanish fort, **San Agustín del Tucson** established in 1775, and the site of an Indian pit house, circa A.D. 800. A more complete description of the area is in WALKING THROUGH THE PAST.

BARRIO HISTORICO

The Barrio is bounded on the north by Cushing (14th) Street, on the south by 18th Street, on the east by Stone Avenue and on the west by the railroad. Believed to be the "best in the west," over 150 old adobes are located here, with a choice collection along Convent Avenue between Cushing and 17th Streets.

As you drive through the area note the colorful walls and doorways, a Mexican tradition. (*See also* PUBLIC ART.) **El Tiradito,** on Main Avenue just south of Cushing Street, is the only shrine in the U.S. dedicated to the soul of a sinner buried in unconsecrated ground. (*See also* WALKING THROUGH THE PAST.)

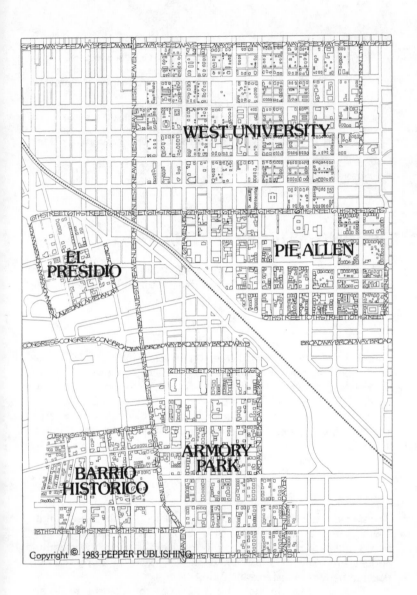

INNER CITY HISTORIC NEIGHBORHOODS

ARMORY PARK HISTORIC DISTRICT

Tucson's first official historic district, established in December of 1974, was developed with the arrival of the railroad in the 1880s and contains numerous homes constructed by both Tucson's affluent and working class citizens of the late 1800s and the first decade of the 1900s. Boundaries are approximately 12th Street on the north, 19th Street on the south, 2nd and 3rd Avenues on the east, and Stone Avenue on the west.

The turn of the century was a period of architectural transition for Tucson. Anglo-American tastes were encroaching on and adding to the Spanish/Mexican building styles. Newcomers added wooden roofs and porches to the Sonoran "mud boxes" as Tucson's adobes appeared to them. Speculators built similar, tract-type homes while private owners built custom houses with an eye for design and craftsmanship. The buildings of Armory Park blend to form an architectural whole that provides a distinguished neighborhood with the grace and textures of yesteryear.

The **Metropolitan Tucson Convention & Visitors Bureau** is located at 130 South Scott Street. They are very helpful and you may wish to stop here for further information on the Old Pueblo.

The **Temple of Music and Art,** a Spanish colonial revival building at 330 South Scott Street, was built as a cultural center in 1920 and had as its first performer, Jascha Heifetz. The first Tucson talkies played here, and recitals and concerts were presented by local artists.

Some restoration was undertaken in 1976 and the building was listed in the National Register of Historic Places. In 1988, the Temple is being rehabilitated as the future home of the Arizona Theatre Company with ATC planning to move in for the 1989 fall theatre season. Plans are also underway for a restaurant and a gift shop.

The **Amado House,** a part of Symphony Square at 16 East 15th Street, is open to the public 10am-3pm Tue-Fri (phone 884-7194). The Tucson Symphony Women's Association is restoring the home and in **The Treasure Exchange** sell antiques and other collectibles. The Amado family, who at one time owned a ranch that stretched from Mission San Xavier almost to Nogales, built the home in 1905.

Armory Park's annual home tour occurs in March or April. Check dates with the Chamber of Commerce.

UNIVERSITY OF ARIZONA CAMPUS HISTORIC DISTRICT

In June of 1986 a portion of the UA campus was listed in the National Register of Historic Places. Eighteen buildings are included, along with the memorial fountain, a volcanic stone wall and the landscaping. All construction occurred between 1885 and 1938.

As the campus is almost auto-free, it is best to park and walk in order to visit this historic portion of the campus.

The sustained use of red brick throughout the campus maintains a continuity even in the newest of buildings. The range of architectural styles includes Territorial Queen Anne and various period revivals: Classical, Renaissance, Italian and Spanish Romanesque.

An additional architectural continuity is due to the limited number of architects commissioned. James M. Creighton, as the first architect, designed several buildings on campus, but only one remains. That territorial gem is thought, by many, to be the best architectural structure in town. Old Main (originally University Hall) housed all functions of the university, including living quarters for the faculty, all classrooms, labs and the library. During the 1960s an effort was made to demolish Old Main, but cooler heads prevailed and it was the first campus building to be listed in the National Register.

David H. Holmes (designer also of the J. Knox Corbett and Rockwell homes) was responsible for three campus buildings, all in classical style.

Roy Place arrived in 1917 and is responsible for a majority of the buildings on campus, along with numerous other landmark buildings in southern Arizona. Mr. Place and J. B. Lyman were designers for my favorite campus building, the old University Library (now the Arizona State Museum, North). This modified Renaissance building with its arched windows and detailed brickwork is similar to buildings at Stanford University designed by an architectural firm for whom Roy Place worked. The second story, which is open to the public, includes an elegant, dignified room with high beamed ceilings and arched glass windows.

An excellent walking tour guide to the Campus Historic District, which includes a map showing building locations, is available for $5 from the College of Architecture. Ask for *Look Around Arizona!*.

WEST UNIVERSITY HISTORIC DISTRICT

Bounded on the north by Speedway Blvd., on the south by East 6th Street, on the east by Tyndall Avenue and on the west by Stone, West University was placed on the National Register of Historic Places on December 12, 1980. The buildings reflect architectural styles from 1890-1930.

The wide variety of architectural styles includes typical tract houses of the era and custom-designed homes by Tucson architects. Trost and Trost, a major southwestern architectural firm, designed four homes and Henry O. Jaastad, one of Tucson's most prolific architects, and one-time mayor, designed some fifty of them. Everything from California bungalows to Pueblo Revival, Tudor Revival, Victorian and Queen Anne styles is available.

The "newest" old gem is the **Geronimo Center**. These buildings, at 736 North Euclid Avenue, were originally the Geronimo Hotel and Lodge. Nine lodges, built in 1919, were considered the finest lodging in town and were occupied by wealthy families from back east who brought their maids and chauffeur to rent the lodges for three or four winter months. The three-story hotel addition opened on October 29, 1929, the day of the stock market crash. The clientele declined through the following depression and the hotel shortly followed suit, until it was scheduled for demolition in 1980.

Through efforts of the city, private developers and the West University Neighborhood Association funding was contributed to save the Geronimo, and architect Frank Mascia provided the expertise to change a run-down eyesore into a neighborhood asset. Retail stores provide a favorite spot for students and neighbors to do a little shopping, enjoy the several eating establishments and relax beside the courtyard fountain.

One of the most outstanding renovated homes is the **Ronstadt House** at 607 North Sixth Avenue. Designed by architect Henry Trost, the two-story structure with its Sullivanesque, neo-classical motifs, is listed in the National Register of Historic Places. Tucson pioneer Fred Ronstadt built the home in 1903 and the Ronstadt family sold it in 1920 (which means Linda didn't live here).

A UA architectural graduate, David Goff, and his parents purchased the home in 1977. Very delapidated, the renovation required a significant amount of work and money. David used drawings and 1920s photographs of the house and conferred with Ronstadt family members to acquire a picture of the home's original layout. His work paid off handsomely in the joy of recreating a dignified, extraordinary building which received the Governor's Award for Historic Preservation in 1984.

Another location with a more unsavory reputation is found at 927 North Second Avenue. In January of 1934, this was the hideout of John Dillinger and his gang and the spot where Tucson's twenty-man police department did what many "modern" law enforcement personnel in other states couldn't do, they caught and arrested Dillinger and three of his most famous accomplices.

The West University Neighborhood Association's annual home tour occurs in the fall. Phone 884-5088 for information.

PIE ALLEN NEIGHBORHOOD

Located near Tucson High School, the boundaries are 6th Street on the north, 10th Street on the south, Park Avenue on the east and 6th Avenue on the west. It is hoped by many that Pie Allen will be the sixth district to be listed as one of Tucson's Historic Districts.

John Bracket (Pie) Allen, who earned his nickname selling pies made from dried apples, laid claim to the area near the railroad tracks in the 1870s, believing the railroad workers and their families would need homes near their jobs. Included are Anglo/Territorial brick homes, several adobe ranch houses from the 1870s, a dozen Sonoran adobe homes from the 1880s, and Mediterranean Revival styles. Many of the original buildings had flat mud roofs supported by heavy vigas, however most of them later had the ceilings dropped for modernization, and hipped and gabled roofs were built over the original roofs.

An apartment complex on the northeast corner of 2nd Avenue and 9th Street was designed by a famous Tucson architect, Josias Th. Joesler and several homes in the area were designed by Henry Jaastad.

Check with the chamber of commerce for dates of the annual historic homes tour.

EL ENCANTO ESTATES

Placed in the National Register of Historic Places in May of 1988, El Encanto is located just east of Country Club Road between Fifth Street and Broadway, with El Con Shopping Center as its east boundary.

Although the neighborhood has had its share of prominent residents and architecturally significant homes, it was accepted in the register due to its unique layout and landscaping.

The circular streets, diagonals and cul-de-sacs were unmatched when developed in 1928 by W. E. Guerin. Hundreds of date and Mexican fan palms were planted along the streets and 157 saguaros are planted in the circular central park.

A variety of eclectic architectural styles are found here, including ranch, mission and Spanish colonial. Fifty-three of the homes qualified for placement in the national register and you will see the designs of many noted Tucson architects, including work by Josias T. Joesler.

I recommend a short drive through El Encanto to enjoy its elegant, distinctive homes along with some of the loveliest landscaping in Tucson. The landscaping lent its distinctive beauty to some wonderful photography immediately following one of our 1987 snows.

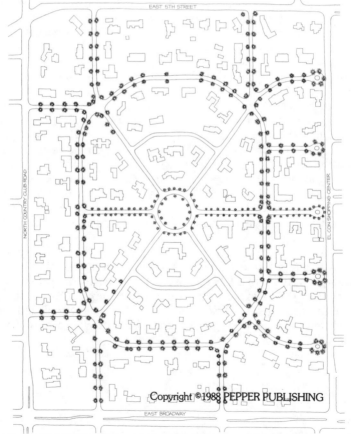

EL ENCANTO ESTATES HISTORIC NEIGHBORHOOD

FORT LOWELL HISTORIC NEIGHBORHOOD

Located just west of Fort Lowell Park on the northeast side of town, Fort Lowell is unlike the inner-city neighborhoods, being distinctly rural. A dense, mesquite bosque extends into the "Y" where the Pantano and Tanque Verde Rivers converge to become the Rillito (Little River), harboring a unique riparian ecology and forming one of the neighborhood's most distinguishing features.

Adjacent to old Fort Lowell, the area includes the old officer's quarters, the Quartermaster and Commissary Storehouse, and the Post Trader's store (which was built by John B. "Pie" Allen of Pie Allen Neighborhood fame). We owe thanks for the early restoration of several of these and other buildings to the Bolsius brothers, Charles and Pete and Pete's wife, Nan, and more recently to Ben and Peggy Sackheim for their exquisite renovation and remodeling of the Old Post Trader's store. Several other old adobes in the area have been lovingly restored by Tucsonans.

In the early 1900s the area was known as El Fuerte (The Fort) and residents supported themselves by farming and selling produce in Tucson. Relatives of these first El Fuerte residents still live in the barrio that is part of the Fort Lowell area. These old-time residents and newcomers to the Fort Lowell Neighborhood are intensely proud of this significant site and are assisted in their protective efforts by the formation of two historic districts in the neighborhood by both Pima County and the City of Tucson. (The area is in both the county and the city and it's nice to see these two government entities do something constructive.)

Once a year, usually in February, the neighborhood hosts its annual *La Reunion de El Fuerte,* a self-guided tour that takes in all of the area, including the Hohokam site on the eastern edge of Fort Lowell Park. Well worth joining, you'll see a Tucson of the past. To paraphrase Shakespeare's quote, "The people are the neighborhood" and they make this neighborhood special. Many will be available to answer your questions.

FORT LOWELL HISTORIC NEIGHBORHOOD

Boundaries are generally north of Fort Lowell Road, south to San Francisco Boulevard, west to Beverly Avenue, and east to include all of Fort Lowell Park. A large portion of the area is entered into the National Register of Historic Places. (*See also* FORT LOWELL MUSEUM.)

Music Hall—Tucson Community Center

I am content to live out my life on the *bajada* of the Santa Catalinas, facing south to the mountains of Mexico. Do I proclaim Tucson to be the heart of hearts? It is obviously not the geographical heart, nor is it the spiritual center, which some say is at Oraibi, Shiprock, or Taos Pueblo. Tucson is to me the intellectual heart and I dwell on its slope because the Southwest's major university and research library are nearby. As a writer, my roots are nourished by the records of the past as well as by the beauty of the present.

An Essay On The Land
by Lawrence Clark Powell

A CULTURED COMMUNITY

Although moderate in size compared to the major cultural centers of the nation, Tucson's cultural activities equal or surpass cities of much larger populations, and the *Wall Street Journal* has stated that Tucson is "becoming a mini-mecca of the arts in a Regional Renaissance."

Part of this renaissance is the newly-formed Downtown Arts District, while another part is the recognition by many of our newly-arrived residents of what we old-timers already knew: we already have a tremendous cultural base. Many of Tucson's exceptional artists have international reputations and Tucson has not only excellent galleries, but is also building a wide selection of public art.

Our professional symphony has provided exceptional musical enjoyment to Tucsonans for over half a century and our professional theatre company is nationally recognized. The drama and music departments of the UA offer an extensive variety of productions, and nationally-known artists and touring theatre troupes appear in concert throughout the year at both the UA and the Tucson Convention Center.

Numerous excellent museums display everything from Renaissance art and 11,000 year-old Clovis spear points to over 130 aircraft and a photographic collection equal to that of the Museum of Modern Art in New York. (*See* LA CIUDAD DE LOS MUSEOS.)

The University of Arizona, Pima Community College and an excellent public library system contribute greatly to the cultural enrichment of our city.

At the end of this chapter are **seating diagrams** for Leo Rich Theatre, the Music Hall and the Arena, located in the Tucson Convention Center complex; and for Crowder Hall, University Theater and Centennial Hall, located on the UA campus.

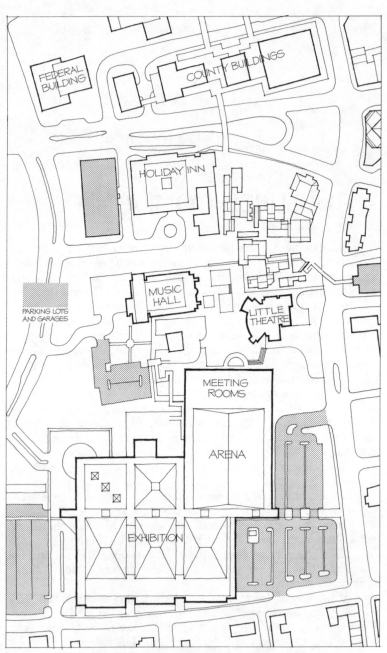

TUCSON CONVENTION CENTER

TUCSON CONVENTION CENTER

South of Broadway
West of Church Street ♿

The Tucson Convention Center complex demonstrates a pleasant melding of contemporary southwestern architecture and historic homesites of yesteryear. Originally designed by CNWC and Friedman and Jobusch, Architects, the blending of the new with the old was perfected amid a tranquil plaza of grass-covered mounds, delightful shade trees, an esplanade and a varied collection of fountains and sculptures.

Facilities include an **Arena** that seats up to 10,000 people for concerts, 8,000 for basketball games and 7,000 for ice hockey. Every seat offers excellent sight lines, with no columns obstructing the view. A 35,000-square foot exhibition hall and meeting rooms provide seating for 50-1,000 people.

Designed by Anderson DeBartolo Pan Inc. and under construction at the time of this writing, are a 100,000 square-foot exhibit hall and a 20,000 square-foot ballroom, scheduled to open in August of 1989. There also will be a new lobby and galleria space with all services moved underground.

The **Music Hall,** home of the Tucson Symphony, provides a perfect setting for ballet, drama, musicals, lectures and concerts and seats up to 2,300.

The **Leo Rich Theatre,** with seating for 575 people, provides excellent space for numerous community groups, along with exhibition space in the lobby for smaller convention groups.

Historic portions of the complex include the **Samaniego House,** built in 1879 and now serving as a restaurant, portions of the old stables, and the **Fremont House Museum/Arizona Historical Society,** a luxury home built in 1858 that has been restored and furnished by the Arizona Historical Society as a branch museum. (*See* THE PAST IS STILL WITH US.)

In the northeast section of the complex is **La Placita Village.** Designed by Architecture One, Ltd. to resemble villages of Old Mexico, it includes offices, several shops and restaurants, and the Arizona Theatre Company box office.

For information on center events, call 791-4911. Ticket information, 791-4266. Charge by phone, 791-4836. (*See also* THE PAST IS STILL WITH US, which includes a map showing parking areas.)

THE PERFORMING ARTS

DANCE

AIRES FLAMENCOS
Various locations   Admission charge

Flamenco music is pure Spain, developing over the years much as blues and jazz has in America, with individual artistic interpretations. Dramatic elegance, combined with the passionate sounds of Spanish music provides a dynamic style of dance form much different from that in the states.

Artistic director Patricia Mahan has been working for many years to provide flamenco dance and music to Tucsonans and to those who enjoy flamenco dancing. Concerts are presented in various locations in town. Check with the Chamber of Commerce or the Convention Bureau for dates and times.

BALLET ARIZONA
Tucson Convention Center
Music Hall

 **El Presidio**
Admission charge

Ballet Arizona was formed in 1986, combining two Phoenix companies with Tucson's Arizona Dance Theatre. Jean Paul Comelin, Artistic Director, provides expertise from his posts as ballet master of the Stuttgart Ballet and artistic director of the Milwaukee Ballet and now defunct Arizona Dance Theatre.

Two programs a year are presented in a mixture of contemporary and classical ballet, in addition to *The Nutcracker Suite* performed with the Tucson Symphony Orchestra during the holidays. Check with the Chamber of Commerce or Convention Bureau for dates and times.

ORTS THEATRE OF DANCE
Various locations

Admission charge
Tickets/info: 744-2375

Organized in the summer of 1985 by director Anne Bunker, ORTS is Tucson's professional repertory modern dance company, providing a mix of avant-garde and accessible pieces. Anne originally stated, "We're dedicated to bringing consistently good contemporary dance to Tucson. We will be tasteful and stimulating."

TENTH ST. DANCEWORKS

Historic Y Building
738 North Fifth Avenue

University
Admission charge
Tickets/info: 628-8880

As Tucson's oldest existing dance company, Danceworks' programs are continual eclectic adventures in dance, music and art.

Several concerts are offered each year with their finest studio works being presented at the Tucson Summer Arts Festival.

UA ARTIST SERIES

This series frequently includes dance performances, such as 1988's Nikolais Dance Theatre and Les Ballets Trockadero de Monte Carlo. See information under MUSIC and THEATRE.

MUSIC

CHAMBER MUSIC

ARIZONA FRIENDS OF MUSIC
University
UA Crowder Hall
Olive Road, south of Speedway

Admission charge
Oct—Apr
Tickets/info: 298-5806

Celebrating their forty-first year in 1988, the Arizona Friends of Music continue to offer their very popular Chamber Music series. Season tickets for the series of six concerts are usually sold out.

CHORALES

TUCSON MASTERWORKS CHORALE
Various locations
293-SONG

Adults	$6
Student/senior	$4
12 & under	$2

Exceptional chorale music, under the direction of Allan Schultz, is presented by this professional-level group of singers includes selections from pre-Baroque to contemporary, often with orchestral accompaniment. Members number 80-100, with a chamber group of 16 singers who perform for concerts and private functions.

An afternoon holiday concert by the 16 Masterworks Chamber Singers is presented on Sat one week preceding Christmas at Mission San Xavier and a dinner concert is presented in the spring. Call 293-SONG or write P.O. Box 41885, Tucson, AZ 85717.

JAZZ

FESTIVAL DE JAZZ AT PUERTO PENASCO
Puerto Penasco, Mexico

$25
May
Tickets/Info: 885-2693

Bring your swimming suit, suntan lotion and head for the beach—and a weekend of jazz. A continuation of jazz parties once held in Paradise Valley, this weekend production enjoyed its sixth successful year in 1988. Traditional Mexican mariachi groups join with numerous jazz ensembles and proceeds from the concert benefit several non-profit research centers in Puerto Penasco.

Additional events include warm-up sessions and barbecues. Contact Thivener & Company Accounting Services, 55 North Avenida de la Vista, 885-2693 for further information.

Puerto Penasco is 215 miles southwest of town. You'll need a Mexican visa and Mexican car insurance.

TUCSON JAZZ SOCIETY
Various locations

Jazz Hotline 623-2463

Established in 1978, this community arts organization was conceived to promote jazz as an art form in southern Arizona. Several separate groups are members of the society, including the **Tucson Jazz Orchestra** an 18-piece "big band" under the direction of Jeff Haskell, and Jazzberry Jam, Tucson's favorite traditional jazz band.

Jazz groups perform at the Society's **Annual Summerset Suite,** the annual free **Jazz Sundae Concert** in May, at the all-female **Primavera Jazz Festival** held in March and at Saturday evening concerts at **St. Philips Plaza,** Campbell and River Roads.

The **Westward Look Resort,** 245 East Ina Road, provides oustanding jazz concerts every Sunday in their Lookout Lounge from 4pm to 7pm. Usually no charge, unless a special concert.

The **Annual Summerset Suite** concert series is heard at the Tucson Museum of Art many Sundays throughout the summer. The bands begin at 7pm and play until ten or so. Admission is $5 or $3 for members of the Tucson Jazz Society and/or the Tucson Museum of Art. Dress is casual, and you'll find ample space to dance. Consider partaking of Janos' Nouvelle Barbeque and Jazz Grill. (*See also* TOMORROW WE DIET.)

The society provides music scholarships and offers workshops, providing those who love jazz an opportunity to share their interests. For tickets/info, write P.O. Box 44163, Tucson, AZ 85733.

OPERA

ARIZONA OPERA COMPANY
El Presidio
Tucson Convention Center
Music Hall

Single: $24—$32
Oct—April
Tickets/info: 293-4336

Tucson-based Arizona Opera Company, a member of Opera America, entered its twenty-first season in 1988, presenting a full opera season in both Tucson and Phoenix.

Four major productions take place each year, with the first in late September/early October. Past productions have included *Aida,* the *La Boheme* and *Barber of Seville.* Bizet's *Carmen* and Verdi's *La Traviata* are on schedule for the 1988-1989 season.

Season tickets are sold through the opera office. Single tickets go on sale one month before the event at all Tucson Convention Center outlets. Contact the Tucson Convention Center Box Office or the Arizona Opera Office, P.O. Box 42828, Tucson, AZ 85733.

SOUTHERN ARIZONA LIGHT OPERA COMPANY (SALOC)
El Presidio
Tucson Convention Center
Music Hall

Single: $8—$15
Subscription discounts
Sep—May
Tickets: 323-7888/884-1212

SALOC celebrates its thirteenth anniversary with the 1988-1989 season, offering *South Pacific, Brigadoon, My Fair Lady,* and *Destry Rides Again.* All performers are local talent, with some semi-professionals, including students, doctors, lawyers, teachers and retired persons. For tickets/info call the Tucson Convention Center Box Office or contact SALOC, P.O. Box 1268, Tucson, AZ 85702-1268.

POPS

CONCERTS UNDER THE STARS

St. Philip's Plaza Courtyard
North Campbell Avenue & River Road

Rillito
Admission free
322-0330

Spring concerts on Saturdays or Sundays are enhanced by the flower-bedecked courtyard and its bubbling fountain. A variety of music is presented, from Dixieland jazz to chamber and Big Band sounds. Concerts are held both in the afternoons and evenings, so best to call for exact times. Seating is limited; you may wish to bring your own lawn chair.

TUCSON POPS ORCHESTRA
El Con
DeMeester Outdoor Performance Center
Reid Park

Admission free
Sun   7:30pm
Info: 791-4873

One of the most popular Tucson Sunday-evening entertainments is **Music Under the Stars.** The sounds of music fill the air six Sunday evenings in May/June and four Sunday evenings in September at the DeMeester Outdoor Performance Center. This delightfull series of concerts by the Tucson Pops Orchestra began in 1954 and up to 9,000 listeners have enjoyed their entertainment.

Pack a picnic basket, take a blanket or chairs and enjoy great pops entertainment. For your choice of seating, best to arrive by 6pm.

SYMPHONIC

PHILHARMONIA ORCHESTRA
OF TUCSON
UA Crowder Hall
Olive Road, south of Speedway

University
 Admission charge
Tickets/info: 323-6565

The Philharmonia Orchestra, an independent group of student musicians, has been performing in Tucson since 1976. The orchestra, with no member older than 25, receives continually great reviews, with more than favorable comparisons to traveling orchestras appearing here. They perform at the **Coronado Music Festival,** a summer arts series and a portion of which is held on Mount Lemmon near the ski slopes.

For tickets/info contact the Philharmonia Orchestra, 2301 East Drachman Street, Tucson, AZ 85719, phone 323-6565.

TUCSON SYMPHONY ORCHESTRA   See prices below
Various locations   Oct—Mar
(See below)   Tickets/info: 882-8585

Tucson's Symphony Orchestra, the oldest continuing symphony in the Southwest, began its sixtieth season in 1988, and also welcomed its new Music Director and Conductor, Maestro Robert Bernhardt.

The season opens in September/October, lasting into late April or May and offers a varied selection of concerts.

The Classic Concerts embrace the rich, opulent sounds we expect in great classical music with some of classical music's most distinguished guest stars. Thu and Fri at 8pm, TCC Music Hall. Single tickets $7, $13, $16.

The Pops Parade marches out the great old favorites, including light classical music, jazz, blues and Sousa's marches. A celebrated performance of *The Nutcracker Suite* is presented each holiday season in association with the Arizona Dance Theatre. Fri and Sat at 8pm, TCC Music Hall. Single tickets $7, $13, $16.

The Joy of Music, a family series, includes comments, demonstrations and stories about the melodies from Conductor Bernhardt. A great musical introduction for children where everyone is invited to participate. Sun at 2pm, TCC Music Hall. Single tickets $6, $9, $11.

The Chamber Concerts and **In Recital.** A series of intimate performances where you become a part of the enchanting music performed by smaller groups. Chamber—Tucson, Fri, 8pm, UA Crowder Hall. In Recital—Tucson, Mon, 8pm, St. Philips Sanctuary, Campbell & River. Chamber and In Recital—Green Valley, Sun, 3pm, Valley Presbyterian Church, 2800 S. Camino del Sol. Single tickets $5, $7, $12.

Single ticket or season series available for any or all performances and can be "mixed and matched," as you desire. Contact the TCC Box Office or the Tucson Symphony Orchestra, 443 South Stone Avenue, Tucson, AZ 85701.

Buses leave from El Con, Foothills and Park Malls, Plaza del Oro and Casas Adobes Shopping Center (call above number or 792-9155 for info). Buses are also available in Green Valley—call 1-625-8989.

UNIVERSITY OF ARIZONA

SCHOOL OF MUSIC
UA Crowder Hall
Olive Road, south of Speedway

 Admission charge
Year-round
Tickets/info: 621-1162

Numerous events during the school year transpire through the School of Music. One or two faculty recitals a month occur on Mon evenings and student and guest recitals are presented during each week.

The school also presents three operas a year, spring, fall and summer, with three evening performances and a Sun matinee.

UA ARTIST SERIES
Centennial Hall
Inside Main Gate
on University Blvd.

Admission charge
Sep—Apr
Tickets/info: 621-3341

For nearly half a century, the UA Artist Series has provided outstanding programs to Tucsonans. With the renovation and opening of Centennial Hall in 1986, an exciting range of entertainment now available to Tucson has included the Philharmonia of London, Mel Torme, Leslie Uggams and Peter Nero, violinist Isaac Stern and Michele LeGrand & Friends. Season tickets are available along with single ticket purchases. Contact Concerts and Public Affairs, 1508 East Sixth Street, Tucson, AZ 85719 or Dillard's Box Office.

THEATRE

a.k.a. theatre
125 East Congress Street
623-7852

El Presidio
$5—$6
Year-round

Avant-garde, and unique, a.k.a. theatre continues to present diverse drama in its Arts District location downtown. Two recent productions were Samuel Beckett's *Endgame* and a horror-filled production of Bram Stoker's *Dracula*. Curtain time at 8:00, but go early and have a light dinner at Magritte's or Cafe Ole. (*See also* TOMMOROW WE DIET.)

a.k.a. has also joined with Tucson Parks and Recreation to present summer theatre at the DeMeester Outdoor Performance Center in Reid Park. Shakespeare's *The Comedy of Errors* and *Lysistrata* by Aristophanes were presented in 1988.

ARIZONA THEATRE COMPANY (ATC)
Tucson Convention Center
Leo Rich Theatre
622-2823 (Box Office)

El Presidio
$13.50—$18.50
Nov—May

Founded in 1967, Tucson's Professional Resident Theatre Company has achieved national recognition from the Ford Foundation, the White House Committee on the Arts, and the National Endowment for the Arts; and the *New York Times* has stated: "Those accustomed to Broadway expertise will not be disappointed." As Tucson's contribution to cultural enlightenment in Phoenix, ATC is the nation's only two-city professional regional theatre, with all productions repeated at that city to the north.

Excitingly adventurous, Gary Gisselman, Artistic Director, and his company offer distinctive, controversial theatre that has produced divided reactions. Subscribers have been known to buy extra tickets for their family or for themselves to participate in a certain play again, while at the same time others have walked out at intermission, demanding refunds and threatening to cancel their subscriptions! You just can't please everyone!

A series of six plays are produced annually and each year over 100,000 Arizonans have enjoyed such plays as *"Master Harold"* . . . *and the Boys, Quilters* and *Galileo.* The 1988-89 season includes Tennessee Williams' *Cat on a Hot Tin Roof, Arms and the Man* by George Bernard Shaw, *Under Milk Wood* by Dylan Thomas, and *Imaginary Invalid* by Moliere.

In early 1988, ATC performed its first original production, *Dreamers of the Day: The Terkel Project.* Conceived and produced by the staff and written by playwright Michael Grady, he called it "an American montage" and I believe it to be one of the greatest plays ATC has contributed to Tucson.

NOTE: Beginning in the fall of 1989, all performances will be held at the Temple of Music and Art at 330 South Scott Street.

GASLIGHT THEATRE
Pantano
In Gaslight Square
7000 East Tanque Verde Road
886-9428

Adults $8.40
Stud/seniors/mil $7.40
12 & under $4.95
Wed—Sun Year-round

Musical melodrama at its greatest! Be sure to take in "The Hottest
Thing to Hit Tucson Since Sunshine" the melodramas at the Gaslight
Theatre. Rip-roaring family entertainment includes indulging yourself
in free popcorn while hissing the villain and cheering the heroine (or
hero). The majority of the light-hearted comedies, which run for six to
eight weeks, are originals, written by local talent especially for the
Gaslight. Take the kids, they'll love it!

Before showtime and during intermission, waitresses serve a wide
variety of snack foods, including pizza, hot dogs, nachos, cheese
crisps, ice cream cones, sundaes, beer, wines and soft drinks.

Special group discounts for twenty or more with dinner options,
are available.

INVISIBLE THEATRE
1400 North First Avenue
882-9721

University
Admission charge
Sep—Jun

Tucson's original experimental theatre (affectionately known as "The
I.T.") has been around since 1971, and for many years the productions
were written by local playwrights. Since the late 1970s, however, it has
become an actor's and director's theatre, under the able auspicies of
Susan Claassen, Executive Director.

Susan has said: "Invisible Theatre refers to the invisible energy
that flows between the performers and an audience during a show,"
and with such recent examples as A . . . My Name is Alice and
Jacques Brel is Alive and Well and Living in Paris, attendees agree with
her.

Performances take place in the theater on North First Avenue, a
small, flexible area with approximately seventy-five seats (depending
upon the arrangement for each performance).

TEATRO EL SOL
El Presidio
308 East Congress Street
882-8011

Adults $5
Stu/seniors $3
Sep—July

Tucson's newest theatre offers bilingual productions in their tiny downtown space. September 1988's opening play is by local playwrite, Silviana Wood, *Anhelos Por Oaxaca (Yearning for Oaxaca)*. If you've ever been to Oaxaca you will understand a person's yearning to return.

PIMA COMMUNITY COLLEGE

DRAMA DEPARTMENT
Anklam Road Campus
884-6973

Tucson Mountains
Admission charge
Sep—Apr

Avant-garde, experimental, and socially critical works are presented by the Pima group in their small theatre on the west side of town.

Programs in 1988 included *The Curious Savage, Talking With* and *Scenes of the Mexican Revolution.*

TUCSON GILBERT & SULLIVAN THEATRE
Plaza Hotel & Conference Center
1900 East Speedway Boulevard
886-9040

University
$17.95 incl dinner
Jan—Apr

Performing in Tucson since 1964, the Tucson Gilbert & Sullivan Theatre has presented a wide variety Gilbert & Sullivan operettas. In 1985 the theatre joined with the Plaza Hotel to present exciting musical drama at Tucson's only dinner theatre.

Four productions are given each winter, including Gilbert & Sullivan and other operettas, with such favorites as *Jazz Holiday, The Desert Song* and *The Mikado.*

All community members are welcome to participate: as performers, crew members, members of the audience or as part of the Board of Directors.

Performances are also presented in Green Valley at the Green Valley Center West. Ticket information through Dillard's Box Office, 293-1008.

UNIVERSITY OF ARIZONA THEATRE PRODUCTIONS

STUDIO THEATRE SERIES
621-1162 or Dillard's 293-1008

Admission charge
Sep—Apr

Some of the best and most inexpensive theatre in Tucson can be enjoyed at the UA's Studio Theatre Series. Frequent sellouts occur with some tickets becoming as prized as those to our basketball games.

Master of Fine Arts candidates are directors of these student produced series, which are not easy tried-and-true productions. The 1986-87 season saw productions of Ibsen's *The Master Builder* and *True West* by Sam Shepard, both excellent productions.

In the fall of 1988, plays will be seen at the Park Theatre, 1030 North Park Avenue. After that date, phone for new location. Ticket prices are minimal, with no advance ticket sales. Curtain time is 7:30pm.

UA ARTIST SERIES
Centennial Hall
Inside Main Gate
on University Blvd.

Admission charge
Sep—Apr
Tickets/info: 621-3341

For nearly half a century, the UA Artist Series has provided outstanding programs to Tucsonans. With the renovation and opening of Centennial Hall in 1986, an exciting range of entertainment in 1988 included *La Cage Aux Folles, Kabuki MacBeth, Cats* and James Whitmore in "Will Rogers, U.S.A."

Season tickets are available along with single ticket purchases. Contact Concerts and Public Affairs, 1508 East Sixth Street, Tucson, AZ 85719.

THE UNIVERSITY THEATRE
UA, University Theatre
Olive Road, south of Speedway
621-1162 or Dillard's 293-1008

Single $8—$9
Sep—Apr
Jun—Jul

The UA Department of Drama continually presents excellent theatre with the sometime assistance of the Faculty of Fine Arts, the School of Music and local citizens participating in various performances.

The outstanding variety of productions has included such examples as: *The Life and Adventures of Nickolas Nickleby* (the only all-student production ever done in the United States and absolutely outstanding), *Caligula* and *Cat on a Hot Tin Roof.* Modern interpretations of Shakespeare's comedies have been presented, along with standard portrayals of his dramas. Frequently quite exceptional, the productions, staging, scene designs and costuming rival the efforts of many professional companies.

In the fall, the London **ROYAL SHAKESPEARE COMPANY** comes to campus to present several public performances, along with workshops and study groups.

SUMMERTIME—AND THERE'S MORE TO DO

Tucsonans used to go quietly into a siesta mode in the summer, with the only action to be found in San Diego. But since 1983 we've enjoyed the **Summer Arts Festival,** in conjunction with the Metropolitan Tucson Convention & Visitors Bureau and the University of Arizona Fine Arts Department and Summer Session and sponsored by Hotel Park Tucson and America West Airlines.

The festival occurs from May to August. Produced by the UA Summer Session and the Faculty of Fine Arts, the festival includes lectures, workshops, concerts, exhibitions, films and three theatre productions.

UA Entertainment in 1988 included *The Lion in Winter,* by James Goldmand, *Present Laughter* by Noel Coward, and Mozart's *Don Giovanni.* Invisible Theatre and a.k.a. theatre had productions and the Tucson Jazz Society presented Summerset Suite 88. Aires Flamencos, Inc., the Orts Theatre of Dance and Tenth Street Danceworks perform, and a series of lectures by distinguished artists are offered. In other words, it may be HOT!, but we're still involved in great entertainment.

For ticket information, phone 621-1162; lecture information, 6217352. Festival Box Office open at the University Theatre Mon—Fri, 1pm—5pm and one hour before each event. Tickets also available at Dillard's and TCC Outlets. Free parking on campus every evening after 5pm and on weekends.

BOX OFFICE AND TICKET INFORMATION

Tucson Convention Center

Downtown ticket office (at Arena) open Mon—Sat 10am—6pm. Visa and Master Card only. Checks accepted with guarantee card. Tickets purchased less than seven days before a performance, without a check guarantee card, require cash. Phone: 791-4266.

El Con Shopping Center (northeast corner of mall by post office) open Tue—Sat 10am—5:30pm. Visa and Master Card only. Checks accepted with guarantee card. Tickets purchased less than seven days before a performance, without a check guarantee card, require cash. No phone.

Eastside City Hall, 7575 East Speedway, Mon—Fri 10am—4:30pm. (Questions answered from 8am—5pm.) No credit cards. Checks with guarantee card. Tickets purchased less than seven days before a performance, without a check guarantee card, require cash. Phone 791-4652.

Dillard's Box Office

Dillard's Box Office has information and tickets for the Tucson Convention Center, UA Centennial Hall, Crowder Hall and Phoenix events.

Tickets can be purchased at Dillard's stores with a 65 cent service fee per ticket. Phone 293-1008.

To order tickets for mail delivery, phone 1-829-5555. Allow at least a week for delivery and add the 65 cent service charge.

Dillards accepts VISA, MC, AMERICAN EXPRESS, DINER'S CLUB and DILLARD'S credit cards.

PUBLIC ART

Travel and Leisure magazine recently stated "There is no better testimony to the vibrancy of Tucson today than the determination of its residents to preserve the city's historical and architectural heritage," and included with that is our determination to have an Arts District.

No longer a dream, Tucson Arts District renovation and redevelopment plans are underway. This downtown location will provide a home for over 100 arts groups, access to the creativity and vitality of our painters, photographers, dancers and musicians and a centralized space for our innumerable ethnic fiestas and fairs.

Generally, the area is bounded by Cushing Street on the south, Alameda on the north, Granada Avenue on the west and Sixth Avenue on the east. It includes the Tucson Convention Center, the old Carnegie Library, the Temple of Music and Art, the new Library Plaza and the Tucson Museum of Art. Hopefully the 4th edition of *This is Tucson* will include a complete rundown.

Several areas in town, besides our art museums and excellent art galleries, provide various forms of outdoor public art. Some of these works have been donated and some are commissioned pieces. If you wish to know more about our Public Art, *The Guide to Public Art in Tucson* is available for $4.50 from the Tucson/Pima Arts Council, 110 South Church, suite 198 or call 624-0595 for mailing information. The guide presently contains work up to 1987, but will be continually updated.

El Presidio

As part of Tucson's **Art in Public Places** program, Mayor Tom Volgy has included exhibits of local artists in his office on the 10th floor of **City Hall.** The public is invited to view these works Mon—Fri, 8:30am—5pm.

The Tucson Convention Center complex contains several sculptures around the Music Hall, the Little Theatre and the Arena: *Arrows* by Fred Borcherdt, *Three Druids* by David Kraisler and *Spherefield II* by George Ehnat. John Heric has done a steel piece in front of the Arena called *The Door is Always Open.*

Three Druids by David Kraisler

The most recent permanent sculpture, designed by Athena Tacha, is located at the east end of the UA mall, just west of Campbell. *Curving Arcades* is a 16-foot high work of upside-down "V" shapes painted in the university colors of red and blue.

The **Arizona Cancer Center** north of the UA campus has the largest art collection of any public building in town (other than our art museums). Through this extraordinary collection of art, the center has achieved its goal of presenting a relaxing, inviting, non-institutional environment when people need it most.

State Fair by Scott Wallace, adjacent to the lobby, reminds one of the loud sounds, sights and colors surrounding state fairs. On the opposite side of the spectrum is Paolo Soleri's tranquil chapel, felt by many to be the most peaceful, meditative indoor space in Tucson. Soleri is best known for Arcosanti, a city being built in the desert north of Phoenix and for his beautiful bronze bells available throughout the Southwest. Hanging in the chapel is a column of 42 of his bronze bells, which you are invited to ring.

Another sculpture is *Solace* by Dennis Jones installed in the walkway connecting the cancer center with the University Medical Center next door.

The numerous prints and paintings in the center's collection will be seen on a revolving basis throughout the year.

El Con

As part of Tucson's **Art in Public Places Program,** the first piece of public art placed in **Reid Park** was a raised relief sculpture, titled *Celebrate the Arts,*1 created as part of the DeMeester Outdoor Performance Center by a husband and wife team, Carole Hanson and Guillermo Esparza. The relief consists of six figures representing music, dance, drama and poetry.

In May of 1988 three new sculptures were dedicated: *Portal With Door and Waves,* by Jim O'Hara is located at the 22nd Street and Lakeshore Lane entrance to the park. The polished aluminum radiates sunlight in the daytime and glows with color at night.

The kids will particularly enjoy two other sculptures. The first is on the northeast side of the lake, *Inverted Pecans in Ceremonial Red* by Roger Asay and Rebecca Davis. Reminiscent of Disney's walking broomsticks in *Fantasia,* these striding tree trunks have been sanded smooth, turned upside down and painted a brilliant red. Great to run through and swing from!

Several fountains and sculptures are found in **El Presidio Park,** all created by local artisans. Architect Mike Lugo designed and Charles Clement created the very attractive sculptural concrete fountain in the center of the park. Southern Arizona's prehistory is set in the concrete base around the pool and the mosaic panels hung about the fountain's structure display the symbols of man's recorded history and influence.

Other fountains in the park include Jack Hastings' in the northeast corner, Don Haskin's stainless steel design in the northwest corner and a stoneware fountain in the southwest corner by Phil Bellomo.

In the north central seating area a serene bronze sculpture imparts Nancy Macneil's interpretation of the human form in its gesture, attitude and feeling.

One of Tucson's foremost ceramists, Barbara Grygutis, designed and created the **Alene Dunlap Smith Garden** at 312 North Granada Avenue, in El Presidio Historic District. The cypress and mesquite-shaded garden blends Barbara's contemporary blue tile walkways and ceramic benches with stonework crafted of volcanic rock quarried from "A" Mountain. Alene was beloved by many and is remembered, among other things, for her perseverance in winning historic status for El Presidio. (*See also* THE PAST IS STILL WITH US.)

Barbara has numerous other sculptures around town. Two major creations are: *Redrock* at the Radisson Suite Hotel at 6555 East Speedway and *Baseline* at the Williams Center Garden Offices just off East Broadway where a major design includes a stream, pools and waterfalls, all incorporated with stoneware arches and columns. Also in this courtyard are two relief carvings sandblasted into the stucco by Andrew Rush. Men, women and children seemingly walking along the corridor give a sense of motion in an empty courtyard.

A large steel sculpture called *A Step in the Right Direction,* by John Heric, is located at **La Entrada,** on the corner of North Granada Avenue and West Paseo Redondo. La Entrada is part of the city's downtown redevelopment plan.

University

Numerous sculptures are located on the UA campus. Several are around the Museum of Art and some are in front of the Union Building, along the mall. The two most famous are at the museum building: *Lesson of a Disaster* by Jacques Lipchitz and *Mujer de pie con manos en la cara (Woman with Hands on Her Face),* by Francisco Zuñiga. Zuñiga's many portrayals of Mexican women are highly prized and awarded throughout the world.

The third sculpture is *Terra* by Carlos Encinas, near the playground next to the bandshell. An eclectic collection of brightly-colored animals in association with an Aztec pyramid that the young ones love to play with. (*See also* REID PARK ZOO.)

Foothills

If you're driving north on Oracle, watch for **6700 North Oracle** and John Heric's *Continuum (Exploring the Pyramid), Black Pool Number One, Black Pool Number Two.* The sculpture consists of three sections, a thirty-foot tall piece through which you may walk and two fountains within the courtyard. Commissioned by the Bohm Company, Jeffrey A. Bohm stated the sculpture "Has its roots in form going back to the Egyptian and Mayan civilization and yet it points forward in a powerful, uplifting way."

MURAL ART

In this hemisphere, the human tradition of the decoration of walls goes back to prehistoric times with embellishments of petroglyphs and pictographs. The history of murals begins with the Aztec and Mayan Indian cultures, and was perfected in the modern Mexican murals produced by such artists as Diego Rivera and Jose Clemente Orozco. As the cultural art of Mexico, these murals, through a multitude of brilliant colors and symbols, depict the loves, passions, trials and tribulations of life, along with the vagaries and erraticism of death.

Santa Cruz

Tucson's Hispanic and Indian neighborhoods continue these traditions with murals breathing life into the various plain stucco exteriors. The **Davis Bilingual Learning Center,** 500 West St. Mary's Road, contains several such murals. Students from the center assisted muralists David Tineo and Estevan Mireles in their wall paintings. The south-facing wall depicts the cultural heritage of Asian-Americans, while the east-facing wall portrays barrio life. The coming together of the two cultures is depicted at the short wall with double doors.

Tineo and Tomas Bandaries, with the help of nearly 100 neighborhood children, painted a mural at the **El Rio Branch** of the Tucson Public Library, 1390 West Speedway. The mural, *Revelation,* is dedicated to Vicki Lynne Hoskinson, Luvia Chavez Garcia and other children who have been kidnapped.

The artists said the mural depicts "the cycle of life and death and the hope for tomorrow." The dominant figures are an angel of death, a cross, and a winged horse, but the most important figure in the mural is a child with a book. "It is important because we have to get rid of ignorance through education," said Tineo.

South Fourth Avenue

If driving on South 6th, at Ajo Way, check the Circle K on the southeast corner (3801 South 6th), where you will see the countenance of Father Miguel Hidalgo staring at you. Hidalgo, known as the "Father of Mexican Independence, was painted by Luis Gustavo Mena.

Mena has also painted three Aztec gods on a wall at the southwest corner of South 4th Avenue and 37th Street. When you head out South 4th for Mexican food, be sure to look for this mural with its bright colors and unique style.

The **Tucson Indian Center** at 120 West 29th Street contains a mural of Chief Joseph, a Nez Perce Indian. The mural, titled *Celebration of the Indigenous Spirit,* was painted by Martin Moreno and four other artists (who call themselves Alambrazo), and was dedicated to a friend of Moreno's.

Many other murals are painted on the walls of the Hispanic and Indian neighborhoods in the downtown area, nearly all of them with the assistance of students or neighborhood kids.

When it was announced in 1885 that Tucson would be the site of the territorial university, the news was not met with joy by most Tucsonans. In fact they were furious and felt cheated. A bartender in one of the saloons summed up the community's anguish: "What do we want with a university? What good will it do us? Who in hell ever heard of a university professor buying a drink?"

Tucson: Portrait of a Desert Pueblo by John Bret Harte

EDUCATION

PIMA COMMUNITY COLLEGE

Pima Community College, a two-year college created in 1970 to serve Pima County, is the largest community college in Arizona, with an enrollment of over 20,000 students. A multitude of classes are held in three main campuses and over fifty off-campus instructional locations.

The **West Campus**, 2202 West Anklam Road, includes a student center, fine arts building and complete library, or Learning Research Center, and is the only campus with a gymnasium and an athletic program. The **Downtown Campus** is located at 50 West Speedway Blvd. and the **East Campus** is at 8202 East Poinciana Drive. All campuses offer a wide variety of credit and non-credit instruction, with two-year vocational and trade programs and two-year preparatory programs for those going on to college.

Each campus provides general education and college transfer courses covering everything from mathematics, English, reading, writing, sociology and history through business and psychology. Occupational programs include secretarial studies, automotive technology, air conditioning, sheet metal, machine tool technology, graphic technology and health careers.

Pima also offers continuing education programs with a wide selection of classes held at over two dozen locations in Tucson. Contact Community Services, 21 East Speedway, Tucson, AZ 85705, 884-6720.

For information on general admissions, contact the Admission Office, Pima Community College, 2202 West Anklam Road, Tucson, AZ 85709, or call 884-6060. (*See also* IF YOU DECIDE TO STAY.)

UNIVERSITY OF ARIZONA

"One Hundred Years, a Proud Beginning" welcomed the University of Arizona to its centennial celebration in 1985. A century before, with an expenditure of $25,000, the UA was established by the Thirteenth Territorial Legislature as Arizona's land grant institution.

Forty acres in the middle of a rattlesnake and coyote infested desert were donated by two gamblers and a saloonkeeper in 1886 and five years later the Territorial University opened its doors with six faculty members, thirty-two students and one unfinished building. The building, which housed living quarters for some of the faculty, all classrooms, labs and the library, is known as Old Main and is located

Old Main

in the center of campus. Designed by C. H. Creighton in a classic territorial style, it is thought by many to be the handsomest building in town.

(In June of 1986, Old Main and seventeen other historic buildings on campus were listed in the National Register of Historic Places. Included are the memorial fountain, the landscaping and the surrounding volcanic stone wall. See also DRIVING THROUGH THE PAST.)

From that humble beginning, the university now covers over 320 acres, includes more than 138 mostly-red brick buildings, and acts as a primary economic source for Tucson, with its student population in excess of 32,000, three-fourths of which are from Arizona.

Campus buildings are designed to preserve or complement the charm of traditional southwestern architecture and as each new building was constructed, planned landscaping included both native and foreign species of plantings. The resulting extensive selection of horticultural plantings includes rhus lancea trees from Africa, growing majestically in front of the Arizona State Museum North Building, and nearly century-old olive trees on North Drive in front of Gila, Maricopa and Yuma Halls.

Following our centennial celebration, the UA geared up for "Century Two," a major fund-raising drive to support the UA's movement into its second century. Numerous future projects are planned.

As part of the centennial celebration, the old auditorium was renovated by John Mascarella and Associates, providing a first-class performing arts center. Originally built in 1936, the entire interior was gutted, rebuilt and reconditioned, including the hanging of ten sensational crystal chandeliers. The stage was increased from 2,000 to 5,000 square feet and a $250,000 sound system added, allowing the availability of cultural events not previously enjoyed. You will have a delightfully elegant experience at Centennial Hall events. (See also THE PERFORMING ARTS.)

Guided by the objectives and mandates of land-grant tradition, the UA maintains an excellent program of public service, research and teaching and is available to assist citizens of Arizona.

As a member of the prestigious Association of American Universities and as one of the top twenty state universities in research funding, the UA is in the forefront of research regarding the Sonoran desert environment. As an example, controlled environmental agriculture, directed by Carl Hodges, is being carried out from the Quechau Indian Reservation on the Colorado River to the shiekdom

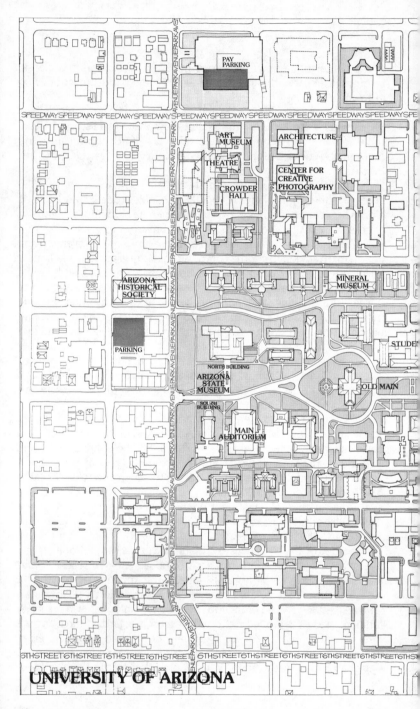

PAY PARKING

SPEEDWAY SPEEDWAY SPEEDWAY SPEEDWAY SPEEDWAY SPEEDWAY SPEEDWAY SPEEDWAY SPEEDWAY SPEEDWAY SPE

ART MUSEUM

ARCHITECTURE

THEATRE

CENTER FOR CREATIVE PHOTOGRAPHY

CROWDER HALL

ARIZONA HISTORICAL SOCIETY

MINERAL MUSEUM

PARKING

STUDEN

NORTH BUILDING

ARIZONA STATE MUSEUM

OLD MAIN

SOUTH BUILDING

MAIN AUDITORIUM

6TH STREET 6TH STREET 6TH STREET 6TH STREET 6TH STREET 6TH STREET 6TH STREET 6TH STREET 6TH

UNIVERSITY OF ARIZONA

FOUNDATION & ALUMNI ASSOCIATION BUILDING

SPEEDWAYSPEEDWAYSPEEDWAYSPEEDWAY SPEEDWAYSPEEDWAYSPEEDWAYSPEEDWAYSPEEDWAYSPEEDWA

CAMPBELLCAMPBELLCAMPBELLCAMPBELLCAMPBELLCAMPBELLCAMPBELLCAMPBELLCAMPBELLCAMPBELL

ADMIN

FLANDRAU
PLANETARIUM

VISITOR
CENTER

VISITOR
PARKING

SCIENCE
LIBRARY

BEAR DOWN

MAIN LIBRARY

McKALE
MEMORIAL
CENTER

ARIZONA
STADIUM

BASEBALL
STADIUM

6THSTREET6THSTREET6THSTREET6THSTREET6THSTREET6THSTREET6THSTREET6THSTREET6THSTR

69

of Abu Dhabi on the Red Sea. The research in this field is headquartered at the **Environmental Research Laboratory** at Tucson International Airport. (*See also* PLACES TO GO AND THINGS TO DO.)

As a world-renown astronomical research center, included are the Steward Observatory, Flandrau Planetarium, the Multiple-Mirror Telescope on Mt. Hopkins and Kitt Peak National Observatory. In 1988, plans are on the drawing board for the largest telescope in the world to be stationed on Mount Graham, to the northeast of Tucson. These numerous projects combine to make Tucson the "Astronomical Capital of the World." (*See also* LA CUIDAD DE LOS MUSEOS and A DAY AWAY.)

The optical sciences program is one of only a few in the United States and the University Computer Center is the most extensive such facility on a college campus. The fields of arid land studies, hydrology, mining, atmospheric physics, anthropology and architecture are all particularly outstanding.

The College of Medicine, located north of the main campus at the UA Health Sciences Center, is noted for its pioneering research in a number of fields, more particularly heart surgery, cancer and arthritis. Programs include the Cardiac Rehabilitation Program (621-4101 or 621-2785), the American Parkinson's Disease Center (626-4019), the University of Arizona Cancer Center (626-6044), the Southwest Arthritis Center (626-6041), the Senior Citizens Clinic (626-6956), and the Risk Reduction and Health Promotion Program (626-7900) an excellent place to begin changing the health risks in your life.

A number of other attractions are associated with the UA: the **Arizona State Museum, the UA Art Museum, Flandrau Planetarium, Mineralogical Museum,** and the **Center for Creative Photography.** The UA's outstanding Drama Department offers an excellent selection of performing arts to the public as does the UA Artists Series. (*See also* PERFORMING ARTS.) The university's athletic teams, known as the **Wildcats,** are members of the Pacific Athletic Conference (Pac 10). Further information on the teams can be found under SPORTS and SEASONAL EVENTS.

The UA mall is closed to vehicles on weekdays from 7am—5pm. Pedestrians have the right of way at all times and the speed limit on campus is 15mph. Check the accompanying map for location of visitor parking lots and garages. WARNING: It appears the UA has found a new source of revenue via parking fines levied on unsuspecting persons. If you park in an unauthorized space or in an unauthorized manner, YOU WILL BE TICKETED.

Student Services provides information and campus tours from the **Visitor Center** located on the southeast corner of Cherry and the Mall. Information desks are located on the main floor of the Administration Building and inside the main entrance to the Student Union Building.

To attend the UA as a resident, a person must live in Arizona for one year. Inquiries regarding admission should be addressed to: Registrar and Director of Admissions, University of Arizona, Tucson, AZ 85721, or call 621-3237 (undergraduate) or 621-3132 (graduate). (*See also* IF YOU DECIDE TO STAY.)

LIBRARIES

TUCSON PUBLIC LIBRARIES

Infoline 791-4010

The City of Tucson has a main library downtown at 200 South Sixth Avenue, thirteen branch libraries and a Bookmobile Service (791-4531). (Presently under construction, a new main library is scheduled to open in mid-1990 at the northwest corner of Stone and Alameda.) A governmental reference library is located on the First Floor of City Hall (791-4041). As the hours vary, check the phone book and call the branch nearest you before venturing forth. Listings are in the blue pages of the Phone Book, Tucson City Government: Library Department.

All branches provide books, records, audio and video cassettes, magazines, newspapers and films and information services. Numerous outstanding programs are offered for all ages: children's story hours, movies for teens, community forums, self-help discussions and visual and performing arts programs.

Public programs support reading comprehension, adult literacy and creative writing and Special Needs Service offers a wide range of resources for the developmentally disabled and physically handicapped.

This Month! published by the Tucson Public Library provides invaluable information on what's happening each month. Pick it up at libraries and city park centers.

I highly recommend the reference department at the Main Library (Infoline number above). They answer over 6,000 questions a month and will find information on anything from the address of a firm in Podunk Center, to the spelling of foreign words and costume styles for ethnic dances. If they don't know the answer, they'll research it and call you back!

A library card is one of your best bargains. Apply for one at the main library or at any branch.

UNIVERSITY OF ARIZONA

Author Lawrence Clark Powell has stated that one of the reasons he lives in Tucson is because of the numerous library facilities available at the UA. The UA's library system includes over 3,000,000 items located in several buildings about campus. They include the following:

MAIN LIBRARY
Cherry Avenue and University Blvd. ♿ 621-2101

The Main Library, designed by architects Friedman and Jobusch, is a pleasant, spacious building occupying nearly 300,000 square feet, with seating for 1,700 persons.

Open stacks provide direct access to the books. More than eighty professional librarians and staff members are available to assist you. The UA Library is a member of the Center for Research Libraries and is one of the approximately one hundred distinguished libraries which comprise the Association of Research Libraries.

A recent addition to the Main Library is nearly 550 cassette tapes containing more than 1,200 old radio programs. These tapes include news, drama and comedy shows dating from the 1930s and are now available in the Media Center of the Main Library.

ARCHITECTURE LIBRARY
College of Architecture Room 101   621-2498

Functions primarily to provide reference service to the architectural students and faculty. Most of this material is duplicated in the Main Library.

ARIZONA STATE MUSEUM LIBRARY
Arizona State Museum North   621-4695

Contains materials on museology, anthropology, the natural sciences and the history of technology, with special emphasis on the southwest region of the U.S. (particularly Arizona and New Mexico) and the northern section of Mexico. (Open 8am-5pm, Mon-Fri.)

CENTER FOR
CREATIVE PHOTOGRAPHY
Olive Road, south of Speedway   621-7968

The center houses a collection of more than 9,000 books about photography as well as photographs and photographer's manuscript archives. References include over sixty photography magazines from around the world. Arizona residents can obtain a borrower's card. (*See also* LA CIUDAD DE LOS MUSEOS.) At the time of publication of *This is Tucson,* the Center is in the process of moving to its new headquarters and will open on February 10, 1989 at the above address.

SCIENCE ENGINEERING LIBRARY
Directly west of Bear Down Gym
across from the Administration Building   621-6384

This library contains books, periodicals and microfilms related to all fields of science and technology.

A **Health Sciences Center Library** and a **Law Library** are located on campus, however, the general user should first seek materials related to health sciences in the Science Library and to the law in the Main Library.

All extensions of the UA Library are available for public use. Persons outside the university community are welcome to utilize all library resources, and those who have special research needs may apply for Special Borrowers cards.

Parking for the main library is directly east of the building. Parking information and permits may be obtained at the Visitor Center located on the southeast corner of Cherry and the Mall. Parking will be available in January 1989 at the parking garage directly north of the Administration Building (entrance on 2nd Street). Metered parking is available at the parking garage located on Speedway just east of Park Avenue with entrances on Park and Helen. WARNING: It appears the

73

UA has found a new source of revenue via parking fines levied on unsuspecting persons. If you park in an unauthorized space or in an unauthorized manner, YOU WILL BE TICKETED.

HISTORY, GENEAOLOGY & ART LIBRARIES

THE ARIZONA HISTORICAL SOCIETY
RESEARCH LIBRARY
University
949 East 2nd Street

Mon—Fri 10am—4pm
Sat 10am—1pm
628-5774

As the largest research center and archive of Arizona history, resources include over 70,000 bound volumes and pamphlets dealing with the Southwest. More than 2,000 collections of private papers, journals, diaries, etc. (many of which are originals), and a tremendous selection of photographic work, including collections from more than 110 photographers are available.

The library and reading room are open to the public. (*See also* LA CIUDAD DE LOS MUSEOS.)

TUCSON GENEALOGICAL
LIBRARY
Pantano
500 South Langley Avenue

Mon Fri Sat 10am—5pm
Tue Wed Thu 10am—9pm
298-0905

Managed by members of the Church of Latter-day Saints, this library serves hundreds of visitors each month intent on researching their ancestry (and you need not be a Mormon to use the facilities). The church has cataloged more than one billion people by name and dates of birth, marriage, death, etc. The central repository for information is in Salt Lake City, however, microfilms from that library may be ordered and reviewed here.

The local library includes an international genealogical index listing all names contained in the LDS church records, the 1900 Arizona census, cemetery records from southern Arizona, books and histories of Arizona and guides to conducting research.

TUCSON MUSEUM OF ART
LIBRARY
El Presidio

Sep—Jul
Mon—Fri 10am—3pm
Closed August
623-4881

The Tucson Museum of Art Library, an integral part of the museum complex, is located in the Education Center on Alameda, just east of the museum. The facility includes 6,500 books, extensive magazine and pamphlet files, and over 23,000 slides relating to pre-Columbian, Spanish, Colonial, Western and twentieth-century European and American art, as well as contemporary southwestern arts and crafts. Included is an ongoing collection of publications from museums and galleries throughout the Southwest and western states and files of information on Tucson artists and galleries.

Members of TMA may borrow materials, others may research in the library. (*See also* LA CIUDAD DE LOS MUSEOS.)

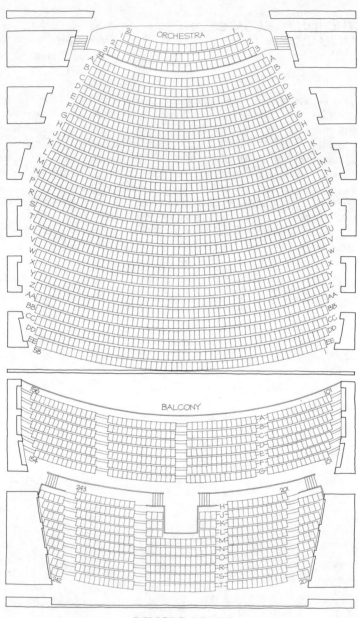

**MUSIC HALL
TUCSON CONVENTION CENTER** ♿

76

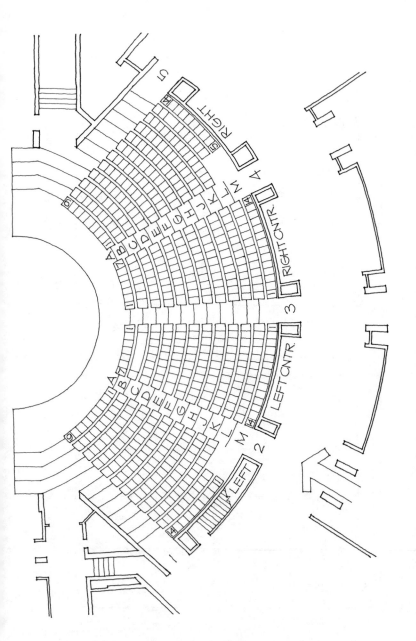

LEO RICH THEATRE
TUCSON CONVENTION CENTER

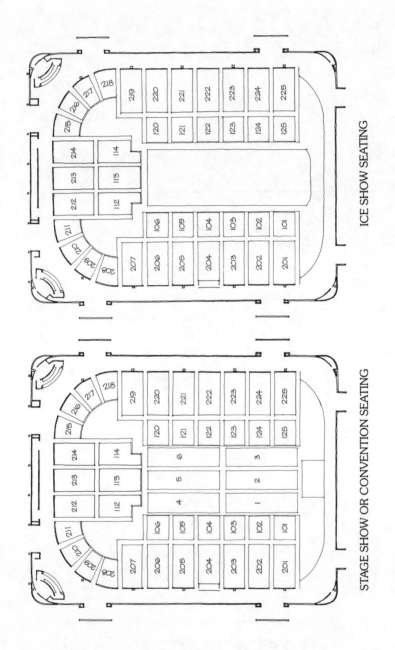

ICE SHOW SEATING

STAGE SHOW OR CONVENTION SEATING

TUCSON CONVENTION CENTER ARENA

78

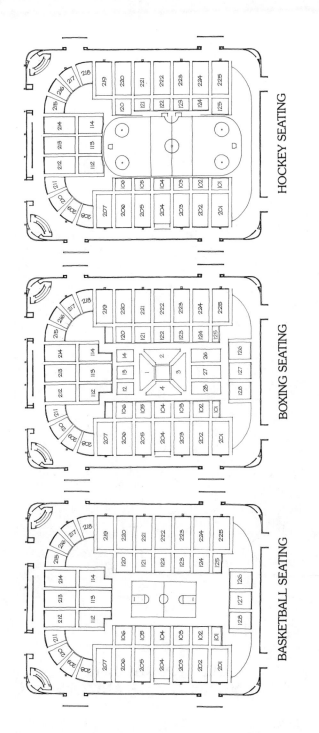

HOCKEY SEATING

BOXING SEATING

BASKETBALL SEATING

79

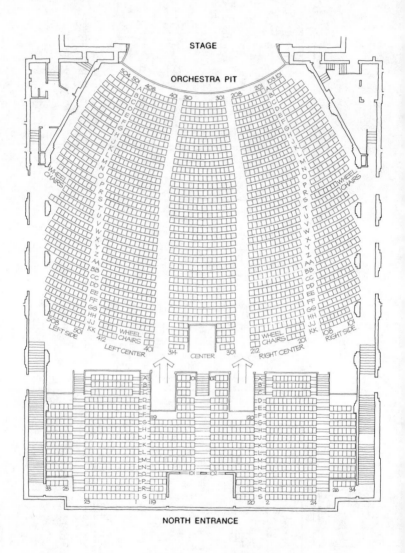

STAGE

ORCHESTRA PIT

**CENTENNIAL HALL
UNIVERSITY OF ARIZONA**

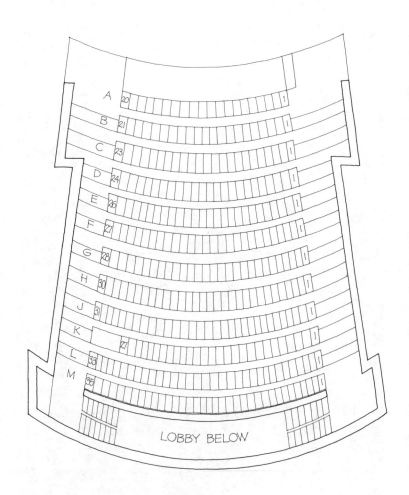

A   20

B   21

C   23

D   24

E   26

F   27

G   28

H   30

J   31

K   27

L   33

M   35

LOBBY BELOW

**UNIVERSITY THEATRE
UNIVERSITY OF ARIZONA**

Standing Woman with Hands on Her Face, 1976 Francisco Zuñga

LA CIUDAD DE LOS MUSEOS

We are truly a City of Museums. Tucson has more museums per capita than any other city its size or larger in the country. Our museums contribute to a variety of interests and several are unique in the United States. From art to astronomy, from children to historical, from insects to minerals and from missiles to photography, you're bound to find a museum for your enjoyment.

If you have time for nothing else, you should visit the **Arizona-Sonora Desert Museum,** chosen by the *New York Times* as one of the most distinctive zoos in the United States. The **Flandrau Planetarium,** one of the major planetaria in the country provides exciting entertainment with its Star Theatre and multi-media affects and the **Center for Creative Photography** is the repository of the world's most extensive collection of twentieth-century photography.

Seventeen museums are in this chapter plus **La Casa Cordova** and the **Fremont House Museum** in THE PAST IS STILL WITH US; the new historical museum at **Mission San Xavier del Bac** in PLACES TO GO AND THINGS TO DO; and the **Parade Museum** (usually open only in February/March during La Fiesta de Los Vaqueros) in SEASONAL EVENTS.

Museums outside of Tucson include several in A DAY AWAY, including **The Amerind Foundation,** and **Museum of the Horse.**

Listed directly under or opposite the name of each Tucson museum is the area in which that museum is located. Check the map on pages 252-253 for assistance in locating.

ART MUSEUMS

CENTER FOR
CREATIVE PHOTOGRAPHY
University
Olive Road, south of Speedway
621-7968

Admission free
Mon—Fri 9am—5pm

(At the time of publication of *This is Tucson,* the Center is in the process of moving to its new headquarters and will open on February 10, 1989 at the above address.)

This world-renown institute stands as an archive and research facility without parallel in the academic world. Major photographic archives housed at the center, along with an extensive collection of over 40,000 master prints, 200,000 study prints and 500,000 negatives, make the center the repository of the world's most extensive collection of twentieth-century photography.

Conceived in 1974 by the late Ansel Adams and Dr. John P. Schaefer, then president of the University of Arizona, Adams agreed to allow the university to safeguard his archives as long as they would be available to the public for research and study. Since then, the center has grown through dedication and love, and Director James Enyeart has said, "There's not enough money in the world to build a collection like the Center for Creative Photography."

By appointment a visitor may view Adams' photographs of Yosemite National Park, Edward Weston's peppers and sea shells, the fashion photographs of Louise Dahl-Wolfe, or any of the works of the more than 1500 nineteenth and twentieth century photographers whose prints and negatives are housed here. Curator Terence Pitts says, "We're the only collection in the world that's as accessible."

Archives of twenty twentieth-century photographers, such as Adams, W. Eugene Smith, Harry Callahan and Aaron Siskind are stored in the center. "Full" archives must be complete, including photographs, correspondence and memorabilia—everything that touches the photographer's life. Included might be the stages of development from negative to print, ledgers regarding the techniques of printing and correspondence between peers and artists. As an example, the Paul Strand collection includes not only prints and study prints, but eighteen shelf-feet of correspondence and personal papers, including more than 100 letters from Alfred Stieglitz.

Main gallery exhibits are changed periodically and may include the center's works or traveling shows from other galleries. A reading room and a print viewing room complete the visitor's access.

The center's uniqueness includes its philosophy of fostering research and allowing total accessibility to its collections through exhibitions, publications and actual first-hand contact. The **Research Library** contains over 9,000 books and more than sixty photographic magazines and periodicals from all over the world, in all languages. A large collection of microfilms and video-taped interviews, lectures and workshops are also available.

Call 621-7968 to set up a print viewing appointment for specific photographs. One hour appointments may be scheduled between 1pm and 4pm Mon—Fri and from noon—4pm Sun. Due to its frequently very personal content, restrictions apply to the viewing of archival materials. These works are accessible, however, to serious scholars.

DE GRAZIA GALLERY
IN THE SUN
6300 North Swan Road
299-9191

Foothills
Admission free
Daily   10am—4pm

This rambling adobe gallery built in the foothills long before the establishment of the hundreds of homes nearby was designed and constructed by the late Ettore "Ted" De Grazia (1902-1982) himself. The numerous rooms are hung with originals showing the development of De Grazia's artistic style through the years.

Besides the main gallery, a small gallery is available for visiting artists and a chapel dedicated to Our Lady of Gaudalupe, the patron saint of Mexico, is located nearby.

De Grazia, known as a kind, generous man, was also a strong individualist. Some of us still remember his revolt against the IRS when, many years ago, with a number of his paintings worth thousands of dollars, he headed for the Superstition Mountains. In protest of the inheritance laws, instead of leaving the paintings for taxes to be paid upon his death, he soaked them with a bottle of Chivas Regal (now that's class!) and set them ablaze.

Shortly after that experience, he created the De Grazia Art and Cultural Foundation to ensure the preservation of his work and the continuing operation of his gallery.

More than a few Tucson homes have walls painted by De Grazia long before he became known as the most reproduced artist in the world's history. His early paintings show the influence of Mexican artists Jose Clemente Orozco and Diego Rivera. However, his most famous paintings are of Indians and wide-eyed urchins, reproductions of which are now found on everything from refrigerator magnets and windbells to plates and note cards.

A 25-minute film produced by the University of Arizona tells more about Ted as an artist. A gift shop offers all types of prints, books, gifts and collectibles.

TUCSON MUSEUM OF ART
El Presidio
North of Alameda Street, between
Main and Meyer Avenues
624-1754

Adults $2
Kids under 13 free
Admission free   Tue
Tue   10am—9pm
Wed—Sat   10am—5pm
Sun   1pm—5pm
Call for summer hours

The Tucson Museum of Art celebrated its fiftieth anniversary in 1987. It is located in the TMA Historic Block, originally part of the site of a Spanish presidio established to protect the missionary priests and settlers of Mission San Xavier del Bac. Tucson's first Mexican and Anglo families constructed their homes and raised their families here and the museum is responsible for the preservation and maintenance of the five nineteenth-century homes on the block. The museum and plaza, along with the restored homes, provides one of the most enjoyable havens in the city, offering a unique blending of art, architecture and history.

Although ultra-modern, the museum melds well into the accompanying adobe structures, having been built down, instead of up, an architectural challenge well met by William Wild and Associates. Visitors to TMA enter at street level and work their way down past the exhibitions by means of a spiraling ramp.

The Upper Gallery and the Main Gallery (located along the ramp) are devoted to changing exhibits. An exhibition of pre-Columbian art, displaying some of the museum's numerous artifacts from the Olmec and Mayan civilizations and areas of Peru, Costa Rica, Panama and

Central Mexico is located on the lower level along with the Ileen B. and Samuel J. Campbell Gallery of Western Art. All exhibits carry bilingual labeling (English/Spanish).

Docents provide scheduled tours on weekdays and will provide group tours, if given a two-week notice. Please call for schedules.

The TMA Library, along with the TMA School and museum offices, is located in the **Education Center** directly east of the museum. A significant collection of resource art material includes 6,500 books, extensive magazine and pamphlet files and over 23,000 slides. Open to the public 10am—3pm Mon—Fri, every month except August. (*See also* A CULTURED COMMUNITY.)

The Museum Shop, on the lower level, features superior selections of arts and crafts by members of the Tucson Craft Guild. Tucson is well-known for its craftspeople and this is an excellent shop in which to discover their creations. (*See also* IMPROVING TUCSON'S ECONOMY.) NOTE: Approximately the first of January, 1990 renovation and expansion of exhibition galleries will occur and the Museum Shop will be moved upstairs. A new plaza will link the Museum and the Education Center. This may outdate some of the above information (and change parking availability).

The **Plaza of the Pioneers,** honoring Tucson's pioneer citizens unifies the museum building and the five historic homes, four of which were constructed over a century ago. The names of many of these hardy pioneers are listed on bronze plaques in the northwest corner of the plaza.

Designed in the Mexican tradition by Lifezones Corporation, the plaza locates the open space in the middle of the block instead of being a meaningless fringe in front of the buildings. The courtyard, with its sculptures, fountain, trees and seating, recreates the gardens of territorial days. Performing arts programs and fiestas occur in the plaza and in the lower level of the museum. Spend a pleasant Sunday afternoon strolling through the museum, enjoying art, music, and conversations with friendly Tucsonans.

A more complete description and historical background on the plaza, the historical homes and their owners is found in THE PAST IS STILL WITH US.

Parking is available in lots on Washington Street and Meyer Avenue (to the north and east of the museum). Have ticket validated in The Museum Shop. (Parking may change after 1990.)

UA MUSEUM OF ART

University
Olive Road, south of Speedway
621-7567

♿ Admission free
Mon—Sat 9am—5pm
Sun   Noon—5pm
Call for summer hours

Acknowledged as containing one of the finest university collections in the United States of Renaissance, European and twentieth-century American art, the UA's Museum of Art had its beginning in the early 1940s when alumnus C. Leonard Pfeiffer donated a collection of American art of the 1930s, including works of Edward Hopper, Stuart Davis and Reginald Marsh.

In the early 1950s, Samuel H. Kress donated over fifty European paintings dating from the Renaissance through the seventeenth century. With the exception of the Kress Collection at the National Gallery, this is acknowledged as the finest in the country. The *Retablo of the Cathedral of Ciudad Rodrigo,* painted in Salamanca by Fernando Gallego and his workshop in the early fifteenth century, is the premier attraction. The twenty-five paintings are the surviving retablos not destroyed by Lord Wellington's canons in the peninsular war and they form a major art treasure in Arizona. Other Kress donations include paintings by Tintoretto, Pontormo, Piazetta and Vigre-Lebrun.

In 1954, Edward J. Gallagher established the Gallagher Memorial Collection in memory of his young son. This collection includes more than 200 paintings, drawings and sculptures by such artists of the twentieth century as Picasso, Rodin, Arp, Maillol and Degas.

A major addition is a collection of sixty-one bronze and plaster models by Jacques Lipchitz, a true master of twentieth-century sculpture. Donated by the artist's widow, the permanent display, presented in an elegant, artistically lighted space, allows a comprehensive observation of the artist's creativity throughout his career.

The contemporary sculptures donated by Gallagher, along with the Lipchitz sculptures and numerous other gifts of statuary make the UA Museum of Art the home of the finest collection of sculpture in the Southwest.

Most of the permanent collections are displayed on the second floor. Due to lack of space, nearly three-fourths of these collections are in storage, therefore the displays are rotated several times a year, allowing Tucsonans and visitors a variety of displays.

The first floor contains the Lipchitz exhibit and changing exhibitions by contemporary artists, including paintings, photography, graphics, crafts and sculpture. In the spring, graduate students in the UA Art Department's Master of Fine Arts program present their thesis exhibition, and in the late fall, a faculty exhibition takes place.

The museum's many educational programs include its Outreach Program for kindergarten through sixth-grade level students. High school seminars and other public events are also presented, including lectures, seminars, music, dance and poetry readings.

Guided tours are provided by appointment only Mon—Fri. Two week advance notice is required.

The Museum Shop offers publications from past and present exhibitions, art periodicals, slides, posters and cards.

The **Joseph Gross Gallery,** located directly north, in the Art Department Building, presents a wide range of exhibits including student work, graduate work and, about once a month, the work of national artists. Hours are 9am—4pm, Mon—Fri.

Metered parking is available at the parking garage across Speedway. Entrances are on Park and Helen. A second garage will open in January of 1989 directly north of the UA Administration Building (entrance on 2nd Street). WARNING: It appears the UA has found a new source of revenue via parking fines levied on unsuspecting persons. If you park in an unauthorized space or in an unauthorized manner, YOU WILL BE TICKETED.

AVIATION MUSEUMS

PIMA AIR MUSEUM

Southeast of Tucson
Wilmot Road Exit off I-10
574-0462
564-0646

Adults $4   10—17 $2
Seniors/Military $3
Kids under 10 free
Daily   9am—5pm
No admit. after 4pm
Closed Christmas

Established in 1967 "in the interest of preserving tangible artifacts of our aviation history for recreational welfare and education of our present and future generations," the Pima Air Museum contains the third largest collection of historic aircraft in the world and is the largest such organization privately financed.

A gigantic 20,000-square-foot display building greets visitors with displays of air paraphernalia, including cutaway engines and several well-preserved aircraft hanging from the ceiling. Many aircraft memorabilia are on display, including models, uniforms, insignia, a

Norden bombsight and an airman's quarters as it would have appeared during World War II (including the ever present photograph of Betty Grable).

After touring the main building, you are free to wander the grounds and visit over 130 aircraft on display. You can see a Boeing B-29 "Superfortress," the type of plane used to drop the first atomic bomb on Japan; a Douglas C-124C "Globemaster," the last large American strategic transport powered by piston engines; a Lockheed P-80, "Shooting Star," the first U.S. combat jet; a North American F-100C "Supersabre," the first jet fighter to exceed the speed of sound in level flight; and a Douglas VC-118A "Liftmaster," that was used as a personal plane by Presidents Kennedy and Johnson.

Due to insurance limitations and safety hazards, visitors are not allowed inside the aircraft, with the exception of the Presidential Aircraft, which is open when volunteer guides are available. Walking shoes are recommended, along with a hat during the summer.

The gift shop has an extensive selection of aircraft models, aviation publications, aircraft prints and posters, T-shirts, caps and jewelry. Snacks and soft drinks are available, as are picnic tables.

To reach the museum from the north, drive east on I-10 to the Valencia exit then 1 1/2 mile east on Valencia; from the east, drive south on Kolb Road, turn west on Valencia; from central Tucson, drive south on Palo Verde and east on Valencia to the museum.

TITAN MISSILE MUSEUM

Approx. 20 miles south of Tucson
Near Green Valley
Res. 791-2929

Adults $4   10—17 $2
Seniors/Military $3
Kids under 10 free
Nov 1—Apr 30   Daily
May 1—Oct 31   Wed—Sun
9am—5pm   Last tour 4pm

The only intercontinental ballistic missile museum in the world is located just south of Tucson at a deactivated Titan II missile site. Originally part of the Strategic Air Command, the missile was one of eighteen located in the Tucson area and was operational from July 15, 1963 until November 11, 1982. The museum is dedicated to those Air Force personnel who spent boring hours sitting in such holes in the ground to ensure the protection of our country.

Approval, not only of the U.S. Air Force, but of local officials, the Strategic Air Command, the Department of Defense and last, but not least, the Soviets was required to maintain the site as a museum. Surprisingly, it cost half as much to convert to a museum as it would have to destroy the missile and its location.

Everything is here except the crew and the missile booster. The numerous many-lighted panels and buttons of the control center display the sophistication of the missile age and the size of the 165-ton Titan, 110 feet long and 10 feet in diameter, impresses the mind with its immensity and possible destructive power.

Previous to touring the silo, you will see a short film on the background of the Titan II. The tour is moderately strenuous, with a stairway of 55 grated steps requiring walking shoes with low heels. Tours are on the hour and half hour, except at 12:30pm, and last approximately an hour. Friendly personnel and volunteers, mostly from Green Valley, will assist you in any way they can. A small gift shop offers souvenirs.

Take I-19 south toward Green Valley to Exit 69 (DuVal Mine Road), go west 1/10 mile past La Canada, turn right.

CHILDREN'S MUSEUMS

TUCSON CHILDREN'S MUSEUM
300 East University
884-7511

University
Admission charge
Tue—Sat 9am—6pm
Sun   Noon—6pm

St. Augustine said that of all the natural wonders, "Man himself is the most wonderful" and this museum clearly illustrates that fact. An excellent museum for both adults and children, you will learn a great deal about that magnificent machine, the human body, as the numerous exhibits explain the workings of the body better than anything else you've seen or read. I especially recommend a tour if your child has surgery pending. The clear, concise exhibits will help allay some of the fears that child may be harboring. And all of us can learn more about the wonderful structure we inhabit.

Located in the Historic YWCA, the Tucson Children's Museum includes the Human Adventure Center and the Southwest Exploratory Children's Center. This center displays "larger than life" models and supergraphics to dramatically explain how our bodies work.

Take ten minutes and listen to TAMi, the Transparent Anatomical Maniken. Electronically programmed in English and Spanish, she lights up and describes the systems of the female human body. Numerous other models adorned with switches, knobs and buttons can be activated to explain divers scientific principles of the human body.

The nervous system and our muscles are clearly shown in separate models. An oversize display of the ear, nose and sinuses helps clarify the mysteries of thse organs of the body.

One of the most fascinating displays is the bicycle-riding skeleton. Watching the interaction of the knee joint as the leg goes up and down truly shows a universal joint that has been hard to copy.

Other exhibits include bas reliefs of the fetus in utero, and small fetal models—wonderful to help explain the miracle of life to your young ones.

The pollen display introduces you to some of the villains that create sinus problems. A shocking statistic is the fact that Tucson has twice the national rate of respiratory allergies. That's from all of those imported flora we've planted through the years of Tucson's immense growth!

Included are Apple computers and several games you can play to determine your health awareness. Check out *Lifestyle*. It will give you food for thought.

Special forums and lectures on medical topics are presented by experts in their fields while programs and learning labs are offered for specific age groups.

A special display from October 1988 through January 1989 is the moving, noisemaking replicas of dinosaurs. Sure to be a special treat.

HISTORICAL MUSEUMS

ARIZONA HISTORICAL SOCIETY, TUCSON
University
949 East 2nd Street
628-5774

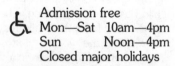

Admission free
Mon—Sat   10am—4pm
Sun   Noon—4pm
Closed major holidays

Known as *the* major historical facility of the Southwest, this is the state's oldest cultural institution. As a research center and cultural museum many displays demonstrate the role of the Hispanic community in the development of our area, reminding us that at one time Tucson was the northern perimeter of Sonora, Mexico. Arizona's history, from the Hohokam to the conquest of the Spanish, through the territorial years and up to the excellent Arizona Mining Exhibit, is displayed in various permanent and changing exhibitions. The 1880-style historic patio includes trees and plantings of that era and the surrounding small rooms, furnished from the same period, present an authentic portrayal of Victorian life at the turn of the century in Tucson.

Over 30,000 artifacts and a half million photographs provide a constantly changing glimpse into Arizona's dramatic past, and a costume gallery displays fashions of the old Southwest. Ongoing efforts are made to obtain materials never displayed before and present them in an exciting and entertaining manner.

Children particularly enjoy the Arizona Mining Exhibit, the largest indoor mining exhibit of its kind in the country, which introduces an eighty-five foot long, two-story example of a "typical" copper mine in operation around 1910 in Arizona. Several walk-in buildings, including a blacksmith shop, with the artifacts associated with that trade, a typical boom-town miner's canvas and wood cabin, and an assay office (known as the "office of heartbreak"), provide the essence of "being there." A mill setup, with original machines used in Arizona during the same 1910 period, includes an ore dumping car, roll crusher, jaw crusher, screen sorter and a 10,000 pound stamp mill. Special audio receivers provide a taped narrative of life in a miner's camp.

If you wish to delve deeper into Arizona history, or if period photographs of Indians or the old Southwest are your interest, visit the library and reading room, where you will find Arizona's largest research center and history archives, including books, magazines, newspapers and an extensive photo collection. Copies of any available prints may be purchased for very reasonable fees. As over forty photographers made their home in southern Arizona in 1875, an excellent selection is on hand. Hours are 10am—4pm Mon—Fri. and 10am—1pm Sat.

The arched portal and rose-window frame in the front of the building is from the facade of the original Catedral de San Agustín, located downtown. The portal was carved in 1882-1883 by a French stone-mason, Jules Le Flein, who was known as El Leon de Piedra (The Lion of Stone) by the Mexicans. (See also THE PAST IS STILL WITH US.) The church was condemned in 1936, and George W. Chambers purchased the stones and frame for $75.00. When the museum was enlarged in 1973, he donated the portal for the main entrance, where it was skillfully integrated into the facade by the architect for the addition, William P. Hazard.

The **Territorial Mercantile Company,** a gift shop reminiscent of the 1870-80s, offers glass and china antiques, Mexican pottery and glassware, old fruit glass, Apache, O'odham and Tarahumara baskets and a collection of old and new books on the Southwest. You quite possibly will find one-of-a-kind articles and affordable collectibles. The shop is operated by the Arizona Pathfinders, Inc., an auxilary to the Arizona Historical Society, and the salespersons wear clothes of the territorial period.

Obtain a token at the society for free parking at the visitors' parking lot located one block west of the society at the corner of 2nd and Euclid.

ARIZONA STATE MUSEUM

University
UA, on University Blvd.
inside Main Gate
621-6302

Admission free
South Building
    Mon—Sat 9am—5pm
    Sun   2pm—5pm
North Building
    Call for hours
Closed major holidays

Established on April 7, 1893 as a Territorial Museum "for the collection and preservation of the Archeological resources, specimens of the mineral wealth, and the flora and fauna of the Territory," the director was offered the municifent stipend of $1.00 per year for his efforts. As an integral part of the Territorial University, the museum became a part of the University of Arizona when Arizona became the 48th state in 1912. Originally located in Old Main, the museum is now housed in two buildings, the South Building and the North Building.

SOUTH BUILDING

The museum staff, particularly concerned about the environment and natural history of the Southwest in relation to the history of mankind, provides permanent and rotating exhibits showing the lifestyle and cultural history of the greater Southwest, focusing on Arizona.

You will see clay, stone and bone objects from the Hohokam (a Pima word meaning "those who have vanished") and artifacts from the Mogollon, Cochise, Apache, Pima, Tohono O'odham (formerly Papago) and Hopi cultures of Arizona. Note that although the Indians lived relatively close together, the items they made and used are quite different. As an example, the Navajo weave woolen blankets, the Hopi weave cotton blankets and the Apache are not blanket weavers at all.

Dioramas show past and present animals and birds. Many of the birds have been with the museum since its origination in 1893, having been assembled by pioneer scientist Herbert W. Brown, who served as curator.

Of particular interest to children is the buffalo, or bison, on the second floor of the building. Obtained in 1930, when the museum was issued one of two permits in a yearly buffalo hunt, the 2,000 pound male is not stuffed, but his skin is stretched over a wooden frame, and the holes in his hide are not bullet holes, but deterioration. Most other animals on display are stuffed with straw. All of the skeletons are real, with the exception of plastic used in the place of cartilage, which, unlike bone, deteriorates with time.

You may see sandpaintings, although the word is a misnomer. Actually "dry paintings," they are composed of crushed flowers, meal, pollen, charcoal and possibly crushed minerals, frequently created on sand.

The presence of man in Arizona over 11,000 years ago is proven by the spear point collection called Clovis Fluted Points, which were imbedded in the ribs, neck and shoulder bones of a mammoth found near Naco, Arizona.

Andrew Ellicott Douglass developed the science of dendrochronology (the study of the annual growth rings of trees) at the UA in the early 1900s and was the founder of the university's unique Laboratory of Tree-Ring Research. The world's largest collection of tree-ring specimens from living trees and ancient timbers is located in the laboratory, with one of those specimens on display in the museum. This tree slice, from a fallen Sequoia in Sequoia National Park, California, is ten feet in diameter and broke into three pieces when it was cut. The rings show the tree began growing in A.D. 212 and fell in A.D. 1915.

The South Building gift shop contains art and gift items from local craftspersons: Navajo rugs, Pueblo pottery, Hopi, Pima, O'odham and Tarahumara baskets and turquoise and silver jewelry, along with a good selection of regional books.

NORTH BUILDING

Designed by Tucson architects, Lyman and Place, this magnificent building was originally the UA Library. Listed in the National Register of Historic Sites, it will ultimately contain all activities and facilities of the museum, including public exhibition halls. While adapting the spaces to their needs, the museum staff is restoring the interior to its original character of the time period 1924-25.

A special exhibit gallery is on the first floor. On the second floor, a particularly handsome room, with its high ceilings and arched glass windows, lends its dignified elegance as an excellent anthropological library and reading room. It is open to the public, with collections of the museum available for study by any accredited individual. Library hours are 8am—5pm Mon—Fri.

Arizona State Museum

Metered parking is available at the parking garage near Speedway and Park. Entrances are on Park and Helen. A second garage will open in January of 1989 directly north of the Administration Building (entrance on 2nd Street). WARNING: It appears the UA has found a new source of revenue via parking fines levied on unsuspecting persons. If you park in an unauthorized space or in an unauthorized manner, YOU WILL BE TICKETED.

A private pay lot is available on Tyndall Avenue and East 2nd Street. (Merchants in the area will give stamps for purchases.)

FORT LOWELL MUSEUM

North Pantano
Craycroft & Fort Lowell Roads
885-3832

Admission free
Winter hours
　　Wed—Sat　10am—4pm
Summer hours
　　Wed—Sat　9am—1pm
Closed major holidays

Located in historic Fort Lowell Park, this area is a reminder of Tucson's difficult and bloody time with the Apache. The original post, established July 29, 1866, was located approximately at the site of the Santa Rita Hotel, downtown. As a temporary post, duties included protection of the Tucson Depot, fighting the Apache and escorting supply wagons (which were frequently joined by civilians looking for protection) to other posts south of the Gila River. By 1872, the proximity of the camp to town had created problems. The area had become "unfit for animals, much less the troops of a civilized nation," the post well was contaminated and there were too many temptations for the men.

In 1873 the camp moved seven miles northeast of town to an area along the Rillito Creek. Although we view the spot as picturesque, the army complained of the terrific wind storms blowing out of the mountain gorges and of the distance from town and from routes of travel, necessitating the furnishing of escorts. They complained of the difficulty of transporting stores and supplies from the city storehouses until such storage was built at the new location and of the necessity of keeping a detached guard at the downtown depot.

Within a year, the hospital, four barracks and the officers' quarters were built, but such niceties as flooring, porches and screens were delayed until 1882. The parade ground ran east and west with the officer's quarters on the south side and the barracks on the north side. A double row of trees in front of the officer's quarters formed Cottonwood Lane.

In 1879 the camp was designated a fort and given permanent status. As its reputation grew and it became the Regimental Headquarters for the Fifth United States Cavalry, the fort became *the* place to be stationed. Walter Reed presided as surgeon of the hospital for a little over a year. Frequent social engagements with the citizens of Tucson transpired, both on the base and in town, with concerts, dances, receptions and dinners occurring weekly. Great military balls were held, with the young women of Tucson invited as guests for the officers and men, while the Fifth Cavalry Band provided music. The several bands stationed at the fort frequently performed concerts in the town parks.

Fort Lowell, established not only as a major supply depot for outlying forts nearer the heart of Apache country, was also expected to help keep and insure the peace on the frontier, resulting in numerous skirmishes with the Apache throughout the life-span of the outpost. The Apache were led by several chiefs, including Natchez and Chato, but the name most feared was Geronimo. Continual Apache raids and the escape by several hundred Apache from the San Carlos Indian Reservation led to a gradual buildup at Fort Lowell and other Arizona camps until at one time nearly one-fourth of the entire U.S. Army was located in Arizona. General Nelson A. Miles assummed command of the Department of Arizona in April of 1886, leading ultimately to Geronimo's surrender to Lt. Charles B. Gatewood on September 4, 1886. Tucson feated Miles with a full week of festivities, including receptions, balls and a parade in his honor on November 8, 1887.

Although a number of small skirmishes between Apache renegades and the soldiers of the fort continued, recommendations for abandonment came in 1889, with such reasons given as the fort's hot and disagreeable location and the constant need for repairs of the adobe buildings. Tucsonans protested, fearing more Apache raids, but orders arrived on January 8, 1891 to abandon the fort; the troops were needed in New Mexico and the northern plains to assist in the pursuit of the Sioux Indians. On February 14, 1891, despite protests, the last troops departed.

Before visiting the museum, walk east of the parking lot, just north and east of the pecan orchard. Here is the Hardy Site and remnants of a Hohokam village. A series of stone slabs describe the site and its prehistoric founders, the Hohokam, who migrated here in A.D. 300.

Walk a bit further east and you will find a riparian woodland. This area mirrors what the banks of the Rillito might have looked like over 100 years ago when the river was a wandering stream, not with steep banks as you see now.

Retrace your steps and head west through the parking lot to find the remains of Fort Lowell. The adobe structures have crumbled in the summer rains until just a few walls are left standing. Walk along Cottonwood Lane where the trees have been replanted as they were in Geronimo's day. The original trees separated the officers quarters and the parade grounds. The structure to the north, under the metal roof, is the remains of the old hospital. Deteriorating adobe walls from the band's barracks are found in the northwest corner of the park and directly east of there are remnants from the cavalry barracks kitchen. Craycroft Road goes through what would have been approximately the center of the fort.

The museum building contains an accurate reconstruction of the commanding officer's quarters with a parlor, dining room, bedroom and the commander's office, furnished in the manner of 1886. Displays include photographs, maps, uniforms and equipment relative to the life that once flourished on the post.

The reconstructed building directly south of the museum (which once served as a kitchen for the commanding officer) contains two archeological exhibits and a revolving photographic display of scenes from Arizona's history.

If you walk a ways west on Fort Lowell Road, you will notice on the north side several adobe structures, all privately owned. These buildings include the Quartermaster Commissary Storehouse and the Post Trader's Store (and local saloon) which was built in 1873 by John B. "Pie" Allen. (*See also* DRIVING THROUGH THE PAST.)

Fort Lowell Park provides comfortable relaxation; you may wish to pack a lunch and enjoy the cottonwoods and the exceptional view of the Catalina Mountains.

OLD PUEBLO MUSEUM

at Foothills Center
7401 North La Cholla Blvd.
742-7191

Foothills—West
Admission free
Open mall hours
Closed major holidays

Believed to be the first museum constructed in a shopping mall, the Old Pueblo Museum has presented excellent exhibits, from carved antique wooden carousel horses to unique models built to the specifications of Leonardo da Vinci's scientific and technical drawings.

Exhibits planned for July, 1988 through July, 1989 include *The Art Quilt, Masks and Costumes by Southwestern Artists, Mexican Textiles: Line and Color/Oaxaca Children's Village, Native American Arts of the Plains,* and *Kites: Sculpture Sky High.*

On permanent display are Sonoran desert minerals, on loan from the Arizona-Sonora Desert Museum, and a reproduction of a Paleo-Indian rock shelter which includes bones of a pre-historic mammoth. The museum theatre also presents multi-image screen productions on southwestern history.

NATURE MUSEUMS

THE ARIZONA-SONORA DESERT MUSEUM

Tucson Mountains
14 Miles west of Tucson
2021 North Kinney Road
883-2702

Adults $6   6—12 $1
Kids under 6 free
Winter
   8:30am—5pm
Mem. Day—Labor Day
   7:30am—6pm
Ticket sales stop one
hour before closing

Selected by the *New York Times* in 1982 as one of the ten best zoos in the world, the Desert Museum was also described as, "Probably the most distinctive zoo in the United States . . ." Our museum is really a desert park featuring live species of insects, animals, plants and fish native to the Sonoran Desert region of Arizona, the Mexican state of Sonora, the Gulf of California and Baja, California.

As Tucson's most popular attraction, it is *the* place to view the natural beauty of our environment, plants, animals and geology. If you have time to visit only one attraction while in Tucson, this should be that place.

Bighorn Sheep—Desert Museum

Nestled in Tucson Mountain Park, the most spectacular route is west on Speedway over Gates Pass. At the top of the pass, spread below and stretching as far as the eye can see, is an unspoiled example of an alluvial desert. (Those who are driving a large motor home or towing a trailer of any size should take the Ajo-Kinney Road route to the museum; Gates Pass has a very steep, narrow road leading into the valley.)

Turn north at Kinney Road and shortly you'll enter a magnificent saguaro forest, ultimately leading to Saguaro National Monument, West. These stately cacti, some of which are over 200 years old and over fifty feet tall, grow nowhere in the world, but in the Sonoran Desert.

Pause for a moment under the ramada entrance and enjoy the magnificent vista of the Avra Valley. On a clear day you can see the mountains of Mexico and even on an overcast day, you should be able to see Baboquivari Peak, 7,730 feet high and the center of the Tohono O'odham Indian universe, and Kitt Peak, home of the world's most advanced astronomical observation facilities. Most of the museum exhibits stretch out at your feet, but they are so well integrated with the desert landscape you barely see them.

Scheduled times of interpretative talks are listed at the ramada and docents are available to answer your questions about our desert life.

Begin your tour at the Orientation Room. The information presented provides an understanding of the creation of the Sonoran Desert and the types of life found here. You may also view some of our most intriguing "critters:" scorpions, Gila monsters and rattlesnakes, all behind glass, of course.

Stop at the Earth Sciences Center and enjoy the simulated limestone cave. Over twenty artists came from throughout the U.S. to work on the cave, using as their examples numerous caves throughout the area. It is the favorite exhibit at the museum and kids in particular love climbing around the stalactites and stalagmites. Before you leave, visit the geologic displays showing the evolution of the earth, including some extraordinary movies of erupting volcanoes.

The newest exhibit is the Mountain Habitats, opened in the winter of 1986. This one-acre man-made site is the home of bears, mountain lions, gray fox, gray wolves, deer and numerous birds. Designed as a natural-like mountain home it's original pristine beauty has changed somewhat due to a couple of very rambunctious bears who have created havoc and mayhem.

When first moved into their new home these two juvenile delinquents made trampolines out of the trees. They broke branches and then systematically shredded them. In an effort to save the plants museum personnel sprayed them with a hot pepper solution—the bears loved it! They found and nearly escaped from the one spot the builders were leary of. They ate everything they could get hold of, including the buried irrigation system. All in all, they nearly destroyed the entire beautiful setting. The museum's curator of large animals, Peter Siminski, took it in stride and said the bears just exhibited their natural behavior and really are very psychologically sound, although the habitat isn't as beautiful as it once was. "In fact," he said, "it looks, well, like we put a couple of bears in there."

A walk-in aviary includes cardinals, quail, and other wild birds of Arizona, along with uninvited rabbits and lizards skittering among the rocks and streams. Take your time or even sit for awhile and look closely among the trees and bushes, as many of the birds will seem hidden from view at first.

A new Hummingbird Exhibit opens in October, 1988. Through the generosity of Mr. and Mrs. Sidney F. Tyler, dedicated museum members, this special aviary will be the finest exhibit of its kind in the world. Captive hummers will be placed in the exhibit, along with plantings to attract wild hummingbirds. As Mount Lemmon, the Santa Rita Mountains and the Nature Conservancy's Mile Hi/Ramsey Canyon Preserve are home to a myriad collection of hummers, this is sure to become a favorite locale for these fascinating, luxuriantly-colored miniatures.

Also reopening in early 1989 is a life underground exhibit which shows what our desert animals do to escape the heat of the day. This exhibit was an original part of the museum's opening and is what put the institution "on the maps."

Our unique desert plants require a new vocabulary and many of the 400 species located throughout the museum are labeled for your identification. Treat our cactus with respect, in particular the cholla or "jumping cactus." You may laugh when told they are an "attack cactus" and will jump right on you, but don't brush too close to find out. Many are those who bear wounds from excessive familiarity.

Over 200 species of animals reside in the museum, including bears, mountain lions, prairie dogs and bighorn sheep. Tunnels lead below ground for underwater viewing of the otters and beavers. Years ago, an employee of the museum related that the filtering of the beaver's pond created no little bit of concern for the beaver. As you know, beavers are builders of dams and good dam builders allow for no leakage. Sure that his dam was leaking at the filtering ducts, every day the beaver filled the skimmers with rocks to stop the leaks, and every day the museum employees removed the rocks so the filters would work. Surely that was the most frustrated beaver in captivity!

Be sure to take notice of the many stones and rocks used in construction throughout the museum. A large majority are man-made, having been built on the grounds by museum personnel to get just the right size and desired effect.

Plan two to three hours for your visit and go early in the day. The animals are more active in the morning, and in the summer months it will be more comfortable. Wear walking shoes, as you will cover quite a bit of territory. In the summer wear a wide-brimmed hat. **Note once again, ticket sales stop one hour before closing.**

Water fountains, public rest rooms and shade ramadas are strategically placed around the grounds. Take advantage of the fountains and drink plenty of water, especially during our hot summer months.

Strollers and wheelchairs are available free for your use and all exhibits can be reached by wheelchair. A cafeteria and gift shop are located at the main entrance, as are public restrooms. In nearby Tucson Mountain Park you will find picnic facilities.

Absolutely no pets are allowed on the museum grounds. If visiting during hot or even very warm weather, **DO NOT** bring your pets and leave them in your car. That not only is a life-threatening situation but is also illegal. (*See also* SUMMERTIME—AND ITS PROBLEMS.)

JANE GOODALL INSTITUTE FOR WILDLIFE, RESEARCH, EDUCATION AND CONSERVATION

Santa Cruz   Admission free
1601 West Anklam Road   792-2075

Newly located in Tucson, the Goodall Institute consists of a United States-based office for Jane Goodall, a library and a museum. Local personnel help arrange Ms. Goodall's annual lecture tour.

A museum opening in the fall of 1988, will include clothing she wore when she first went to Lake Tanganyika in 1960, chimpanzee nests and, hopefully, a garden of the vegetables grown in Gombe, Tanzania, East Africa, Goodall's African home. (Personnel are not yet sure those vegetables grown in Africa will also grow here.)

As the only Jane Goodall Institute in the world, you will find her scrapbooks of chimpanzee behavior for the past 28 years. Videotapes of chimpanzees in Africa and of chimps in general are available for viewing.

SONORAN ARTHROPOD STUDIES, INC.

North University

2437 North Stone Avenue

884-7274

Adults $1

Kids under 5 free

OPEN FALL '88

"This Bug's For You" is Steve Prchal's jaunty motto. SASI, an "insect museum," with no equal anywhere in the country has taken Tucson by storm and Steve's stated purpose of increasing public awareness of and appreciation for the arthropods is being fulfilled.

Steve has been interested in animals, birds and snakes since he was a child (I know, because I've known him and many of his pets since that time). At the age of 19 he realized a long-time goal of working at the Arizona-Sonora Desert Museum and when he left 16 years later he was assistant curator of small animals.

But before he left he had become immensely interested in arthropods, which includes all invertebrates with segmented bodies and joined limbs—"bugs" to you and me. He also became an expert on those many insects some of us would rather not deal with, and his museum provides a world of information which might change your mind about bugs.

Exhibits are continually changing. The first major exhibit was "Incredible Insects" from the Oakland Museum and a more recent exhibit was "Ants, Bees and Fun Things to See." When fire ants invaded the museum shortly after the opening of his first exhibit, he built a cage for them and made them part of the show.

Educational outreach programs to schools and children will possibly allay the early-on fears many adults never quite get rid of. The natural curiosity of children will be reinforced and Steve hopes they'll carry their interest on into adulthood.

Many Legs Trading Post, SASI's gift shop offers insect-oriented gifts and books, T-shirts and inexpensive scopes for viewing insects.

Membership in SASI includes free admission, use of the library, 10% off at the gift shop, discounts on field trips and workshops and *Backyard BUGwatching,* a stimulating publication worth the price of membership alone. Write SASI, P.O. Box 5624, Tucson AZ 85703.

SCIENCE MUSEUMS

FLANDRAU PLANETARIUM

University
UA, Cherry Ave on the Mall
621-4515
621-7827 (Program Info.)

Science Halls: Free
Theatre:
Adults $3.75   Kids $3
Mon—Fri   10am—5pm
Sat—Sun   1pm—5pm
Tue—Sun 7pm—10pm
Closed major holidays

Located at the center of "The Astronomical Capital of the World," the Grace H. Flandrau Planetarium is one of the major planetaria in the country. Dramatic shows in the Star Theatre, space age exhibits in the science halls, a 16-inch public telescope, educational programs and The Astronomy Store combine to interest and delight visitors of all ages.

SCIENCE HALLS

Open free to the public, exhibits include those on optical sciences, space sciences and astronomy, many of which visitors can manipulate themselves. Moon rocks on special loan from NASA are on display as well as one of the 1.8 meter mirrors made for the Multiple Mirror Telescope on Mount Hopkins. (*See also* FRED LAWRENCE WHIPPLE and MMT OBSERVATORIES.) Among other experiences, you may touch a meteorite whose origin may date back to the formation of the solar system five billion years ago; use lenses and mirrors to bend, magnify and distort light; and explore the invisible spectrum of light from x-rays to radio waves.

16 INCH PUBLIC TELESCOPE

The observatory houses the largest telescope in Arizona intended solely for public use. Weather permitting, the Cassegrain telescope is open Tuesday through Sunday evenings allowing a close-up view of the Arizona skies from dusk to 10pm. Camera adaptors are available for most 35mm SLR cameras should you wish to try some celestial photography. There is no charge for use of either the adaptors or the telescope.

STAR THEATRE

The Flandrau presents no ordinary show normally associated with a planetarium but offers the perfect environment for communicating science to a non-science oriented public through the universal language of art.

105

Shows take you on journeys through time and space to the far reaches of the universe. The Star Theater employs multi-media effects using slides and special effects, the Minolta star projector, Omniphonic sound, and the Cinema 360 fisheye film system that surrounds you with the beauty of natural wonders, both on earth and in space. The 50-foot diameter dome includes over 100 projectors encircling the theater which, together with the star projector and fisheye film system, create magnificent effects as you sit comfortably gazing starward.

Call for program information and schedules of performances. Admission is charged for the theatre and children under five years are not admitted. There may be slightly higher admissions for some programs. Discounts are allowed for seniors and students.

The Astronomy Store features educational and fun merchandise for everyone from the serious science enthusiast to the curious layman. (*See also* MUSEUM SHOPS.)

Visitor parking is available south of the planetarium. Parking information and permits may be obtained at the Visitor Center directly across the mall from the Planetarium. Parking will be available in January 1989 at the parking garage directly north of the Administration Building (entrance on 2nd Street). WARNING: It appears the UA has found a new source of revenue via parking fines levied on unsuspecting persons. If you park in an unauthorized space or in an unauthorized manner, YOU WILL BE TICKETED.

MINERALOGICAL MUSEUM
University

UA, Geology, Mines & Metallurgy Bldg.	Admission free
On North Drive	Mon—Fri 8am—4:30pm
621-6024	Closed some holidays

This 2200-square-foot museum on the first floor of the Geology Building contains one of the most impressive collections of fossils, minerals and stones in the world, including excellent samples of the extraordinary minerals for which Arizona is famous. A curtained booth in the museum allows the viewing of some specimens under black, or ultraviolet light, revealing the hidden magnificence of fluorescent colors.

A fossil display includes a preserved rhamphorhynchus, a flying reptile of 140 million years ago, and a dinosaur footprint, estimated to be seventy million years old, found in the rocks of southern Utah.

TAXIDERMY MUSEUM

INTERNATIONAL WILDLIFE MUSEUM

Tucson Mountains
4800 West Gates Pass Road
624-4024

Adults $4   6—12 $1.50
Kids under 6 free
Winter:
    Daily   9am—5:30pm
Summer:
    Mon—Thu 8:30am—6:pm
    Fri—Sun 8:30am—8:30pm

I was raised in Denver and spent many youthful hours frequenting the Museum of Natural History in City Park, studying hundreds of animals portrayed in their natural habitats and enjoying the beauty of these settings. So, having been raised on stuffed animals and dioramas, I wondered about the surrounding furor of the opening of the Tucson's Wildlife Museum.

Well, believe me, Denver has nothing to worry about. The building, reminiscent of a medieval fort, is dismal and does not belong in this foothills location. A huge sculpture of a mountain lion by Lorenzo Ghiglieri is a slightly saving grace, however.

Inside are several dioramas, but what educational benefits they offer, along with those of the weak "Scientific Classification of Animal Skeletons" and a conservation videotape, do not make up for the overall depressing atmosphere, accentuated by the McElroy Collection and its room of heads, heads, heads, including that of an elephant, mounted on all four walls. Additionally, the poster announcing that a National Heads and Horns collection is coming didn't improve my melancholy.

As a friend has stated, this is a "Monument to Big Game Hunting" and if that is your interest, you will probably enjoy the museum.

A film is shown every hour on the hour in the Wildlife Theatre. The one I viewed on Cheetahs in Serengeti National Park, Tanzania, Africa, narrated by Bing Crosby, had some wonderful photography of beautiful live animals. It almost improved my mood.

The Garden Restaurant provides inexpensive snacking, although the stuffed birds situated in glass cages about the room didn't create an urge to dine. A gift shop offers imported and domestic animal-related items, along with posters, cards and books.

Drive west on Speedway (which becomes Gates Pass Road) to Camino de Oeste. The museum is approximately six miles from Stone & Speedway.

107

Reid Park Zoo

In 1947, the municipal airfield moved to the new location . . . . The airport's move deprived Tucsonans of at least one pleasant summer recreation. On hot evenings, many people liked to go out to the civilian edge of Davis-Monthan, where it was grassy and cool and there were lawn chairs. There they would watch for one regularly scheduled evening plane to arrive. It was a cheap, enjoyable, and comfortable way to spend what might otherwise have been an unpleasantly oppressive evening.

Tucson: Portrait of a Desert Pueblo by John Bret Harte

PLACES TO GO AND THINGS TO DO

Tucson's sightseeing includes some of the most unique in the nation, from the **Reid Park Zoo,** known as one of the finest of the smaller zoos in the United States to **Colossal Cave,** our own underground natural wonder, and **Mission San Xavier del Bac,** the finest example of mission architecture in the United States.

Things to do include ballooning, gliding, bingo and wine tasting tours. And if you're looking for tour guides, several are listed in this chapter, from walking historic tours to hiking, bus and Sonoran mission tours.

Of course everything in *This is Tucson* is somewhere to go or something to do, but in particular be sure to check THE GREAT OUTDOORS and A DAY AWAY and the previous chapter, LA CIUDAD DE LOS MUSEOS, which includes the one attraction all visitors to Tucson should have on their "must see" list, the **Arizona-Sonora Desert Museum.**

Listed directly under or opposite the name of each recommended sight or activity is the area in which that sight is located. Check the map on pages 252-253 for assistance in locating.

PLACES TO GO

"A" MOUNTAIN
Santa Cruz
Just west of I-10   Daily 7am—10pm

This is the "dark mountain" from which rock was taken to construct several of Tucson's early homes, and the base of which, centuries ago, was home to a Pima Indian village.

Located only five minutes from downtown, the 3,100 foot mountain (700 feet above the city) was originally known as Sentinel Peak, when the settlers of territorial days used it as a lookout for Apache raiders (who *Star* Columnist R. H. Ring calls "the first anti-growthers").

UA students, in celebration of a football victory in October, 1915, introduced the whitewashing of the "A". Now, whitewashing the "A" prior to our first football game is part of the initation period of UA freshmen.

The mountain provides a panoramic view of Tucson, which is especially attractive at night, and a striking vantage point to view our kaleidoscopic sunsets. To reach "A" Mountain, take the Congress Street exit west off I-10 to Cuesta Street, then go south onto Sentinel Peak Road.

COLOSSAL CAVE
Rincons
Colossal Cave Park
22 miles east of Tucson
791-7677
Call for summer hours

Adults $4   11—16 $3
6—10 $1.50
Kids under 6 free
Oct 1—Mar 31
Mon—Sat 9am—5pm
Sun   9am—7pm

Arizona's greatest underground natural wonder is set deep into the Rincon Mountains. One of, and possibly, *the* largest dry caverns in the world, this limestone cave has been a home for ancient peoples, Indian tribes, outlaws and explorers, and was the setting for *The Outlaw Cats of Colossal Cave,* as seen on The Wonderful World of Disney.

Many are the legends of gold being hidden deep in the caverns, although none has yet been found, or no-one has admitted to discovering same. Some people will go a long way to keep secrets from the IRS!

Stalactites, stalagmites and calcite columns abound in the cavern's crystal halls. Hidden lights illuminate spectacular formations such as the Frozen Waterfall, Drapery Room and Kingdom of the Elves. You may see other structures to newly designate.

The fifty-minute tours are three-quarters of a mile long and begin every five to twenty minutes. Recommendations are that you stay with the guides and don't wander off; the end of the cave has never been found and you might become an unwilling permanent resident.

No special clothing is needed, as the year-round temperature is 72°. If visiting during the summer, the cave is a great place to spend a couple of hours as a respite from our summer heat.

A snack bar serves hamburgers, hot dogs, chips and soft drinks and the gift shop is well stocked with jewelry, Indian handcrafts and other desert and western items.

Drive out Old Spanish Trail, eleven miles past Saguaro National Monument or take I-10 to the Vail-Wentworth exit, then five miles north. The cave is located in 500-acre Colossal Cave Park, which has free picnic areas and campgrounds.

ENVIRONMENTAL RESEARCH LABORATORY
Tucson International Airport

Admission free
Tuesday   1:30pm

The University of Arizona's arm of environmental research is limited not at all by the wildest imagination. Ongoing accomplishments of ERL research, both locally and worldwide, are opening new vistas of opportunity that will affect us all.

With buildings originally funded by Rockefeller money, the ERL now thrives on foundation or corporate structure funding, along with moneys earned by the lab in their own agriculture and aquaculture research. Applications of ERL knowledge are operating in Arizona, California, Mexico, Abu Dhabi, Egypt, Kuwait, Sharjah, Saudi Arabia and Dubai and those of you who have visited the Land Pavillion at EPCOT Center at Disneyworld have already previewed some of their agricultural research.

The tour of about one hour will provide insight into ERL's ventures in conservation and their incomparable use of land, air and both freshwater and seawater. There's not a great deal of walking, but as some of it is through sand and gravel, it is best to wear flat-heeled shoes.

In the laboratory's controlled-environment **agriculture** greenhouses you'll find plants requiring no fertile soil and little irrigation. General requirements for food crops are 1400 square foot of land per person, ERL uses half of that space to obtain the same quantity of food.

To me, one of the most exciting experiments is that of using dirt and plants to clean the air through a "soil bed reactor." Simply stated, bad air is fed into dirt beds, microbes use the air, giving off carbon dioxide and water and providing nutrients for plants, which provide oxygen for humans. Application of this system could help solve our pollution problems and provide the beauty and shade of trees at the same time: large fans installed in planters at street corners would suck in polluted air, using it to feed trees and bushes; patches of trees, flowers and grass-filled dirt could replace bare ground above and around underpasses and tunnels; and companies could direct the fumes from their copy rooms to planters providing plant life in their offices.

Controlled environment **aquaculture,** oversimplified, is placing fish ponds into greenhouses to control fish growth and yield. Temperature and radiation levels are controlled, feed is manufactured like livestock diets and scientific disease prevention is utilized. Once again, the crop yields are astonishing. ERL pioneered the raising of shrimp in Mexico and in 1984 opened a large commercial shrimp farm in Hawaii.

The development of their extremely successful shrimp nutrition was accomplished in the Fleischmann Laboratory. Here they also maintain ongoing pathology studies on shrimp, offering these findings and studies free to those who need them.

More recently, in an effort to help meet the worldwide demand for seafood, they are "farming" Tilapia. A hearty fish that grows either in fresh or salt water, and reported by professional chefs to be excellent, Tilapia is being raised as a gourmet fish. A 50-acre fish farm, under construction near Yuma, Arizona will use waste water to fertilize and irrigate 1,000 acres of alfalfa, jojoba and other crops.

Another new venture is the growing of plants in dirt fed by water in which fish are maintained. Microbes in the water change amonia to nitrogen; the plants use the nitrogen, clean up the water and provide the fish with fresh water. In this experiment, if the plants show a need for minerals, the minerals are fed to the fish!

For seawater-based communities, the study of **halophytes** offers bright new futures. (halophytes are plants native to salty estuaries and deserts that will thrive in extremely high salinity concentrations.) Since 1978, the lab has been collecting halophytes from around the world and their collection now includes over 1000 different entries. One such plant, an oilseed known as SOS-7 (Salicornia Oilseed, 7th year of selection), is being grown and harvested in Mexico, Egypt and the United Arab Emirates. It produces a safflower-like cooking oil, protein seed meal for chickens and forage for either cattle, sheep or goats.

Besides providing both human and animal food, halophytes can be grown as grasses for marinas and golf courses, as trees for shade and as hedges to act as sand fences. Their multiple colors and lovely flowers are perfect for patios, and in all cases, they act as a foil toward erosion. Halophytes are being planted in Arabian countries in traffic "roundabouts," replacing fresh water plants requiring costly distillation of seawater.

Last on the tour is the **Solar Oasis**. This refreshing retreat suggests a new method of cooling desert communities. The space includes flowers, vegetables, protective shading and a "cool tower" which provides cool air at the cost of running a 1/16 hp pump. A similar complex is planned to open in early 1990 in Phoenix Civic Plaza, where an entire city block of scorching concrete will be transformed into a cool, shady oasis.

Take Tucson Boulevard south from Valencia Road toward the airport, then turn left on the air freight road and go 1/10 mile to the laboratory entrance. Reservations are required for groups of ten or more. Phone 621-7962 for information.

(Having just toured the ERL on the 1988 summer day that scientists announced the "Greenhouse Effect" has arrived, I feel scientific endeavors such as those accomplished here are more important than ever if we are to survive what damage we are doing to Planet Earth.)

BIOSPHERE II

"All life known to humankind exists within the context of a biosphere, the biosphere of planet Earth: a stable, complex, evolving system containing life, composed of various ecosystems operating in a synergetic equilibrium, essentially closed to material input or output, and open to energy and informational exchanges.

". . . Biosphere II [will be] essentially isolated from the existing biosphere by a closed structure, composed of components from the existing biosphere. Like the biosphere of planet Earth, Biosphere II will be a stable, complex, evolving, materially closed, life closed, energetically and informationally open system containing five kingdoms of life, at least five biomes, plus humankind, culture and technics."*

The application of the Environmental Research Laboratory's many experiments are being put to extraordinary use in the planning and building of **Biosphere II,** north of Tucson.

*Copyright 1985, 1986, 1987, 1988 by *Space Biospheres Ventures.*

Covering approximately two acres, the ground is lined with stainless steel planned to last 100 years. Arizona soil will be placed over the steel, creating all aspects of earth's life zones: desert, marshes, ocean, savannah and a rainforest. The innauguaration in mid-1990 will see eight individuals enter a completely-contained space from which they will not withdraw for two years.

Imagine the scenario. All food must be grown in the environment. Sufficient animals, fish, fowl, plants and insects (for pest control) to provide food for several humans for two years, must be available, without access to Biosphere I! (And you thought a camping trip required planning!)

As a pristine environment, no chemicals will be used. Plants will change and might die and possibly animals too, but the atmosphere will be kept livable. There will be storms and there might be drought. We will learn physically and scientifically to keep air clean and people alive. The tremendous educational value of creating a new "world," with its natural checks and balances offers future benefits to all. "We will," as Beth Hodges of Planetary Design Corporation, says, "become stewards of the planet—the 1990s will become the educated 1960s."

A Visitor Center will be open sometime in the mid-1990.

GARDEN OF GETHSEMANE

Santa Cruz

On Congress Street   Admission free
just past I-10   Daily   9am—4pm

The focal point of Santa Cruz River Park (*see also* PARKS & RECREATION) is **Felix Lucero Park,** a small site located at the northeast corner of West Congress Street and Bonita Avenue. The park is named for the sculptor who created the Garden of Gethsemane and other life-sized religious statues located here.

Lucero, a World War I veteran, vowed while he lay wounded on the battlefield that if he survived, he would donate twenty years of his life to God by building religious statues. He arrived in Tucson in 1938, lived under the old Congress Street bridge for many years and constructed his statues from concrete, sand and debris from the river bed, on land he didn't own.

The statues include the Last Supper, the baby Jesus with Joseph and Mary and Jesus on the cross and in the tomb. Originally on a site deeded to the city in 1948, they were shifted when the new bridge was constructed in 1971.

To reach the Garden, drive west on Congress, just past I-10 and turn right on Bonita. Free parking is available.

114

Mission San Xavier del Bac

MISSION SAN XAVIER DEL BAC

San Xavier
9 miles southwest of Tucson
294-2624

Admission free
Daily 6am—sunset
Nominal fee for
Historic Museum

This magnificent baroque church is the *piece de resistance* in any visitor's schedule. Incorporating Spanish, Byzantine and Moorish architecture, it is the spiritual center of the Tohono O'odham (formerly known as the Papago) Indian Reservation, the home of 7,000 native Americans. Declared a Registered National Historic Landmark in 1963, it is considered by many to be the finest example of mission architecture in the United States.

When you first see the mission, standing majestically in the barren desert with its backdrop of purple-hued mountains, you will comprehend the church's other title, "The White Dove of the Desert" and sense the same awe 19th-century travelers must have felt when this imposing building appeared before them.

Intertwined with the mission's history is that of Father Eusebio Francisco Kino, the Jesuit priest who traveled through the uncharted deserts of Sonora and established many missions, the most famous of which is San Xavier. He first visited this area in 1692 and laid out the foundation for the first church in 1700. That first church, however was destroyed and its actual location remains a mystery. It is believed construction of the present building began about 1783 by Father Juan Bautista Velderrain and was finished about 1797 by Father Juan Bautista Llorenz.

We know the church was built almost entirely of local materials, with wood used only for grills, altar rails and the pulpit. The walls, domes, arches and cross vaults were constructed of a primitive Spanish brick called tabique, which has a higher clay content and is considerably stronger than fired adobe. The floors were of polished mortar. The structure was plastered with lime for preservation.

The structural system is remarkably sophisticated; the roof of the church is spanned with shallow elliptical vaults, which are in fact parabolic. The walls at the base of the towers are three to six feet thick, sized to support the weight above, but also to enclose tunnel-like stairways which wind around the inside of the walls.

Legends abound regarding the unfinished tower. Was the building left incomplete to preclude the payment of taxes to Spain (true these days in Egypt)? Or did the architect who designed the church fall to his death from the tower and it was left unfinished as a memorial to him? In 1970 additional mystery was added to this legend when strong evidence showed the stairway leading upward to the tower had been sealed at the time the church was built. Bernard "Bunny" Fontana, in his "Biography of a Desert Church: The Story of Mission San Xavier Del Bac", printed in *The Smoke Signal* (Spring, 1961), states the most likely reason is the builders ran out of money!

As you ponder the legends of the tower, and approach the front entrance of the mission, look closely at the ornate carvings above the doorway. A cat sits on one side and a mouse on the other, evidently chasing each other. Like the story of the ravens leaving the Tower of London, tradition says that when the cat catches the mouse we will see the end of the world.

Even on Tucson's hottest days, a cool, serene interior will greet you past the weathered mesquite doors. The thick walls and small window openings cool the church in the summer and help warm it in the winter.

The baptistry and its 300-year old hammered copper baptismal font from Mexico are on the left, along with the stairs to the choir loft and the completed west tower. As your eyes become accustomed to

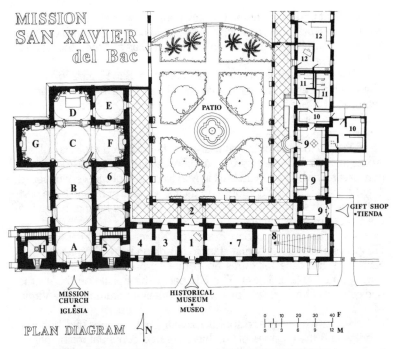

MISSION
SAN XAVIER
del Bac

PATIO

GIFT SHOP
•TIENDA

MISSION
CHURCH
•
IGLESIA

HISTORICAL
MUSEUM
•
MUSEO

PLAN DIAGRAM ⊸N

0 10 20 30 40 F
0   3   6   9   12 M

GUIDE TO CHURCH
GUÍA A LA IGLESIA

A CHOIR LOFT ABOVE •
SOTOCORO Y CORO
(ARRIBA)
B NAVE
C TRANSEPT WITH DOME •
TRANSEPTO CON CÚPULA
EN EL CRUZERO
D SANCTUARY • PRESBITERIO
E SACRISTY • SACRISTÍA
F CHAPEL OF THE EPISTLE •
COLATERAL DE LA
EPÍSTOLA
G CHAPEL OF THE GOSPEL •
COLATERAL DEL
EVANGELIO
H WEST TOWER: BAPTISTRY •
CUBO DE LA TORRE
PONIENTE: BAUTISTERIO

GUIDE TO MUSEUM
GUÍA AL MUSEO

1 ENTRANCE AND ORIENTATION • VESTÍBULO
2 ARCADE & CLOISTER • DEAMBULATORIO
DEL CLAUSTRO
3 INTRODUCTORY EXHIBIT • SALA DE INTRO-
DUCCIÓN GENERAL
4 EXHIBIT • SALA DE EXHIBICIÓN
5 EAST TOWER: EXHIBIT • CUBO DE LA TORRE
ORIENTE: AREA DE EXHIBICIÓN
6 CHAPTER ROOM (CHAPEL, REFECTORY,
LODGING . . .) • SALA CAPITULAR
7 REVOLVING EXHIBIT: TOHONO O'ODHAM
LIFEWAY • SALA DE EXPOSICIONES
TEMPORALES
8 AUDIO-VISUAL HALL • AUDITORIO
9 GIFT & BOOK SHOP • LIBRERÍA Y TIENDA DE
REGALOS
10 STAFF & STORAGE • AREA DE PERSONAL Y
BODEGAS
11 PUBLIC RESTROOMS • SERVICIOS
SANITARIOS
12 CURATOR'S OFFICE • OFICINA DEL CURA-
DOR: AREA DE CONSERVACIÓN

DELINEATION BY ROBERT VINT, ARCHITECT

117

the dim light you will note the building abounds with statues, carvings, painted designs and frescos, similar to ornate eighteenth-century Mexican churches, although you'll note time has softened the lusture of once dazzling gilt and color.

The statue directly above the altar is that of San Francisco Xavier. The retable, behind the main altar, has been acclaimed as the finest example of a Spanish retable north of Mexico. Once dazzling in its display of color, it is perhaps more unique than others due to its rare Moorish-style construction.

Directly in front of the altar are two handcrafted replicas of lions stolen in 1986. Donated by Gloria Giffords, Tucson art historian and conservator, who had them built in Mexico, the replicas were unveiled July 17, 1988. The original lions and their enigmatic grins had been part of the church since its dedication in 1797 and were legendary among the O'odham parishioners.

Vows are made to San Francisco Xavier in the Chapel of the Gospel on the west. It is long-standing tradition to pay homage to San Xavier to intercede for cures and other favors, as did Father Kino during a nearly-fatal illness. The Chapel of the Epistle on the east is dedicated to Our Lady of Sorrows and contains a statue of The Virgin Mary.

Moisture damage and soot damage from thousands of devotional candles and the vagaries of age have created continual maintenance and preservation problems, making the story of San Xavier, of necessity, one of ongoing restoration. From work undertaken by Bishop Granjon at the turn of the century to the venture by Tucson architect, Eleazar D. Herreras, FAIA, and Father Celestine Chin, O.F.M., in the 1950s and to the 1988 restoration by THE NBBJ/ GRESHAM LARSON architectural group, upkeep and preservation is an ongoing concern.

Present fundraising efforts are underway to raise $1 million for a complete restoration of the interior. As the mission operates as a Roman Catholic church serving the Tohono O'odham, it is ineligible for government money and must rely on private funds. (If you are interested in participating, donations may be sent to the Patronato San Xavier, Route 11, Box 645, Tucson, AZ 85746.)

After your visit, exit the church and walk east to the **Historical Museum** (1), once the convento. A nominal fee will admit you to the museum, a magnificent arcade and plaza, and the gift and book shop. (You may also enter the gift shop at the east side of the building [9]. Gift shop hours are daily 9am—6pm.) Evolving displays (3, 4, 5 and 6) may include architectural exhibits, period vestments, and a typical missionary's living quarters, including period furniture and personal effects. Note in (5) (the base of the east tower) the stairway built into the tower walls. A Tohono O'odham Lifeway exhibit is in (7) and in the Audiovisual Hall (8) a three-projector dissolve unit and tape recording give you a more detailed history of this architectural gem.

One of the most delightful results of the present restoration is access to the beautiful arcade (added by Bishop Granjon in 1905) and the inner courtyard, which for so many years have been off-limits to visitors. Formerly the site of a corral, a windmill and a frame house, the present garden and fountain were dedicated to the Pew Family in 1968 for their contributions to previous restoration projects of San Xavier Mission. New wrought iron surrounding the arcade was copied after that of the Mortuary Chapel and was donated by Escamilla Welding, while that company's workers donated their construction time.

The rooms housing the museum give us an opportunity to view the massive mesquite timbers and saguaro rib ceilings thought to be from the earlier Espinoza Chapel built by Father Alonzo Espinoza and older than the mission itself. These buildings are all of raw adobe, not the Spanish brick, tabique.

To the east of the mission is the **Hill of the Cross,** a replica of the Grotto of Lourdes, France. This is an excellent site from which to view the church in early morning sunlight or to watch the sun sink behind the Tucson mountains in the evening. BE SURE TO BRING YOUR CAMERA. San Xavier is a photographic mecca. Early morning and late evening hours offer the best photography; daytime sun can be too glaring. Drive around in back—some outstanding images have been captured here.

The Mortuary Chapel is to the west of the church. Under the floor of the chapel are the remains of two pioneer missionaries of the area. Traces of other ancient buildings are found west of the church. Also due west of the mission are the foundations of the Espinoza Chapel, predecessor to the current church.

Across the square is **San Xavier Plaza,** built by the Tohono O'odham in 1979. Here you will find arts and crafts and, frequently Indian fry bread. You may even be lucky enough to see some traditional Indian dancing.

MASSES

Weekdays   8:30am
Saturday   7pm
Sunday   8am 10:30am

Sunday noon is a high mass
with participation by the
San Xavier Mariachi Group

119

FESTIVALS

Wa:k Powwow   March weekend

Tribe members from as far away as Michigan celebrate **Wa:k Powwow** at San Xavier. (Wa:k is the original O'odham name for the San Xavier village.) As one of Arizona's largest festivals, various cultures are shared, both among the Indians and with the general public, who is invited to all events. Activities include calf roping, dancing, races, games and craft sales.

San Xavier Pageant & Fiesta   Easter season

The founding of the mission is commemorated during a dramatic evening of pageantry with Tohono O'odham and Yaqui Indian dancing and the arrival of robed friars, pilgrims and mounted Spanish lancers. Call the Tucson Festival Society, 622-6911, for the dates of this yearly event and keynote of the Tucson Festival. (*See also* SEASONAL EVENTS.)

Craft and food booths open around 10am, with various events during the day. If you come only for the pageant, arrive no later than 6pm to ensure a good view. The only charges are for parking. As our early spring nights are usually cool, you'll need a jacket and if you wish to sit, bring your own chair.

St. Francis of Assisi   October 3 and 4

Indians begin gathering about sunset for prayer and celebration. Fire works are set at the foot of the Hill of the Cross and the towers and facade of the church are illuminated.

Feast Day of San Francisco Xavier   December 3

This major event includes the decoration of the interior of the mission with tinsel and lighted candles. Prayers, processions and fireworks are similar to the October celebrations.

To reach San Xavier, drive south on I-19; you'll notice the mission ahead and to the right just after you pass the Valencia Road turnoff. Take San Xavier Road, exit 92. You can also reach the mission by driving west on Ajo Way and taking Mission Road south.

Old Tucson

OLD TUCSON
Tucson Mountains
201 South Kinney Road
883-0100

Adults $7.95   4—11 $4.50
Pima Cnty Resident $6.95
Kids under 4 free
Daily   9am—5pm

"Twelve Miles and 100 Years From Town" will put you in Old Tucson, the famous movie location created in 1939 for *Arizona*, the movie home of many of your favorite stars while filming in Tucson and the second most popular visitor attraction in Arizona.

Lee Marvin, Jack Palance, Shirley MacLaine, Burt Reynolds, John Wayne, Robert Mitchum and the pioneering Chaparral family have all appeared in this frontier town of the old west. A re-creation of 1860 Tucson, the town is built of sun-baked adobe bricks, dirt streets and board sidewalks. Employees dress in authentic middle-1800s western clothing and, several times daily, blazing gunfights occur, with local actors portraying those vengeful, ruthless characters of yesteryear.

Amusement rides include an authentic stageline and a narrow-gauge railroad which travels through the sets of hundreds of motion pictures. A trip through the haunting Iron Door Mine and a spin around the 1940s 24-horse carousel is a delight for all ages. Tour the sound stage, the gift shops, a saloon and restaurants. You might even be lucky enough to catch stars and a camera crew shooting a new movie or television special.

Musical melodrama is a summer tradition. Check to see what may be on stage while you are in town.

Old Tucson is at the intersection of Gates Pass and Kinney Road. Drive west on Speedway over Gates Pass to Kinney Road or west on Ajo Road until you reach Kinney and turn north. (If you are pulling a trailer or driving a large motor-home, I recommend you take the Ajo Road route.)

REID PARK ZOO
El Con
Gene C. Reid Park
1090 South Randolph Way
(North of 22nd Street)
791-4022

Adults $1.50   5—14 $.50
Kids under 5 free
Winter hours
    9:30am—5pm
Summer hours
    M—Th   8:30—4pm
    F—Su & holidays   8:30—6pm
Closed Christmas & New Years

Tucson's zoo is known as one of the finest of the smaller zoos in the U.S., but don't let that "smaller" keep you away. Reid Park Zoo epitomizes the saying that "good things come in small packages." Emphasizing natural environments, you will see an African Veldt with zebras, addax, marabou storks and ostrich; an Asian Grassland with blackbuck, nilgal, muntjac and sarus cranes; and an Australian Outback with wallabys and emus. (See map on page 130.)

Still more animals to see are giant anteaters, huge Galapagos tortoises, tigers, elephants, a rhinocerous in a mud wallow and a rare pigmy hippopotamus resting in her own pool. Shaba and Connie, the zoo's elephants may be performing some of the tricks they have been taught. Not only will the kids enjoy it, but you will too. Exhibits are clearly marked with definitions, breeding information and places of origin.

Another interesting display is the waterfowl and gristmill exhibit with over thirty species of waterfowl, including flamingos, parrots and several forms of fish life.

Located across from the zoo school is *The Ark* by Charles Clement, an early piece of public sculpture. The resemblance of a zoo to Noah's Ark is strong when one realizes that Noah also was concerned with education, conservation, research and entertainment.

A shady veranda welcomes you to the snack bar and a gift shop offers a large selection of stuffed animals and a collection of carved wooden animals from Africa. Strollers for small children may be rented at the snack bar. Tour guides are available at no charge to groups with reservations. Rest rooms are located next to the snack bar.

TUCSON BOTANICAL GARDENS
El Con
2150 North Alvernon Way
(South of Grant)
326-9255

Adults $2
Kids under 12 free
Sep—May
> Mon—Fri 9am—4pm
> Sat 10am—4pm
> Sun Noon—4pm

Call for summer hours

Originally a private estate, this five-acre site was donated to the city in 1968 by Rutger and Bernice Porter "for the enjoyment of the people of Tucson." The intricate layout, set off by paths, statuary and fountains, makes the gardens seem "delightfully like visiting an eccentric relative's backyard."

Although space is limited, you will see a large selection of plants, including roses, desert plants, wildflowers, a southwestern native crops garden featuring corn, cotton, beans and melons, an herb garden and a tropical greenhouse containing coffee plants, sugar cane, macadamia nuts and papaya.

In keeping with the Garden's desire to interpret the plants of the world and their relationship to mankind in the Southwest, the patio contains species of evergreens from China, California and New South Wales, Australia. An iris garden contains more than 300 varieties, and a large number of trees, including cork oak, olive, ironwood, palo verde, fig, cypress and giant eucalyptus offer shade. Bougainvillaea and hibiscus provide a riot of color throughout the year.

The tour begins at the old adobe house built in the 1930s. A gift shop sells gardening books, notecards, baskets, flower seeds, handicrafts, fine art from local artists and other southwestern gifts. Pamphlets delineate a self-guided tour or on Saturdays and Sundays you may attend a tour led by a docent.

Spring and fall activities include an annual plant sale by TBG and an art show sponsored by the Southwestern Art League. The Gardens offer numerous classes and workshops, including: Container Gardening, Backyard Birding, Planting and Care of a Cactus Dish Garden and the very popular **Gardening in Tucson for the Newcomer,** which is offered every month.

THINGS TO DO

BALLOONING

Anyone seeing a resplendent, multi-colored hot-air balloon floating silently through the air surely has had at least a momentary desire to participate in ballooning. From the beginning inflation of the balloon to the ascension, flight and ending champaign celebration, this extraordinary experience is available in Tucson.

All flights are subject to F.A.A. limitations and pilots are commercially licensed and experienced. Flights occur early morning or evening hours and only during fair weather, as pilots prefer winds of less than 10mph. The duration and distance is subject to weather conditions and landing areas, although the usual flying time is 1 to 1 1/2 hours.

A crew member drives a chase vehicle following the balloon's path, maintains radio contact and then returns passengers to their vehicles after the balloon descension.

Tucson also has its own Balloon Festival—*see* SEASONAL EVENTS.

FOX BALLOON ADVENTURES
Rincons $125/person
886-9191 Mid-Sep—Mid-June

Reservations and deposits are requested. Due to desert thermals in the summer, no balloon flights take place in July or August.

The balloons take off from the east side of Tucson, just off Houghton, near Speedway and Tanque Verde Loop Road. Write P.O. Box 17733, Tucson, AZ 85731.

SOUTHERN ARIZONA
BALLOON EXCURSIONS
$100/one $180/two
624-3599 Year 'round

This group operates year round in the Tucson Mountain area. In the summer the only flights are at sunrise, so plan on an early trip. In the cooler times of the year occasional late afternoon flights occur near sunset. Write 926 West Grant Road, Tucson, AZ 85705.

124

BRIDGE

One of the largest groups in Tucson is the American Contract Bridge League with over 875 members living in or near Tucson. Open games are played in Tucson, Green Valley, Nogales and Sierra Vista. Invitational events are held in both Tucson and Green Valley.

Organized **Duplicate Bridge** is played throughout the week at the Adobe Bridge Club, 3727 East Blacklidge, 881-7242 (the largest privately-owned facility for duplicate bridge in the state); the Bridgecenter, 3131 East First Street, 881-5691; and at 110 La Creciente 325-5068. A majority of the games are non-smoking. They also offer bridge lessons; call for information.

Tournaments include the Desert Empire Regional, the Copper State Sectional, Tucson Winter Sectional and Tucson Spring Sectional. Unit Grand National Events include North American pairs and Grand National Teams.

GLIDING

TUCSON SOARING CLUB
Marana
El Tiro Gliderport
West of Marana
Ans Serv 296-3069

$20/person	All day
Sat & Sun	Afternoon
Wed	10:30—4:30pm
Winter	9:30—4:30pm
Summer	

Rides are available all day Saturday and Sunday and Wednesday afternoons. You can buy "gift certificates" which will give you a "reservation" or you can go out to the glider port and take your chances on a first-come, first-served basis.

The desert thermals provide exciting soaring experiences and the adventure of quietly soaring at 10,000—14,000 feet over the magnificent landscape surrounding Tucson is hard to beat. Rides last twenty to forty minutes, depending upon the available winds.

If you buy a gift certificate in advance, a member will call you Friday to set up your flight time. Otherwise, you can just arrive at the gliderport and wait your turn. For further information or reservations, call 296-3069.

Take I-10 north to the Marana exit. El Tiro gliderport is located eleven miles west. Signs at every turn show you the way.

MOVIES

Tucson's conventional movie theatre schedules are presented daily in the local newspapers. Those who wish to view classic, unusual or nostalgic films, however, have several other choices.

CLASSIC/FOREIGN FILMS

THE CLASSIC FILM SERIES &
THE INTERNATIONAL ARTS SOCIETY Sep—Dec
University   Varying days & time
UA Modern Languages Auditorium   621-1044

The Classic Film Series entered its twelfth year in 1988, while the International Arts Society celebrated its thirty-fourth year. Films have included *To Catch A Thief, Sahara, Animal Crackers, The Crime of Monsieur Lange, Five Easy Pieces,* and *Roman Holiday.* If there's a movie you wish to see again, or one you've missed, these two series may possibly show them.

Individual or season tickets are available.

NEW LOFT THEATRE
University
504 North Fremont   624-4981

Located one block east of Park, just off Sixth Street, the Loft presents old classics and foreign art films at reasonable prices. It's a small theatre, so you may have to wait in line or come back for the next showing. Check the newspapers for films and times.

If you're looking for something different any Friday or Saturday at midnight, wander over to the loft and you can catch *The Rocky Horror Picture Show,* now in its tenth year of weekly presentations.

SHOWCASE THEATRE
El Con
3233 East Speedway Blvd.   326-2425

Art and foreign films are frequently presented. The theatre to check out for those unique movies.

OLDTIME WESTERNS

ARIZONA HISTORICAL SOCIETY
University
949 East Second Street
628-5774

Nominal admission
Summer & Winter
Wed   7:30pm

The Historical Society runs various western and historical films throughout the year. Summer of 1988 included Charlie Chaplin in *The Face on the Bar Room Floor,* Daffy Duck in *Daffy Duckaroo* and Peter Ustinov and Jonathon Winters in *Viva Max!.*

RERUNS OF RECENT FLICKS AND OLD TIMERS

GALLAGHER
University
UA Student Union

During school year
621-3102

The Gallagher presents fairly recent movies you may have missed first time around. Summer '88 films included *Raising Arizona, Broadcast News, Star Wars, Manhattan* and *Psycho.* Movies usually run only two or three days.

TRAVELOGUES

SUNDAY FORUM
TRAVEL ADVENTURE SERIES
El Presidio
Tucson Convention Center
Music Hall

Adults $4.75
Kids under 12 $3
Jan—Mar
326-7577

Whether you wish to relive a favorite holiday, preview an upcoming vacation or vicariously enjoy a unique location you may never visit, the **World Geographic Society** and its Sunday Forum Travel Series offers tempting tableaus of our fascinating world.

World travelers and explorers present and narrate their own travel adventure documentaries. Past arm-chair traveling has provided tours of Scotland, China, Mexico, Ireland and Australia. The 1989 season includes Germany, Spain, New Zealand, Hawaii, Egypt and the Greek and Roman World of St. Paul.

Season tickets available at a 20% savings. Contact Carolyn Lutz at 2839 East La Cienega, Tucson, AZ 85716.

PARKS AND RECREATION

Parks and Recreation Administration
900 South Randoph Way (Reid Park)

Over eighty parks are sprinkled throughout Tucson and the metropolitan area. Some are city maintained, some are county maintained and several are privately owned. I have included just a few as a sampling. (*See also* TUCSON URBAN FISHING, SPORTS and PICNICKING, HIKING AND CAMPING.)

Tucson Parks and Recreation Department offers numerous year-round classes for children, teens and adults including lessons in piano, yoga, needlepoint, calligraphy, ceramics, photography, stained glass, belly dancing and backpacking. The following phone numbers will assist you in using our city parks:

Randolph Recreation Complex
100-200 South Alvernon Way   791-4560

Information   791-4873

Class Registration   791-4877

Concerts   791-4079

Facility Rental   791-4873

Recreation Centers   791-4382

Four times a year Tucson Parks and Recreation publishes *The Tucson Parks & Recreation REVIEW* through our local newspapers. This information-filled pamphlet is also available at park centers and libraries.

BEER PERMITS

In an effort to control the abuse of alcohol in our parks, without completely prohibiting its use, city ordinance prohibits the consumption of beer, *without a permit,* and the use of ANY glass containers in city parks. (Drinking wine and hard liquor in city parks is prohibited by state law.) There is a mandatory minimum $10 fine for bringing glass containers into the park.

Beer permits costs $3.00 for 100 persons or less, and the day of use must be specified. Permits may be purchased on weekends, for use the day they are issued, at the Reid Park Zoo snack bar or the park lake snack bar. Monday through Friday from 8am—5pm they may be purchased at the Parks Administrative Office, 900 South Randolph Way; Park Service Center, Park and Ajo; Downtown City Hall; Eastside City Hall; and all Council Offices or call 791-4583 for further information.

J. F. KENNEDY PARK   Tucson Mountains—South
Ajo Way and Cholla Boulevard   CITY PARK

Located in the southwest corner of Tucson, Kennedy Park's main attraction is a 10-acre lake which allows fishing and boating, but no swimming or wading. Boat rentals and a snack bar are available as is a launch ramp for saleboats. You will also find a number of windsurfers using the lake. (*See also* TUCSON URBAN FISHING.)

Picnic areas include ramadas and barbeque grills and the recreation area provides tennis courts, playgrounds, a swimming pool, and baseball and little league fields.

A number of Mexican fiestas are held in May and September, celebrating Cinco de Mayo and Diez y siez de Septiembre. The first is a celebration of May 5, 1862, when a small band of poorly organized Mexican patriots defeated the French at a battle in Puebla, proving that Mexico could fight off the encroachment of foreign powers, and the second celebrates Mexico's Independence from Spain on September 16, 1821. Festivities at these affairs include mariachi and folklorico groups both from Mexico and Tucson and local bands. Saturday is usually children's day with puppet shows, games and pinatas.

Drive west on Ajo to Mission Road and turn north on Mission one block to the park entrance.

GENE C. REID PARK   El Con
Between Broadway & 22nd Street   CITY PARK
and Country Club Road & Alvernon Way

Located in the center of the city, this major urban park has a zoo, two 18-hole golf courses (*see also* SPORTS), a lake, a rose garden with more than 2,000 plants, a concert band shell, loads of picnic tables and sixteen ramadas. The Handi-Dog Pavilion, located in the northwest corner of the park, at East Camino Campestre and South Country Club Road, was designed for the physically disabled and restrooms nearby have wheelchair access.

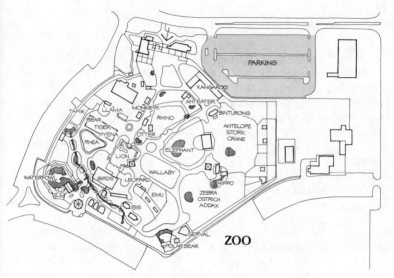

ZOO

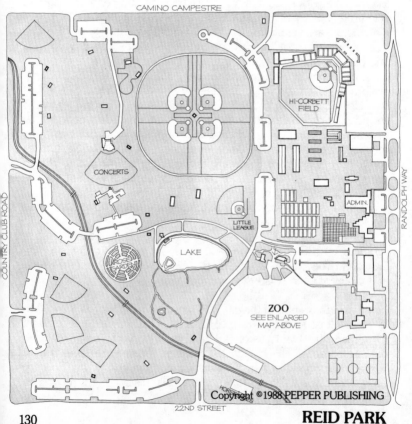

CAMINO CAMPESTRE

HI-CORBETT FIELD

CONCERTS

LITTLE LEAGUE

LAKE

ROSE GARDEN

ADMIN.

ZOO
SEE ENLARGED
MAP ABOVE

COUNTRY CLUB ROAD

RANDOLPH WAY

HORSE

22ND STREET

REID PARK

The lake is stocked and fishing is allowed for kids under 14 years. A daily fishing permit may be purchased at the snackbar near the lake on weekends and at the snackbar at the zoo on weekdays. (No swimming or wading). (*See also* TUCSON URBAN FISHING.)

The **Randolph Recreation Complex** (791-4560) on the Alvernon side of the park, includes tennis and racquetball courts, a swimming pool, therapeutics clubhouse and several buildings incorporating crafts shops, photography labs and performing arts spaces. A new gymnasium includes a weight training area and gymnastics center.

THE FOLLOWING TWO PARKS ARE ESPECIALLY FOR WALKERS, JOGGERS AND BIKERS THEY EXTEND ALONG TWO OF OUR RIVER BANKS AND PROVIDE A RURAL EXPERIENCE IN TOWN

RILLITO RIVER PARK
Between North Flowing Wells and
North Campbell Avenue

Rillito
COUNTY PARK

Averaging 50 feet on each side of the river, this linear park includes bike and jogging paths, horse trails, benches and picnic areas. Over 4,000 mesquite, cottonwood and ash trees are planted along the riverbank, along with 3,000 shrubs and bushes and over 1,000 cacti.

On the northern bank of the Rillito in the area between North Flowing Wells and North Oracle Road is the **Children's Memorial Park.** This park is dedicated as a memorial to deceased children.

SANTA CRUZ RIVER PARK
West bank—Speedway north to Grant
East bank—St. Marys Road north to Speedway
Mission Lane and St. Marys Road

Santa Cruz
CITY PARK

Future plans for this linear park include returning the river to its original greenbelt of native vegetation and creating a wildlife habitat. Remains of a Hohokam village will be incorporated into an Indian cultural center as the focal point of the area. At this date, you will find a bike and jogging trail, picnic tables and a softball field near Speedway and Grant.

If we've had some rain and you are near the river, you might note that one of its pecularities is that it flows north instead of south.

It's more likely the river will be dry, and if so, keep your eyes open for our **Santa Cruz River Sand Trout.** Jim Griffith, Director of the Southwest Folklore Center at the UA says he has seen a goodly

131

number of them. They live quite close to the surface, with their eyes peering out from tall stalks and they're not prone to swimming very far because the friction on the hot sand burns their hides.

Prickly pear or cholla pads make good bait, but horned toad is best. Put the leader around the toad's middle and as he walks down river, the sand trout will grab him and the neck spikes will catch the trout. Reel the fish in quickly and the hot sand will skin and cook him. Then give a sharp snap, allowing the horned toad to break loose. Remember, horned toads are protected so you can't injure them, but no one says you can't take them for a walk!

Rumor has it that Jim's story is really academic, however, as the Ichthyology Department of the UA claims the entire population of sand trout drowned in the floods of 1983. (Have you read the story about the EPA treating the Santa Cruz like a gamefish river? Honest! Which proves the government seldom knows what it's doing.)

Even though you may not be lucky enough to see our sand trout, you may be present at the break up of the ice on the Santa Cruz. Tradition has it that this occurs the first day the temperature in Tucson hits the 100° mark, normally around the end of May.

SPORTSPARK
6901 North Casa Grande Hwy
West Ina Road & I-10

Santa Cruz—North
Adults $8.75
Info: 744-9496

Along with a miniature golf course, bumper and race cars, horseshoes, softball fields, volleyball courts and an 18-hole miniature golf course, Sportspark Softball-Volleyball Complex includes three hydrotube rides, the steepest and fastest of which is "The Whip" a 350-foot ride taken after an eleven flight climb up a 47-foot tower! (*See also* SWIMMING.)

TOHONO CHUL PARK
7366 Paseo Del Norte
742-6455

Foothills
Donations requested
Daily 7am—sundown

Surrounded by residential neighborhoods, Tohono Chul (Desert Corner in O'odham) is located immediately north of the intersection of Ina and Oracle Roads. This privately-owned 35-acre desert park includes nature trails, picnic tables, botanical gardens, an exhibit hall and gallery, a greenhouse and a gift shop. The park is a gift to the people of Tucson from Richard and Jean Wilson, owners of The Haunted Bookshop. They wish the area to be considered as a museum to provide the public an opportunity to learn more about desert plants and wildlife.

This desert sanctuary includes wandering paths (which are wheelchair-accessible) leading to shaded ramadas, surprising caches of water, numerous nooks and crannys filled with a variety of plants, and countless birds and other desert life. The weather station informs you about our desert climate and a geology exhibit includes rocks from the Santa Catalina Mountains.

Bird-watching and guided tours may be arranged by calling 742-4109. The exhibit hall is open 9am—5pm seven days a week, and the park gift shop is open 9:30am—5pm Tue—Sun. Tours of the park are conducted by docents Wed at 9:30am. Free to members, a $2 admission contribution is suggested for non-members. Desert Discovery Days are held for children with walks through the park, art, storytelling and hands-on activities. Call 742-6455.

One of Tucson's legendary book stores, **The Haunted Book-shop,** is also located at this site, as is the **Tohono Chul Tea Room.** (*See also* BOOKSTORES and LIGHT EATING.)

IF YOU NEED A GUIDE

HISTORIC WALKING TOURS

FREMONT HOUSE MUSEUM/
ARIZONA HISTORICAL SOCIETY   Nov—Mar
151 South Granada Avenue   Sat 10am
622-0956 $3.00/person

Winter walking tours are provided of the downtown historic areas. Professional guides take you past twenty some homes in a 1 1/4 mile tour of El Presidio Historic Neighborhood, with an emphasis on Tucson history, architecture and the lives of our pioneers. (April through October tours are possible with a minimum number of fifteen persons.) A 15-minute slide show before the tour introduces visitors to some of Tucson's history. (Plans are in the making for a similar tour of the Armory Park Neighborhood.)

Prior reservations are required. Please call the above number. (*See also* THE PAST IS STILL WITH US.)

TUCSON/PIMA COUNTY
HISTORICAL COMMISSION
Info: 791-4121 $1.00 donation

Tours are scheduled on request for a minimum of twenty persons. At least two-hours is required and preferably three hours. Morning hours are best, beginning at 8:30 or 9:00am.

Norma Niblett, commission member, will be your guide. You may contact her at the above number or at 5837 North Paseo Ventoso, Tucson, AZ 85715.

TWILIGHT WALKING TOURS
P.O. Box 50501
Tucson, AZ 85703-1501   323-9290

Enjoy the translucent light of a Tucson summer evening along with a tour of the El Presidio Historic District with Ken Scoville. Along with visiting our earliest homes, Ken provides a sociological overview of those early settlers, their history, families and architecture. Reservations are required and Ken prefers groups of 8—10.

HIKING TOURS

DESERT TORTOISE OUTINGS
8912 Camino Coronado
Tucson, AZ 85707   Res/info: 888-1557

Much of the surrounding beauty of Tucson is hidden from the person who travels only by motor. To participate in that beauty it is necessary

Desert Tortoise Outings' knowledgeable guides will take you into mountain canyons accessible only by foot trails. There you'll enjoy magnificent views, and secluded pools and waterfalls while learning about our desert flora and fauna.

Hiking experience or stamina is not necessary, but comfortable clothing and footgear are. Call Karyle Klasz.

DO IT YOURSELF DRIVING

"TALKING TOURS"
577-3466 $8.95/cassette

If you have transportation, but would like explicit directions to some of Tucson's attractions, you will be interested in auto-tape tours developed by Diane Weintraub.

These tapes allow you to go at your own pace and receive points of information you might not receive otherwise.

One tour of approximately two hours is a 35-mile loop of Tucson. You'll pass many points of interest with explanations of what you are seeing. Optional side trips are also described.

The second tour includes the Arizona-Sonora Desert Museum, Old Tucson and Saguaro National Monument-West.

BUS AND VAN TOURS

ARIZONA STAGECOACH COMPANY
4520 East Grant Road
Tucson, AZ 85712   Info: 881-4474

The tour division of Arizona Stagecoach provides tours for individuals or groups. Depending upon group size, transportation is available by van, minicoach or motorcoach.

Knowledgeable, qualified, certified driver/guides and step-on escorts will bring the territory alive for you.

Tours are taken to Old Tucson, Arizona-Sonora Desert Museum, Mission San Xavier, Sabino Canyon, Colossal Cave, Nogales, Bisbee and Tombstone.

For further information, call Mary Ann Coe or Doug Kramar, Arizona Stagecoach Arrangers.

CLASSIC TOUR & TRANSPORTATION 3568 North Campbell Tucson, AZ 85719 Res/info: 327-3333	Summer: 9:15am 9:30am Winter: 1:15pm 1:30pm	Tue, Thu, Sat El Con Mall Carlos Murphys Daily El Con Mall Carlos Murphys

You say you thought you saw an English double-decker bus going down the street yesterday? Well, you probably did. Although for over 27 years, it rode through the streets of London, it belongs here now; and what better way to tour Tucson Town?

The double-decker (without air conditioning) is driven on summer Saturdays, while an air conditioned van is used on summer Tuesdays and Thursdays. During the winter (considered to be about October 1 through June 1), the double-decker is used every day.

The two-hour tour covers downtown historical districts, "A" Mountain, the University of Arizona, El Encanto, the Catalina Foothills, De Grazia Studios, La Paloma and Fort Lowell Park.

Beginning in October, daily tours to the Arizona-Sonora Desert Museum and Old Tucson are offered, with pick-ups at the same spots.

El Con pick up is at the main bus stop. Motel/hotel pick up is available for two or more for a small fee; please phone at least two hours prior to tour departure.

GRAY LINE TOURS

P.O. Box 1991
Tucson, AZ 85702   622-8811

Gray Line Tours/Citizen Auto Stage Company has several tours operating year-round.

Monday, Wednesday and Friday tours include trips to the Arizona-Sonora Desert Museum, Old Tucson and Mission San Xavier. Tuesday, Thursday tours go to Nogales, Sonora, Mexico.

Numerous year-round trips are planned for destinations in northern Arizona and bordering states.

Pickups are made at many leading hotels, motels and bus terminals. For reservations and further information, call above number or see the Gray Line agent in your hotel or motel.

PLEASUREBENT TOURS

P.O. Box 7868
Tucson, AZ 85731   Res/info: 884-0777

Amy Maffeo escorts you on these tours, some of which are fairly extensive, including jaunts to Scottsdale for Fifth Avenue Shopping, Canyon de Chelly and Gallup, New Mexico, Santa Catalina Island off the coast of California and Ensenada, Mexico. Tucson area tours include trips to Kitt Peak, Mount Hopkins and Nogales, AZ. There is also a tour of the Tucson Art Museum, De Grazia's Gallery in the Sun and Hacienda Del Sol Ranch.

Tours are scheduled every month or so. Call to find out what tours are available while you are in Tucson. Advance reservations are very important.

SONORAN MISSION TOURS

KINO MISSION TOURS $195/person
Southwestern Mission Research Center   888-4037
UA, Arizona State Museum   Apr and Oct

Four tours of the Kino Missions of Sonora take place in the spring and fall every year. The tours require three-day weekends, leaving Friday at 8am and returning Sunday evening about 6pm. Tour guides include some of the area's most interesting academics who combine history, past and present, with cheerfulness, relaxation and much hilarity. It's a tremendous way to enjoy the beautiful Mexican countryside and also learn more about our cultural background.

The tours visit the missions of Cocospera, San Ignacio, Magdalena, Tubutama, Oquitoa, Pitiquito and Caborca. Members of the SMRC take care of all reservations and the obtaining of Mexican tourist cards. Tucsonans who have taken the tours rave about the education, the enjoyment and the camaraderie of the groups.

You must have with you documentation to prove your nationality in order to travel into Mexico; this may be a birth certificate or passport.

Reservations are required. Call Marjorie Gould at 888-4037 or write her at 101 West River Road, #251, Tucson, AZ 85704. The 1988 fee of $195 covered bus transportation from Tucson, picnic lunches and overnight accommodations.

Sabino Canyon

SPORTS

BIKING

Tucson's wonderful weather and level terrain provides two necessities for good biking and, supposedly, we have more bicycles per capita than any other city in the U.S. Actual bike paths, however, are few and far between. Recent legislation provides that all new roads and those under repair will have wide paved shoulders or signed bike lanes, which should improve matters.

Two very popular out-of-town routes are through Sabino Canyon and Saguaro National Monument—East (you can pick up maps at the visitor centers). (*See also* CAMPING, HIKING AND PICNICKING.)

Two new bikeways are the 2 1/2 mile bike path through the **Santa Cruz River Park** which can be combined with a picnic and/or looking for Santa Cruz River Sand Trout (*See also* PARKS) and **Rillito River Park**. A free bikeways map produced by the Pima Association of Governments provides bikeways and selected bikeable streets. Look for it at most bicycle stores or write to PAG, 100 North Stone Avenue, Suite 1100, Tucson, AZ 85705, phone 628-5313.

Bike Tours in Southern Arizona by Ed Stiles and Mort Solot will greatly assist you. A compact, excellent guide for the avid biker, it includes maps, mileages, restaurants, motels, museums and other local attractions. The Greater Arizona Bicycling Association sponsors free rides each month and also publishes a newsletter listing rides and other events in Arizona cities. Most bike stores carry free copies, or write to the association, Box 43273, Tucson, AZ 85733. Speedway Bicycles, 3025 East Speedway Blvd. carries the book and newsletter and also provides bicycle rentals.

BOWLING

Several good bowling lanes are found in Tucson. Check the yellow pages for addresses and phone numbers. The members of the Professional Bowlers Association make a stop in Tucson early each summer at Golden Pin Lanes to play the Tucson Open, which celebrated its 27th year in 1988.

GOLF

One of the Old Pueblo's most popular sports is golf. Our winter visitors know they can enjoy golfing any day of the year and our retired population realizes that golf is a sport that can be played all the years of your life.

We regularly host the **Tucson Open,** part of the men's PGA Tour. At this writing, the home of the men's tour is the Tournament Players Club at StarPass, adjacent to Tucson Mountain park on the west side of town. This course, designed by Jack Nicklaus' company, Golforce, features the stadium golf concept, with each hole built to provide spectator viewing. I am not sure this course will remain the tourney location. (*See also* SPECTATOR SPORTS.)

Tucson also hosts the increasingly popular **Circle K LPGA Open,** played at Randolph's north eighteen holes. Both events are sponsored by the Tucson Conquistadores. For further information, call the Conquistadores at 792-4501.

Our public courses, although heavily used, are exceptionally well-maintained. The one disappointment may be during that period when the summer bermuda greens are seeded in winter rye. The person taking your reservations will usually warn you that the course is on temporaries, which means that a patch of fairway has been mowed to serve as a makeshift green until the rye grass has become a decent putting surface.

Information on fourteen public courses follows. Listed opposite each course name is a generalized area location and each course is coded to the map on pages 148-149.

TUCSON PARKS AND RECREATION operates five municipal golf courses. All are full service facilities, open to the public every day of the year. Each course offers a resident P.G.A. professional, lighted driving ranges, practice greens, clubhouse, food and cocktails, pro shop and electric or gas carts. Three of the courses, Randolph North, Randolph South and El Rio are extremely busy at all times.

RESERVATIONS are not required, but may be made seven days in advance. Reservations for weekend play will be accepted on Monday ONLY from valid holders of Tucson Resident passes and City of Tucson Senior Citizen cards. Weekend reservations for non-card golfers are taken on Tue-Fri. Weekday reservations may be made one week in advance. **Call 791-4336.**

RESIDENT CARDS are issued Mon—Fri, 8:30am—4:30pm, at 900 South Randolph Way. The fee is $5 and an Arizona Driver's License with a Tucson address or an Arizona Identification card issued by the Motor Vehicle Division is required. RESIDENT SENIOR CITIZEN GOLF PROGRAM is also available. Phone 791-4873 for information.

MUNICIPAL GOLF COURSES

GREEN FEES: (effective June 1, 1988)
   9 Holes: $7 (Randolph North $.50 extra) ($2 disc with res. pass)
   18 Holes: $12 (Randolph North $1   extra) ($3 disc with res. pass)

Suntan Rates: (Noon—4pm, Mon—Fri)
   9 Holes $3   18 Holes $5.50

Electric/Gas Golf Carts
   9 Holes $7   18 Holes $12

   A.   **El Rio Municipal Golf Course**   **Santa Cruz**
        1400 W. Speedway   Starter: 791-4229
        18 hole, 6,464 yards—70 par

   B.   **Fred Enke Golf Course**   **Pantano—South**
        8250 East Poinciana Drive   Starter: 791-2539
        18 hole, 6,809 yards—par 72

   C.   **Randolph Municipal North Course**   **El Con**
        602 S. Alvernon Way   Starter: 791-4161
        18 hole, 6,893 yards—72 par

D. Randolph Municipal South Course   **El Con**
       602 S. Alvernon Way   Starter: 791-4161
       18 hole, 6,418 yards—70 par

E. Silverbell Golf Course   **Santa Cruz—North**
       3600 N. Silverbell   Starter: 791-4297
       18 hole, 6,264 yards—72 par

SHORTER COURSES FOR BEGINNING AND
SLOWER GOLFERS

F. Dorado Country Club   **Pantano**
       6601 E. Speedway, 885-6751
       18 hole, 3,680 yards—62 par

G. Cliff Valley Golf Course, par 3   **Foothills**
       5910 N. Oracle Road, 887-6161
       18 hole, 2,223 yards—54 par

FURTHER OUT AND LESS CROWDED

H. Arthur Pack Golf Course   **Foothills—West**
       9101 N. Thornydale Road, 744-3322
       18 hole, 6,800 yards—72 par

I.   Santa Rita Golf Course   **Rincons**
       Benson Highway & S. Houghton Road, 623-9556
       18 hole, 3,109 yards—72 par

AT NEARBY COMMUNITIES

J. Canoa Hills Golf Course   **Green Valley**
       1-648-1880 and 791-2049
       18 hole, 6,599 yards—72 par

K. Desert Hills Golf Course   **Green Valley**
       1-625-5090
       18 hole, 6,183 yards—72 par

L. Haven Golf Club   **Green Valley**
       1-625-4281
       18 hole, 6,868 yards—72 par

M. Tubac Valley Country Club   **Tubac**
       Tucson phone 624-5857
       18 hole, 7,151 yards—72 par

A recent trend is for some Tucson resorts to open their courses to the public. This includes:

N. El Conquistador Resort Golf Course   **Foothills**
       10000 North Oracle Road, 297-0404
       9 hole, 3,029 yards—35 par

HORSEBACK RIDING

What better way to enjoy Tucson's picturesque surroundings and relive those stores of the old west? Our numerous, spectacular trails through wilderness areas draw many to horseback riding. Several stables in town rent horses, provide lessons, and have steak rides, hay rides, sunset rides, moonlight rides, breakfast rides and champagne rides.

Prices run from $10/hr to $30 for steak and champagne.

Foothills—West

El Conquistador Stables, 10,000 North Oracle Road, Tucson, AZ 85704, 742-4200. Horse-drawn hayrides available along with breakfast and dinner rides.

Westward Look Resort Stables, 245 East Ina Road, Tucson, AZ 85704, 742-1889 or 742-6283.

Pusch Ridge Stables, 11220 North Oracle Road, Tucson, AZ 85704, 297-6908. Breakfast, sunset, steak, full moon and hayrides; moonlight carriage rides for two.

Tucson Mountains

Tucson Mountain Stables, 6501 W. Ina Road, Tucson, AZ 85743, 744-4407. (East side of Tucson Mountains, 2 miles SW of I-10.) Hayrides, breakfast, dinner and full moon rides.

Rincons

Tanque Verde Trail Rides, 15000 East Reddington Road, Tucson 85619, 749-1515 or 749-2387. The Tanque Verde Guest Ranch is the winter home of the Grand Canyon mules. Being sure-footed and trail-wise, mules are extremely well suited to the rugged terrain of the Tanque Verde area.

SKIING

MOUNT LEMMON
SKI VALLEY
Altitude, 8,250

Open daily/
Snow permitting
Dec 21—Apr 1

Although hard to believe, skiing is just thirty-five miles away and an hour and a half from town, at Mount Lemmon Ski Valley. The season usually starts in late December and runs through early April, depending upon Ol' Man Winter. The quantity and type of snow varies greatly, with powder snow in the early and late parts of the season and packed snow in February and early March. Ski Valley had one year of over 300 inches of snow and also a year or two when they haven't opened at all.

Two rope tows take beginners to gentle slopes while the Heron Double Chair Lift, one-half mile long, takes the more advanced skiers to the moderate and expert slopes, such as the Hot Dawg and Lemmon Drop trails. A ski school operates daily with a professional staff furnishing group and private lessons. Equipment rental is available and a small retail shop also provides waxes, gloves and goggles. Both professional and National Ski Patrols cover the slopes.

A snack bar is located near the chair lift and the **Iron Door Restaurant,** across the road, offers its famous homemade chili and cornbread in a chalet-type atmosphere, or if it's a warm day, you might prefer to eat on the patio and watch the action on the slopes.

Parking is limited and carpooling is suggested. The paved road is plowed by county snowplows, although as chains are sometimes required, it is best to call the Sheriff's office at 882-2800 for current road conditions. (*See also* CAMPING, HIKING AND PICNICKING.)

Mount Lemmon Ski Valley
P.O. Box 612   Ski Report   576-1400
Mount Lemmon, AZ 85619   Office   576-1321

SWIMMING

CITY PARKS   Adults $.50
                                       Kids 17 & younger $.25

As spring turns into summer and the weather gets warm, or should we say pretty darned hot, many Tucsonans head for the nearest swimming hole. Twenty-three public pools are available to help you cool off, usually opening around the first or second week in June and staying open until school begins in the fall. Lessons are available for children and adults.

May of 1988 saw the opening of a 133-foot-long water slide on Tucson's southside, at Freedom Park, 5000 East 29th Street. The city hopes to put slides in other city-owned pools.

Hours vary so best to call the individual pools listed in the blue pages of the telephone directory under Tucson City Government, Parks & Recreation, Swimming Pools or Reid Park, 791-4873.

WATER SPORTS

THE BREAKERS WATERPARK
Foothills—West
8555 West Tangerine Rd.
792-1821

Taller than 48″ $7.95
40—48″ $5.95
Under 40″   Free
Daily 10am—5pm
Mem. Day—Labor Day

The Breakers Family Waterpark advertises itself as "The Beach That's Easy to Reach."

The park's main attractions are the 44,000 square-foot-wavepool (the world's largest), with a maximum depth of six feet and gentle waves that reach 34 feet in height, and two 350-foot long water slides.

Ramada-shaded picnic areas and snack bars provide indoor and outdoor eating. Glass, alcohol and barbecues are not allowed, nor are inner tubes or "boogie" boards. You may bring a raft or rent one at the park. Certified lifeguards are stationed at the pool.

Changing rooms, lockers, a video arcade and a gift shop add to all you might need for a day's excursion.

Drive north on I-10 to Tangerine Road, turn east one-half mile to the entrance.

JUSTIN'S WATER WORLD
Tucson Mountains
3551 South San Joaquin Road
883-8340

Adults $5.95
Kids under 6 free
Thu—Sat & Holidays
   10am—5pm
Late May—Labor Day

Described as a "desert oasis," this 43-acre park includes eight pools and seven giant water slides of varying degrees, including the 275-foot-long, 3-story high White Water Slide, the 250-foot-long, 3-story high Blue Twister Slides; and the 150-foot-long, 3-story high Kamikaze Tunnel. It is estimated that a person reaches a speed of 40mph at the end of this 7.4-second ride!

Picnickers can relax under shaded ramadas, although be sure to bring plastic dishware as no cans or glass containers are allowed in the park, nor are barbecue grills or alcohol.

A snack bar keeps you out of the kitchen and a gift shop and games room are available for those who tire of the water.

Drive west on Ajo Way three miles past Kinney Road and turn north on San Joaquin Road. The park is 2 1/2 miles further, just north of Bopp Road.

SPORTSPARK
6901 North Casa Grande Hwy
West Ina Road & I-10
744-9496

Santa Cruz—North
Adults $8.75

Along with numerous other sports features, Sportspark includes three hydrotube rides, the steepest and fastest of which is "The Whip" a 350-foot ride taken after an eleven flight climb up a 47-foot tower! Not too long ago, I would have tried this one out, but I think I'll let my granddaughters tell me about it instead. Ed Severson, *Arizona Daily Star* journalist said "The first time it feels like you're starring in a burial at see." He also added that the kids love it and some of them can't get enough—screaming all the way down. (*See also* PARKS AND RECREATION.)

TENNIS AND RACQUETBALL

We have over 220 public tennis courts in every area of town and over half of them are lighted. Several private clubs offer excellent tennis opportunities. One of the largest tennis facilities in the country is the Tucson Racquet Club at 4001 North Country Club Road, with thirty-four lighted courts.

Several tennis tournaments are held throughout the year. Check with the Chamber of Commerce or Convention Bureau.

Following are thirteen public courts and nineteen public school courts. The numbers are coded to the map on pages 148-149. Randolph Tennis Center (791-4896) does not take reservations. Himmel Park (791-3276) will, with a $2 surcharge over the regular fee, but they suggest the wait is seldom long. Fees are charged at Randolph, Fort Lowell and Himmel Park courts, all of which have lights.

PUBLIC COURTS

1. **Jacobs Park**   Santa Cruz—North
       3300 North Fairview, at Navajo
       2 light courts

2. **Manzanita Park**   Santa Cruz—South
       5300 W. Nebraska at Westover Rd.
       2 lighted courts

3. **Mission Park**   Santa Cruz—South
       6200 S. 12th Avenue
       2 courts

4. **Kennedy Park**   Tucson Mountains
       Ajo Way at Mission
       2 courts

5. **Himmel Park**   El Con
        100 North Tucson Blvd.
        at 2nd Street, 791-3276
        8 lighted courts

6. **Randolph Tennis Center**   El Con
        100 S. Alvernon Way, 791-4896
        24 courts, 21 lighted
        10 raquetball/handball courts, all lighted

7. **Fort Lowell Park**   Pantano
        2900 N. Craycroft Road, 882-2680
        8 lighted courts

8. **Palo Verde Park**   Pantano
        300 S. Mann
        2 courts

9. **Pantano Park**   Pantano
        400 S. Sarnoff
        1 court

10. **Stefan Gollob Park**   Pantano
        401 South Prudence
        4 lighted courts

11. **Wildwood Park**   Foothills—West
        6201 North Parsley
        1 lighted court

12. **Marana Park**   Marana
        Marana High School
        4 lighted courts

13. **Thomas Park**   Airport
        2945 S. Forgeus
        2 lighted courts

PUBLIC SCHOOL COURTS

14. **Flowing Wells High**   Santa Cruz
        3725 North Flowing Wells Road, 887-1100
        6 courts, 5 lighted

15. **Flowing Wells Jr. High**   Santa Cruz
        4545 North LaCholla Blvd., 887-1100
        6 lighted courts

16. **Pueblo High**   Santa Cruz
        3500 South 12th Avenue, 791-6524
        10 courts

17. **Sunnyside High**   University
        1725 North 2nd Avenue, 791-6700
        12 courts, 4 lighted

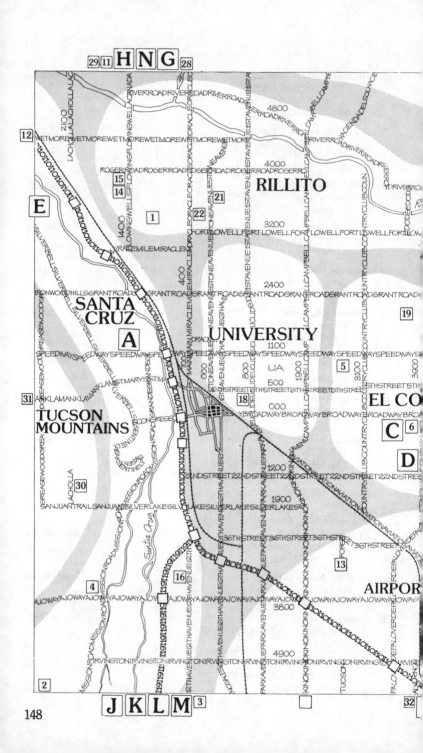

The large free-form ovals, each with an identifying title, delineate specific valley areas to which each subject in the text is referred.

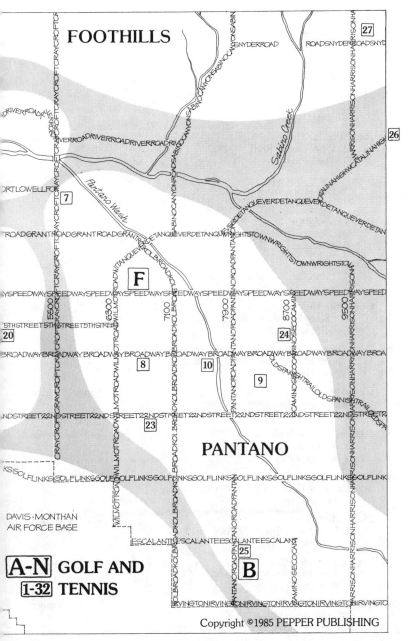

149

18. **Tucson High**   University
    400 North 2nd Avenue, 791-6700
    9 lighted courts

19. **Catalina High**   El Con
    3645 East Pima, 791-6300
    10 lighted courts

20. **Rincon High**   El Con
    422 North Arcadia, 791-6612
    10 courts

21. **Amphitheater High**   Rillito
    125 West Yavapai Road, 887-3183
    12 lighted courts

22. **Amphitheater Jr. High**   Rillito
    315 East Prince Road, 887-3183
    2 lighted courts

23. **Palo Verde High**   Pantano
    1302 South Avenida Vega, 791-6411
    10 lighted courts

24. **Sahuaro High**   Pantano
    545 North Camino Seco, 296-3201
    10 courts

25. **Santa Rita High**   Pantano
    3951 South Pantano Road, 791-6804
    10 courts, 6 lighted

26. **Emily Gray Jr. High**   Foothills—East
    4201 North Melpomene Way, 749-3838
    2 lighted courts

27. **Sabino High**   Foothills—East
    5000 North Bowes Road, 749-5000
    9 courts

28. **Canyon del Oro High**   Foothills—West
    25 West Calle Concordia, 887-3183
    12 lighted courts

29. **Cross Jr. High**   Foothills—West
    1000 West Chapala Drive, 887-3183
    3 lighted courts

30. **Cholla High**   Tucson Mountains
    2001 West 22nd Street, 791-6309
    9 courts

31. **Pima Community College**   Tucson Mountains
    2202 West Anklam Road, 884-6005
    8 lighted courts

32. **Chapparral Jr. High**   Airport
    3700 East Alvord Road, 746-3188
    2 courts

SPECTATOR SPORTS
BASEBALL, BASKETBALL, FOOTBALL

The majority of these three spectator sports involve the UA and our great **WILDCATS**. The UA Wildcats play in the Pacific Athletic Conference, better known as the Pac 10. Loud and loyal fans urge the Cats on against such teams as: UCLA, Washington State, Washington, Oregon, Oregon State, Stanford, UC at Berkeley, University of Southern California and, of course, Tempe Normal (better known as Arizona State University), with whom we have our biggest rivalry. Although if ASU makes it to the finals and we don't, we'll cheer them on to a win.

Games are played at **Arizona Stadium, McKale Center** and **Wildcat Field.** In an effort to eliminate alcohol, a ban on ALL beverage containers or beverage-related containers, such as ice chests and thermoses is in affect. You will not be allowed to enter any of the stadiums with those containers and if your handbag or knapsack appears large enough to contain any such beverages, it will be searched.

ALSO, parking is at a premium (especially at football games) when 14,000 to 50,000 people head for the UA. Plan on arriving early if you do not have a reserved parking space.

UNIVERSITY OF ARIZONA

BASEBALL   Wildcat Field
Tickets/info: 621-2411   Feb—May

Jerry Kendall's **Baseball Cats** have won the national title at the College World Series three times in eleven years: 1976, 1980 and 1986. Even in 1986 after a slow start, they won the necessary NCAA games and went on for that third win in Omaha against Florida State. No other coach has had that kind of success.

When playing at home, the Baseball Cats can be seen at 9,000-seat Wildcat Field, just south of McKale Center.

BASKETBALL   McKale Center
Tickets/info: 621-2411   Dec—Mar

After the 1987-88 basketball season, Lute Olsen's **Basket Cats** have *the* place in Tucson's Hall of Fame. Even those Tucsonans whose previous thoughts had never turned to basketball became fans of one of the greatest teams the UA has nurtured. We won the Pac 10 conference with thirty-five wins and three losses. And with the roar of "Ste-e-e-ve Ker-r-r" being heard on television sets throughout the nation, we went to the NCAA Final Four in Kansas City. We didn't come back with the national championship, but you couldn't tell that from the reception the team received when they came home.

It was a wonderful year and we think 1988-89 will be even better. Tickets will be as rare as icebergs in the Rillito, if at all available. The basketball games (played from December through March) are held in 14,000 seat McKale Center, located on McKale Drive, just west of Campbell and north of East 6th Street.

FOOTBALL
Tickets/info: 621-2411

Arizona Stadium
Sep—Nov

Coach Dick Tomey and the **Football Cats** also played great last year with four wins, four losses and three ties. Football is played in 57,000-seat Arizona Stadium located at East 6th Street and North Cherry Avenue. Most games are night games (it's still pretty hot in September and October) and are played from September through November.

PROFESSIONAL BASEBALL

CLEVELAND INDIANS
El Con
Reid Park/Hi Corbett Field
900 South Randolph Way

Tickets 325-2621
Admission charge
Mar—Apr

The American League's Cleveland Indians make Tucson their home for their spring-training sessions. You can see them play such teams as the San Francisco Giants, Milwaukee Brewers and San Diego Padres.

Enter at Randolph Way, (between Country Club and Alvernon Way) from either Broadway or 22nd Street.

TUCSON TOROS
El Con
Reid Park/Hi Corbett Field
900 South Randolph Way

Tickets 791-4906
Admission charge
Apr—Aug

The Tucson Toros, a Class AAA Pacific Coast League affiliate of the National League's Houston Astros, make their home in Tucson. Games are scheduled from April through August at Hi Corbett Field.

GOLF

Tucson's PGA tourney epitomizes my frustration in trying to keep *This is Tucson* current. Since I began record keeping, the tourney's name has changed six times, with the newest, coming up in 1989, of the **Tucson Open.** To add to my confusion, tournament play changed from January to fall and now, for 1989, back to January again.

Also, in previous years, the tournament course was Randolph's north eighteen holes. In 1987 play was at the Tournament Players Club at StarPass. Designed by Jack Nicklaus' company, Golforce, it features the stadium golf concept, with each hole built to provide spectator viewing. However, it is thought to be too far out of town by many and consideration is being given to moving the tourney back to Randolph's north eighteen holes!

I believe you can plan on the 1989 tournament being played at StarPass, but Corky Simpson, *Citizen* Sports Columnist is pushing for moving it back to Randolph, a much more accessible location for everyone. Hang in there, at least it's not been just the same old thing all the time!

Whatever happens, **The Tucson Conquistadores** sponsor the PGA and the LPGA every year. (I'm assuming this won't change.) The women's tournament is known as the **Circle K LPGA Open** and is usually in the spring. For information and tickets call the Conquistadores at 792-4501 or the Chamber of Commerce.

GREYHOUND RACING

TUCSON GREYHOUND PARK
South 4th
South 4th Avenue at 36th Street
884-7576

Admission charge
Year-round except
July 5—August 5

The greyhounds race in Tucson year-round with a month off from approximately July 5th to August 5th and two weeks off during the Christmas holidays.

The Clubhouse has reserved seats with restaurant service or grandstand seats where you can snack on hot dogs, popcorn and beer. (Reservations for the Clubhouse are a must.)

For information on racing dates, post time, reservations and bus service, check the newspapers or call 884-7576.

HORSE RACING

RILLITO DOWNS
4504 North First Avenue

Admission charge
Winter

Although it had been closed to racing since 1982, a section of Rillito Downs was entered into the National Register of Historic Places in 1986. The chute concept of racing quarter horses was developed at Rillito Downs and that 660-yard straightaway chute (built in 1943) received the designation. It was at Rillito that regulated quarterhorse pari-mutuel betting was first permitted and during the 1940s and '50s the track carried the title of "Quarter Horse Capital of the World." Rillito's historical background also includes the pioneering of the electronic timing device that led to modern photo-finish equipment.

A short racing period was held in 1987-88 and hopes are high for future quarter horse and thoroughbred racing. For information, call the Chamber of Commerce or the Convention Bureau.

SONOITA HORSE RACES
Santa Cruz County Fairgrounds

Admission charge
Sonoita, AZ

Quarterhorse and thoroughbred racing are held the last weekend in April and the first weekend in May. May's weekend includes a racing day combined with the Kentucky Derby. The races are part of the Santa Cruz County Fair and include betting on the Kentucky Derby itself. Mint Juleps are available and you can pretend you're sitting in bluegrass country urging on your favorite.

POLO

PIMA COUNTY POLO CLUB
Mariposa Field
624-1389

Rincons
Nominal charge
Jan 1—Apr 15

The Pima County Polo Club holds it tournaments from just after the first of the year until tax day. Practice begins a month or so before hand. Both match and tournament games are held Sat and Sun. I'm told plans are in the works for resurrecting the old UA Polo Team, once a stalwart of polo teams in the U.S.

Take Tanque Verde Road 1 1/4 miles past Bear Canyon. Turn south on Bonanza Road. Signs will direct you further.

RUGBY

ESTEVAN PARK
1000 North Main

Santa Cruz
Oct—Apr

Rugby began in Tucson in 1969 and numerous fans enjoy the games played at Estevan Park, located north of downtown, just south of the intersection of Speedway and Main Streets.

Halloween brings us the Michelob-Continental Rugby Classic Schedule, which enjoyed its 14th year in 1988. Played at Hi Corbett Field, tickets are available at Tucson Optimist Clubs, the McKale Ticket Office, through youth athletic groups and through Tucson's four rugby clubs.

ADDITIONAL SPECTATOR SPORTS

Tucson's sunny, year-round weather encourages a number of spectator sports, from tennis and golf to numerous university and junior college athletic programs.

The **UA Wildcats,** members of the Pac-10 Conference, not only play baseball, basketball and football, but field varsity teams in many men's and women's sports. These sports include swimming, golf, tennis, track, volleyball and field events. The **UA Icecats,** members of the Pacific Intercollegiate Hockey Conference, play home games at the Tucson Convention Center with the season running from early November through early March. For information on any of the preceding, call the ticket office at McKale Center, 621-2411 or Media Relations, 621-4163.

Pima Community College also offers varsity competition in cross country, archery, baseball, basketball, track, wrestling and golf. Both men's and women's varsity teams compete. For information, call 884-6005.

The Tucson Convention Center features many events throughout the year, including professional hockey games and basketball. Call them at 791-4266.

Sabino Canyon

THE GREAT OUTDOORS

Tucson's desert beauty is complemented by the majesty and grandeur of the mountain ranges surrounding our city. Like stalwart guardians, the Catalinas, Rincons, Santa Ritas and Tucson Mountain encircle Tucson, while in the distance can be seen the Tortolitas, Whetstones, Huachucas and Sierritas. It is but an hour's drive north or south to leave cholla, palo verde and creosote and be in juniper, piñon and ponderosa pine country, with accompanying weather changes. Our mountains provide not only summer and winter playgrounds, but contribute greatly, with their runoff, to the table of groundwater on which Tucson's life depends.

This beauty entices many to "head for the hills" but I recommend you take a few precautions while hiking in those hills. First of all, take a buddy. Wise scuba divers always have a diving buddy and hikers should follow the same rule. Accidents do happen and having a friend to get help may save your life. Notify someone where you will be going, what route you're taking and when you plan to return. If you're not back when expected, help can be summoned.

Summertime and our heat can be dangerous, especially for those not prepared. The most important item to carry is water. Even if not thirsty, you should drink at least a gallon a day. It is very easy to become dehydrated, which is dangerous and painful. A hat, appropriate walking shoes and periodic applications of sunscreen should be a given. Pack a small signal mirror. Getting lost is no fun, but it happens every year to numerous campers and the flash from a mirror can be seen over 40 miles away. If you do get lost, stay put and be prepared to signal at correct times. (*See also* SUMMERTIME—AND ITS PROBLEMS.)

Summer also brings out numerous "critters," including rattlesnakes. Don't stick your hands or feet in spaces you can't see. If bitten, get to first aid as quickly as possible. Elevate the wound and do not treat with ice, incising or tight tourniquets. A light constricting band may be applied above the wound.

Although it may be quite warm in Tucson, expect sharp climatic changes if driving into the nearby high mountains, especially in the wintertime. Summer temperatures will be approximately 30° cooler than in Tucson. Take along a sweater or jacket and be prepared for rain in the summer and snow in the winter; and year 'round don't forget to take extra water.

CAMPING, HIKING AND PICNICKING

North

CATALINA STATE PARK   Day fee $3/car
11570 North Oracle (U.S. Highway 89)   Night fee $5/car
9 miles northwest of town   628-5798

This 5,500-acre preserve proves what can be accomplished with perseverance and a lot of hard work. When developers tried to rezone this area to house a community of 17,000, environmentalists and outdoor enthusiasts formed a coalition; after a ten-year effort and approval by voters of a bond issue, the land was acquired and in May of 1983 dedicated as a state park.

This dense part of the desert includes a mesquite bosque which provides shelter for much of the park's bird population, including golden eagles and peregrine falcons. Pusch Ridge, to the south, is the home of about seventy desert bighorn sheep.

Numerous trails include a special 1-mile nature loop built with birders in mind that winds through the mesquite bosque. Tucson's Audubon Society regularly schedules walks here; phone 629-0510.

The best time to visit the park is from September to May. As the elevations range only from 2,650 to 3,000 feet, it will be hot in the summer. If it is too hot, head up the trail to Romero Canyon where you will find pools shaded by sycamore and oak. Do bring drinking water.

A trail map is available at the visitor center near the entrance to the park. Trails are open to horses (except the nature trail) and a corral and parking area is available for horse trailers. Pusch Ridge Stables, one-half mile south of the entrance rents horses; contact them at 11220 North Oracle Road, Tucson 85704, 297-6908. Other nearby stables are at the Sheraton El Conquistador and Westward Look resorts. (*See also* HORSEBACK RIDING.)

The Hohokam once farmed this area and pit houses and ball court ruins are found amidst the verdant growth. Water and toilet facilities and nearly 100 picnic tables and grills are included with the fifty-five camping spaces. Quiet hour for campers is 10pm. Wood fires are forbidden; be sure to bring charcoal.

As the paved road is very short, don't plan on driving through in your car to sightsee. You must park your car and get out and hike. Although only four miles of roads are paved, the more than seven miles of hiking trails lead to numerous waterfalls and pools; to Sabino

Canyon, sixteen miles on the other side of the mountain; and to the top of Mount Lemmon. The park manager has said, Mount Lemmon is "only 12.6 miles away, but about 6,000 feet up."

PEPPERSAUCE CANYON

This canyon, on the back side of Mount Lemmon, is approximately a 90-minute drive from the northern edge of Tucson. Take highway 89 north and then highway 77 to Oracle (which, incidentally, was once the home of Buffalo Bill Cody). Past Oracle follow the signs to a five-mile dirt road leading into the mouth of the canyon. Although a steep, winding road, it is passable for ordinary vehicles.

The 4,400-foot altitude brings some snow in the winter and temperatures in the 90's in the summer. However, the large amount of shelter provided by the black walnut, sycamore and oak trees keeps the climate comfortable. A no-fee campground provides running water and toilets.

Approximately two miles from the campground is **Peppersauce Cave,** a well-known haven for local spelunkers. A large cavern inside the cave is forty feet high, however, the only way to enter the cave is through a twenty-inch opening or by using ropes to descend from above. Caution is urged for the inexperienced adventurer.

The road continues up the back side of the Catalinas. It is not maintained and becomes barely navigable by four-wheel drive vehicles shortly after you leave the canyon.

PICACHO PEAK	Day use	$3
45 miles northwest of Tucson	Park & sleep	$5
1-466-3183	Tent sites	$6
	With electricity	$8

Erupting out of the desert to an altitude of 2,000 feet, you can see this spire for miles. It is an attractive area, particulary in February and March, when winter rains have encouraged the desert flowers to bloom their bright yellow, orange and blue colors. Tucsonans frequently make the drive just to enjoy the wildflowers in their burst of color.

The 3,400-acre park provides picnic tables, both primitive and RV camping (with electric hookups), drinking water, showers, rest rooms and barbecue grills. Several nature study and hiking trails are included, one of which leads to the summit of the peak. Peregrine falcons, redtailed hawks and other native birds and animals make their home at the peak, along with about forty-five head of Sicilian miniature burros who were imported to the area before the park was established.

The only civil war battle in the State of Arizona and the westernmost battle, occurred near Picacho Peak in April of 1862, when Union troups lost three men. The battle is re-enacted each spring at Black Mountain just north of the park.

To reach the peak, drive north on I-10 through Marana and Red Rock.

SABINO CANYON   **Foothills**
North Sabino Canyon Road

Located in the foothills of the Catalinas, only thirteen miles from downtown Tucson, Sabino Canyon is an ideal retreat for either a quick picnic or an all-day visit with cottonwoods, sycamores, ash and willows providing shaded sanctuary among the quiet pools fed by Sabino Creek. In the second century, A.D., Hohokam Indians built irrigation dams along the creek but now the creek tumbles over cascading waterfalls and under arched stone bridges, built in the 1930s by C.C.C. workers.

Numerous picnic spots and trails are available. A favorite of Tucsonans is the 4 1/2 mile round trip hike to Seven Falls that takes about three hours round trip. This not-too-strenuous climb begins at Lower Bear Canyon Picnic Ground and terminates at a singularly picturesque setting. The waters of Sabino Creek cascade over a series of rock formations into a large, tranquil pool that has been rated as one of the best natural swimming holes in the U.S.

Another more accesssible swimming hole is not too far up Sabino Canyon, one that was also enjoyed by the pony soldiers from Fort Lowell in the 1870s.

The area is closed to automobile traffic, allowing travel only by bicycle, horseback, shuttle bus or shanks' mare. The shuttle, an open air tram, makes a round trip of about seven and a half miles through Upper Sabino Canyon. You'll cross over nine one-way bridges before reaching the top, providing delightful views at every turn. An informative talk, given by the driver, will apprise you of the vegetation and natural history of the area. You may alight anywhere along the way and return on a later tram, or walk down, if you wish. A shuttle bus is also available for Bear Canyon.

During the full moon, April through December, romantic moonlit rides are available by reservation. Steering only by the light of the moon, you'll see silver saguaros standing as sentries along the route and hear owls hooting their nighttime songs. The moonlit reflections of trees and rocks in the tranquil pools add enchantment to an already bewitching location. The rides fill quickly, so call ahead several days for reservations.

Drinking water is not available in either Upper Sabino Canyon or in Bear Canyon. You are advised to carry an adequate supply. No pets or guns are allowed in the canyon. No glassware of any kind is permitted: no bottles or drinking glasses and no overnight camping is allowed.

To reach Sabino Canyon, take Tanque Verde Road east to Sabino Canyon Road; turn north, the entrance to the canyon is only 4.5 miles. From the north and west, take Sunrise Drive which ends at the Sabino Canyon Visitor Center.

Sabino Canyon Visitor Center
8am—4:30pm
Tucson, AZ 85715
749-3223

Sabino Canyon Tours, Inc.
Route 15—Box 280
Tucson, AZ 85715
749-2861 Info/Tour schedule
749-2327 Moonlight res.

The **Sabino Canyon Shuttle Bus** runs every 30 minutes from 9am—4:30pm (Adults $4, kids 3—12 $1.25, under 3, free). The **Bear Canyon Shuttle Bus** runs hourly from 9am—4pm (Adults $2, kids $1). Buses operate daily and the round trip through Upper Sabino Canyon takes 45 minutes. Shuttle personnel will assist the disabled and have a means of transferring individuals to a wheelchair for the ride through the canyon. Please call for specifics.

If coming from the south, you might wish to stop at the **Hidden Valley Inn,** 4825 North Cabino Canyon Road and pick up a picnic lunch or have some mesquite-broiled steaks or ribs. It's more than just a restaurant, sort of an Old Tucson—East. You'll find old-time buggies, covered wagons and thousands of carved miniatures in a replica of the Cole Brothers Circus.

Northeast

SANTA CATALINA MOUNTAINS

Road Construction Hotline: 749-3329

Thirty-four miles and an hour away from Speedway and Wilmot, you can enjoy the same flora, fauna and climatic conditions as our far-away neighbors in Canada. It is a fact that every 1,000 feet of elevation in the Sonoran Desert is equal to traveling 300 miles closer to the north pole. As the Santa Catalina range towers above Tucson at 9,000 feet it's the same as being 2,100 miles north of Tucson.

Both the range and its most famous peak, **Mount Lemmon,** were named for women. Father Kino named the mountains after his sister, Catarina, which later became Catalina, and Mount Lemmon was named after Sara Lemmon, a woman who spent her honeymoon climbing the north side of the range on horseback. Her diary described mountain lions, bobcats, bears and wild parrots.

As the highest mountain in the range, Mount Lemmon reaches skyward 9,157 feet. You'll find a lake, campgrounds, picnic grounds, meadows full of wild flowers, cool dark forests and over 150 miles of improved trails for hiking. You probably won't see any wild parrots but you will see many species of hummingbirds AND numerous raucus Steller's jays. Once-in-awhile a mountain lion has been known to wander into town, but more likely you'll see only skunks and squirrels chasing around the trees with maybe a fox or deer in the distance.

WARNING: Most of the two-lane road is built on a narrow ledge along mountain slopes with numerous sharp curves and limited visibility of oncoming traffic. As one of the more dangerous roads in Arizona, it is wise to follow the posted 35mph speed limit. Road improvements begun in 1988 will continue during every even-numbered year for eighteen years. During this construction, you may find the road closed for several hours at a time, or if open, incur minimal delays. The road will be open Fridays, Saturdays and Sundays. Call the Mount Lemmon Highway Reconstruction Hotline, 749-3329, for hours of closings. Also, there are no service stations on Mount Lemmon, so refuel before leaving town.

Drive east on Tanque Verde Road and turn north on the Catalina Highway. From this intersection to Summerhaven is 29.5 miles. Shortly you'll find yourself in 4,500-foot high Molino Basin campground, with scrub oak, cottonwoods, willows and ashes and if you're sharp-eyed, you may see raccoons, turtles and flitting hummingbirds. Hundreds of years ago the Hohokam used this area as a campground.

As you continue climbing, the low shrubs and manzanita will be replaced by junipers and piñon pines and you'll begin to see those bright blue Steller's jays. Numerous Arizona cypress grow at Bear Canyon and the tallest cypress ever recorded is near the canyon crossing. Both Bear Canyon, and General Hitchcock Camp nearby are forests of juniper and oak. If you see a squirrel with a large, fluffy tail it is probably an Abert squirrel.

Approaching Windy Point Vista, you'll notice large outcroppings of granite growing out of the mountain and overhanging the hills. The elevation here is 6,600 feet and the view of the Tucson valley and ten mountain ranges in the distance is spectacular. If it's a very clear day, you should be able to pick out the twin towers of Mission San Xavier thirty miles to the southwest. Nightime views, with the lights of Tucson twinkling in the distance, are particularly beautiful.

Shortly past Windy Point is Geology Vista Point, with explanations of how the mountain was created many eons ago. This is also an excellent spot to view the Rincon Mountains to the east.

At 7,000 feet, you'll be in ponderosa pine country and just after milepost 17, you'll see the turnoff to Rose Canyon Lake. A large campground provides spaces for trailers and mobile homes and the 11-acre lake is stocked with trout. Unless you're under 14, you'll need a fishing license. (See also FISHING AND BOATING.)

San Pedro Vista, a little further up the road offers a wonderful view of the San Pedro Valley with the river in the distance—another side of the mountain.

Just before milepost 20 and the Palisade Ranger Station is Organization Ridge, the location of summer homes and campgrounds of scout and church groups. The air begins to become cooler and thinner with White and Douglas fir trees mingling with the pines. There are more campgrounds, some with springtime streams. In the summertime, you'll find columbine and wild roses blooming and with a sharp eye you may find wild blackberries.

Spencer Canyon Campground is near milepost 21 at an elevation of 7,700 feet. One of the larger campgrounds on the mountain, the area is closed in the winter.

Bear Wallow picnic ground, a favorite retreat of the Audubon Society, is located after milepost 22 at 7,600 feet. Birders have recorded sightings of nearly 200 species. As you continue your climb, you'll pass numerous summer home areas and campgrounds and soon, to your right, (after milepost 25) is the 1.5 mile road to Mount Lemmon Ski Valley.

The Iron Door Restaurant (576-1400), across from the ski run, offers lunch and early dinners. If the weather is good, the outdoor terrace is a pleasant spot to enjoy refreshments and a view of the ski slopes. The lift runs when weather permits and is a great way to enjoy the exceptional views of the surrounding mountains and forests. The round-trip ride takes about twenty-five minutes. (See also SKIING.)

Just past the turnoff to Ski Valley is **Summerhaven,** the year-round home of a number of families and the summer home to many Tucsonans who retreat to the cooler air every year. Here you will find **The Alpine Inn** with its grocery store, restaurant and pub. (Try their Alpine Bavarian Grill—it's wonderful.) They also operate as a Bed and Breakfast if you wish to spend more than just a day on the mountain. (Call 576-1500 for reservations.)

There are rental cabins, however their availability is unpredictable. Check listings in the business white pages of the Tucson phone book under Mount Lemmon cabin rentals.

Several shops offer a variety of gift items. On the left is **Timeless Treasures,** with antiques and collectibles and **Kimball Springs** offers a country theme with crafts, toys, gifts and old fashioned rock candy. **The Living Rainbow** is on the right, a little further down the road. Debbie Vought has books and cards along with unique handmade items, including pottery, windchimes and crystals.

Less than a mile further on is the road leading to Marshall Gulch, one of the loveliest picnic areas on the mountain. Picnic tables, grills and toilets are available. Also, several hiking trails begin from this area.

Both the novice and the expert will find many miles of hiking trails. An excellent guide for hikers is *Trail Guide to the Santa Catalina Mountains* by Pete Cowgill and Eber Glendening.

Wintertime brings little snow to Tucson, but there is a ski run in the Catalinas and that means a lot of snow, which means the road to Mount Lemmon can be impassable, or at least chains will be required. The road is usually cleared quickly, but if we have had bad weather, contact the Pima County Sheriff's Department for road conditions before you start.

Santa Catalina Ranger District
Mt. Lemmon Info: 749-2855
Sabino Canyon Info: 749-3223

Road Conditions
Pima County Sheriff
882-2800

Mount Lemmon Ski Valley
576-1400

The Alpine Inn
576-1500

ROY P. DRACHMAN—
AGUA CALIENTE PARK
4002 North Soldier's Trail
(Between East Prince & East Limberlost Roads)

Rincons
882-2680
COUNTY PARK

Orange groves, native fan palms and a bosque of mesquite trees growing around four spring-fed lakes make this a true desert oasis, preserved in its natural state. Known for its wildlife, you'll also see ducks, birds and maybe a heron or two, along with fish swimming in the lagoon.

This ancient Hohokam site, and in the 1800s a cattle ranch, includes several picnic areas, with tables, grills and water available. Reservations are necessary on the weekends and there is a charge; on weekdays there is no charge and tables are available on a first-come, first-served basis. Equipment for lawn games is provided by the park staff.

This is a quiet park, more for contemplation and relaxation than for the sports-minded. There is a volleyball court and horseshoe pits, but you'll not find softball diamonds and soccer fields.

One- to three-day arts and crafts workshops are held in a building on the property. For information on workshops, or to reserve a picnic table, call 882-2680.

East

THE RINCON MOUNTAINS

The three major peaks of the Rincon Mountains east of Tucson, are: Tanque Verde Peak, Rincon Peak and Mica Mountain, the highest elevation at 8,666 feet, and the mountain you see when driving east on Speedway. The one outstanding feature of the Rincons is that there are no roads. Over seventy trails, winding through 58,000 acres of wilderness, provide some rugged hiking. Day hikers have no restrictions, however backpackers need a permit, which is free.

The closest you can drive to the Rincons by car is:

**SAGUARO NATIONAL
MONUMENT—EAST**
296-8576

    ♿ $3/vehicle $1/person
Daily 8am—sundown

Saguaro National Monument is divided into two segments, on opposite sides of Tucson. The Rincon Mountain unit, containing 99 square miles, was established in 1933, and is the oldest of the two units. Several picnic areas are provided and Cactus Forest Drive, a scenic nine-mile loop road, takes you through the lush vegetation of the monument.

The saguaro is unique to the Sonora Desert, towering to heights of fifty feet or more and living to the ripe old age of nearly 200 years. May or June will find the ends of the saguaros covered with white flowers and the blooms, which are the state flower, give the impression of elegant white hats. The ripe fruit produced each year is harvested by the O'odham and Pima Indians.

Many other types of desert vegetation are found in the monument, along with javelinas (wild pigs), coyotes, bobcats, foxes, badgers, Gila monsters, snakes and the desert tortoise.

A quarter-mile wheelchair accessible tour, with plants labeled for easy identification, provides access for the disabled. Numerous programs and guided tours are offered at various times. Check with the monument personnel for schedules.

Picnic grounds, rest rooms and barbecue grills are available, but no water and no camping allowed. A visitor center at the entrance includes dioramas and exhibits showing the geological, botanical and human history of the monument. To reach the monument, drive east on Old Spanish Trail, about five miles from the intersection of Broadway and Old Spanish Trail.

If visiting the monument around lunch or dinnertime, you may wish to stop at **Saguaro Corners Restaurant** just across the road. At their unique location, you'll find large picture windows overlooking watering holes and may, while enjoying a meal, see anything from coyotes and rabbits to javelinas or bobcats.

South

SANTA RITA MOUNTAINS

Located south of Tucson, the Santa Ritas include 9,453 foot Mt. Wrightson (also known as Mt. Baldy), the highest peak near Tucson, along with a summer retreat known as:

MADERA CANYON

To reach Madera Canyon, which is about fifteen degrees cooler than Tucson in the summertime, drive south on I-19 to Green Valley, then take state route 93 through Continental to the Madera turnoff. Only twelve miles southeast of Green Valley, the road is a very gradual climb, favored by those who don't enjoy the usual steep mountain roads.

You will find two picnic areas and a campground, at Bog Springs, for which there is a charge. Over seventy miles of hiking trails provide varying lengths and difficulties, including an eight-mile hike to the summit of Mt. Wrightson. The forest is made up of oak, juniper and sycamore trees, with Ponderosa pine, fir and aspen in the higher elevations. Trail maps can be purchased at the Continental Store in Continental and at the Nogales Ranger District Station, 2480 Tucson-Nogales Highway in Nogales, AZ.

The canyon is a wildlife refuge that becomes home to over 200 species of birds in the summertime, along with thousands of birders who haunt the canyon to view those birds. Included are owls, hawks, eagles, and twelve hummingbird species. Deer, fox, bobcats, mountain lions, squirrels, coyotes and black bear also make their home in the canyon.

Sadly, one of those mountain lions created a stir in May of 1988 when it attacked several dogs who were accompanying their hiking masters along Old Baldy Trail. When the cougar grabbed and ran away with his miniature schnauzer, one hiker chased the cat, hitting it with his walking stick and a rock, before the cat dropped his dog. The dog survived after a trip to the vet's, however another dog wasn't so lucky.

As it was believed the cat wasn't a threat to humans, immediate plans were to let the cat alone, however after another hiker opened his eyes during meditation and found a cat sitting 20 feet away staring at him, and then had her stalk him as he backed down the trail, a mountain hunter from New Mexico was called in. Numerous letters to the editor protested this decision, but several days later a young cougar was killed. The conflict between nature and civilization goes on.

Santa Rita Lodge, in the canyon, offers rooms and cabins, all with kitchenettes. Reservations are suggested year-round, but particularly during the busy summer season; many birders make reservations a year in advance. For information, call 1-625-8746.

PATAGONIA LAKE STATE PARK

This 600-acre park provides primitive and R.V. camping with hookups, picnic areas, a swimming beach and the largest recreational lake in southern Arizona. It's located 70 miles southeast of Tucson. For further information see FISHING AND BOATING.

West

TUCSON MOUNTAIN PARK

Managed by the Pima County Parks and Recreation Department, this 17,000-acre high desert and mountain area west of town includes not only the Arizona-Sonora Desert Museum and Old Tucson, but many miles of hiking and riding trails, picnic sites and a campground. To reach the area, drive west to Kinney Road, either from Gates Pass or Ajo Way and on toward the Arizona-Sonora Desert Museum. (Those who are driving a large motor home, or towing a trailer of any size, should take the Ajo-Kinney Road route to the park; Gates Pass has a very steep, narrow road leading into the valley.)

These mountains are quite different from the other ranges and not nearly as high, with Wasson Peak being the top elevation at 4,687 feet. But, in many ways, the Tucson Mountains are much more dramatic with their sharp, volcanic peaks, their sparse desert vegetation and a number of prehistoric Indian petroglyphs throughout the area. In early spring of 1988 a hiker found part of a huge leg bone thought to be from a hadrosaur, a type of duck-billed dinosaur that lived sometime between 65 million and 200 million years ago. Other identifiable parts found include two knees and a few vertebrae.

Ocotillo, palo verde, mesquite and many saguaro populate the landscape. Very little natural water is found, but a riot of color transpires when the wildflowers bloom after a rainy winter. The area is exceedingly representative of our desert and great for winter and spring picnics, with April being an ideal month to visit and enjoy the frequent desert blooms. A charge is made for the Gilbert Ray campground and all day-use sites close at 10pm. Alcoholic beverages are prohibited by law and the area is patrolled.

SAGUARO NATIONAL MONUMENT—WEST
883-6366

 ♿ Admission free

The western section of Saguaro National Monument is located two miles beyond the Desert Museum, off Kinney Road. These magnificent cacti sometimes reach an age of 200 years and grow to a height of fifty feet. They are protected by state law and by the National Park Service. The O'odham and Pima Indians of our region have permission to harvest the saguaro's sweet fruits in the early summer continuing a tradition of many generations.

This 24-square-mile site contains a much more vigorous forest of young saguaros than those on the eastern side of Tucson. You might also find javelina, coyote, deer and bobcats. Note how many of the saguaro grow adjacent to a palo verde. Saguaros are quite tender to the sun when they are young and must have protection, tending to root in the shade of a palo verde or other stronger desert plant.

The six-mile Bajada Loop Drive wanders past two picnic areas and Indian pictographs on canyon walls. A twelve-mile dirt road leads to four picnic areas and over sixteen miles of hiking trails. Picnic areas include tables, shelters, restrooms and barbecue grills, but you'll need your own firewood; and the only water is in the visitor center. Self-guided auto and nature trails are provided, along with a short, wheelchair-accessible trail.

A slide program and talk about the surrounding area is given at 7:30pm Saturdays, at the Gilbert Ray campgrounds in Tucson Mountain Park.

CLEVELAND INDIANS
Reid Park/Hi Corbett Field
900 South Randolph Way   Admission charge

The American League's Cleveland Indians make Tucson their home for their spring-training sessions. Enter Randolph Way, which is midway between Country Club and Alvernon Way, from either 22nd Street or Broadway.

For ticket and game information, call (602) 325-2621.

SPRING/SUMMER

TUCSON TOROS
Reid Park/Hi Corbett Field   Admission charge
900 South Randolph Way   April—August

The Tucson Toros, a Class AAA Pacific Coast League affiliate of the National League's Houston Astros, make their home in Tucson. Games are scheduled from April through August at Hi Corbett Field. For information, call (602) 791-4096.

ADDITIONAL SPECTATOR SPORTS

Tucson's sunny, year-round weather encourages a number of spectator sports, from tennis and golf, to numerous university and junior college athletic programs.

The UA Wildcats, members of the Pac-10 Conference, not only play football, basketball and baseball, but field varsity teams in many men's and women's sports. These sports include swimming, golf, tennis, track, volleyball and field events. The **UA Icecats**, members of the Pacific Intercollegiate Hockey Conference, play home games at the Tucson Community Center with the season running from early November through early March. For information on any of the preceding, call the ticket office at McKale Center, (602) 621-2411 or Media Relations, (602) 621-4163.

Pima Community College also offers varsity competition in cross country, archery, baseball, basketball, track, wrestling and golf. Both men's and women's varsity teams compete. For information, call (602) 884-6005.

The Tucson Community Center features many events throughout the year, including professional hockey games and basketball. Call them at (602) 791-4266.

SANCTUARY COVE   **Tucson Mountains**
744-2375   Daily 8am—sunset

Bounded on the south and west by Saguaro National Monument, the Cove is a spiritual sanctuary open to the public. Numerous trails through the surrounding 80 acres provide extraordinary views of the Santa Catalina and Tortolita mountain ranges. Amid numerous cacti, you'll find towering saguaros, wildflowers and a variety of birds. A small stone chapel is open all day offering a meditative atmosphere for the purpose of spiritual meditation and retreat.

Picnics, horses, alcohol, dogs and mountain climbing are prohibited. Bring your own drinking water.

To reach the cove, take I-10 to the Ina Road exit and turn west to Silverbell Road. Turn right and follow the signs to Pima Farms Road. Turn left on Pima Farms Road and left again on Scenic Drive to the entrance.

FISHING AND BOATING

Although Southern Arizona is officially a desert, several lakes in Tucson's urban area and others within a day's drive offer seasonally excellent fishing. All lakes are stocked by the Arizona Game and Fish Department and are stocked during the warmer months. For current fishing conditions, consult the weekly Friday fishing report in the local Tucson newspapers' Sports and Outdoors sections.

Everyone 14 years or older must have an Urban Fishing Permit for fishing in Kennedy, Silverbell or Lakeside Lakes. This license is good for one year. The daily bag and possession limit is four trout and four catfish. Unlicensed juveniles under 14 years may take two trout and four catfish. State fishing limits apply on other species. Reid Park fishing intended only for kids under 14. Permits are available at marina store.

Everyone fourteen years or older must have an Arizona Fishing License for fishing in rural lakes. This license may be purchased for one day, five days, nine days or a year.

Arizona licenses are available at most sporting-goods stores, fishing tackle shops and most rural park concessionaires. Urban Fishing Permits are sold at sporting goods stores near the lakes and both state licenses and urban permits are available from the Game and Fish office at 555 North Greasewood Road. For further information, call the Arizona Game and Fish Department, 628-5376.

TUCSON URBAN FISHING

Four lakes within the urban vicinity of Tucson offer fishing: Lakeside, Kennedy, Silverbell and Reid Park. Kennedy, Lakeside and Silverbell are stocked with rainbow trout from November to March and with channel catfish from April to October. Bluegill are common and occasional catches of largemouth bass are reported.

KENNEDY LAKE   Tucson Mountains
Mission and Ajo Roads   Sunrise—10:30pm

J. F. Kennedy Park has a 10-acre lake for fishing and boating without motors, with a maximum boat size of 14 feet and a maximum canoe size of 17 feet during daylight hours only. A lot of sailboat action occurs on weekends and anglers can catch trout in the winter and channel catfish, largemouth bass, tilapia and bluegill during summer months. Snack bar and boat rentals are available. No campfires or open fires along shoreline. No swimming or wading allowed. No dogs allowed in lake.

Drive west on Ajo to Mission Road. Parking access from Mission Road or La Cholla Boulevard.

LAKESIDE LAKE
Lakeside Park   **Pantano**
Stella and Sarnoff Roads   Sunrise—10:30pm

Lakeside Park includes a 14-acre landscaped lake and island bird shelter, a soccer field, lighted ramadas and picnic tables. The lake is stocked in winter with trout and in the summer with channel catfish.

Maximum boat length 14 feet, maximum canoe length 17 feet during daylight hours only. Electric trolling motors up to 1 hp may be used. Gasoline motors are prohibited. No swimming or wading. No campfires or open fires along shoreline.

Drive east on Golf Links Road (located one mile south of 22nd Street) to Pantano Road. Turn south, drive one-half mile to Stella and east on Stella to the park.

SILVERBELL LAKE
Silverbell Park, Silverbell Road   **Santa Cruz—North**
between Camino del Cerro & Grant Roads   Sunrise—10:30pm

This 13-acre lake, located in Silverbell Park at 4600 North Silverbell Road, allows boats 14 feet and under and canoes up to 17 feet. Electric trolling motors up to 1 hp may be used. Gasoline motors are prohibited. Surrounded by desert landscape you can fish for tilapia, bass, bluegill and trout. No swimming or wading allowed due to large pumps which have the potential to draw you down. No campfires or open fires allowed along shoreline.

A large area has been set aside for model plane enthusiasts. Weekends will find the reverberating sounds of those engines filling the desert air.

REID LAKE
Gene C. Reid Park

El Con
Sunrise—10:30pm

This 2-acre lake, centrally located near 22nd Street and Country Club Road, is the smallest of the city lakes, It is intended only for children under 14 years. A daily fishing permit may be purchased at the snackbar near the lake on weekends and at the snackbar at the zoo on weekdays. The lake is stocked with tilapia, sunfish and an occasional bass. Each winter, normally during January, the Parks and Recreation Department sponsors a Trout Fishing Derby for children with prizes, etc. Trout are stocked here only for the derby. No swimming or wading allowed

Take 22nd Street and enter the park at Lake Shore Lane which is across from McDonalds and between Country Club Road and Randolph Way.

ROSE CANYON LAKE
Santa Catalina Mountains   7,000 foot elevation
33 miles NE of Tucson   Entry fee

This small 7-acre lake is stocked with trout in the spring, summer and fall. It is closed in the winter. A large forest service campground provides drinking water, rest rooms and grills. As there are no concession facilities, you may wish to pick up supplies before you start up the mountain. Some supplies are available at Summerhaven ten miles further on. No boats are allowed, so you'll have to fish from shore.

Many scenic trails from the lake area to the southwest overlook tree-covered mountainous terrain, and the valley and city of Tucson. (*See also* SANTA CATALINA MOUNTAINS.)

RURAL SOUTHERN ARIZONA FISHING

The following lakes, all within a day's drive, are from seven to 260 acres.

ARIVACA LAKE
60 miles south of Tucson   Elevation 3,750 feet

Located in one of the most beautiful areas of southern Arizona, this remote spot requires a real desire to get there due to poor road conditions. Rest rooms and a launch ramp are provided, but only two parking areas and no concessions at this 90-acre lake.

Drive south on I-19, past Green Valley fourteen miles. Turn west at Arivaca Junction and then drive twenty miles to Arivaca, where you may wish to purchase supplies. Take county road 39 (a dirt road), five miles south to a sign on the left, which states Arivaca Lake is two and a half miles further on. The last mile of this section is narrow, bumpy, and can be very dangerous if wet or washed out. Take your time and enjoy the scenery.

If you have extra time and an inclination to wander, take county road 39 south, for an additional twenty miles, through the picturesque countryside to Pena Blanca Lake.

PARKER CANYON LAKE   Elevation 5,400 feet
75 miles southeast of Tucson   Day use $3/car
                                             Campsite $5

Parker Canyon Lake's 125 acres are primarily known for trout fishing during the five winter months, however, catfish, bluegill and largemouth bass may also be caught. At the entrance, a map shows roadways and directions to the launch area, concession, campsites and picnic grounds of this crescent-shaped fishery. The United States Forest Service maintains the picnic and camp areas with picnic tables, grills, restrooms and refuse dumpsters for public use, and collects the common honor system fees.

The concessionnaire sells fishing licenses, bait, limited groceries and has boat rentals. There is a maximum limit of eight horsepower on outboard motors and you can launch free from the boat ramp. Try fishing from the bank at points and mouths of coves for some good catches.

173

Located in a mile-high valley, the lake is encircled by grassy, rolling hills and mountains with Mexican pine, manzanita, yucca, mesquite and oak trees. Cooler evening temperatures soothe hot summer days, with good camping year round, although you may find it a bit cold during the winter months, when there may be a little snow.

Parker Canyon Lodge, 3/4 mile from the lake, has four housekeeping cabins. For reservations, call 1-455-5351 or 1-455-5367.

To reach Parker Canyon Lake, drive east on I-10 to exit 281, south on state route 83 through Sonoita on a winding road, which turns south and east to a dirt road, twenty miles from the lake. The dirt portion is well maintained, but suffers damage due to weather, so if towing or in a passenger vehicle, take your time.

PATAGONIA LAKE

Patagonia Lake State Park	Elevation 4,000 feet
70 miles southeast of Tucson	Dev campsites (110) $6/car
1-287-6965	Undev campsites (14) $5/car
	Elect hookups (10) $8/car
	Day use $3/car

Picturesquely set in the middle of rolling ranch country, 9,000 foot mountain peaks south and north of this creek-fed 275-acre lake rise majestically in the distance. Seven miles from Patagonia and 12 miles from Nogales, the lake is part of 600-acre Patagonia State Park which also features primitive and R.V. camping, electric hookups, restroom-shower facilities, picnic areas with ramadas, and a swimming beach. The marina provides free boat launching and has a dock and fish-cleaning station. Camping and fishing supplies, canoe and gas boat rentals and fishing licenses are available (phone 1-287-6063).

The largest recreational lake in southern Arizona, Patagonia Lake provides fishing, skiing, boating, swimming, sightseeing and plain old relaxation. You'll see ducks, an occasional crane, and if you're lucky, a few deer in the early morning. Fish here for trout in the winter, largemouth bass, crappie and catfish year-round. Bluegill are prevalent and can also be caught anytime. At 4,000 feet, the nights are slightly cooler than Tucson, but the days are similarly hot, with colder temperatures in the winter.

You may water-ski on the lake's east end; the west is reserved for fishing. Sailboats and motorboats are allowed, with no limits on mast or motor size. If you are boating, note that after exiting from the marina cove a sign designates a no-wake speed to the north or to your right, but no restriction to the south or to your left.

Drive east on I-10 to exit 281, south on state route 83 to Sonoita; take state route 82 six miles past Patagonia to the lake turnoff, then west four miles on a graded dirt road. (*See also* PATAGONIA, ARIZONA.)

PENA BLANCA LAKE

70 miles south of Tucson

Elevation 4,000 feet
Campsites $5
Electric hookup $7

Pena Blanca, or White Rock Lake, averages 45-acres and features twenty camping units with drinking water, restrooms and provisions for R.V.'s and tents without electricity. Temperatures are usually 10—15° cooler than Tucson, so this lake, long known as a fisherman's favorite, is also a great place to survive our warm summers. Fish for bass, crappie, bluegill, catfish and in the winter, trout.

The Pena Blanca Lake Resort offers rooms, meals and a bar, along with groceries, fishing supplies and licenses. If you wish to stay in the lodge or rent any part of your fishing gear, including rowboats and paddle boats, it's best to make reservations: call 1-287-5251. Only boats with electric motors 1 hp or less are allowed on the lake.

To reach Pena Blanca Lake, drive south on I-19 approximately 60 miles, take the Ruby Road exit, then west on state road 289 (which is paved), about ten miles.

> In many ways the desert mountains are more tantalizing than others. Rising high out of the heat and sand, their crests darkened by trees, they suggest a different and more congenial world. The oven-heat of a desert summer is not so unbearable if you know that with a car and an hour you can be in sweater weather. Then the mountains become a refuge, offering the sound of wind in pine tops, the smell of sun on pine needles, and cool shadows. In the winter they offer snow and icicles to the curious and nostalgic, skiing to the sportsman.
>
> *Home is the Desert*
> by Ann Woodin

El Presidio Park and Pima County Courthouse

CALENDAR OF EVENTS

Numerous seasonal activities occur year 'round, although the most active months are from September through May. Although ol' sol's domination results in less summer activity, things have been changing since 1983, with the **Tucson Summer Arts Festival** providing a number of events.

Fairs, festivals and rodeos know no bounds with new ones appearing every year. Sports include the Cleveland Indians and those wonderful UA Wildcats. The PGA and the LPGA make stopovers, as do several tennis tournaments.

The Calendar of Events includes not only Tucson, but numerous out-of-town activities. Those with bullets—•—in front of them are set forth in this chapter; those with asterisks—*—are discussed elsewhere.

For further information on any event, contact either the sponsor, the Metropolitan Tucson Convention and Visitors Bureau, 130 South Scott Avenue, Tucson, AZ 85701, 624-1889 or the Tucson Metropolitan Chamber of Commerce, 435 West St. Mary's Road, Tucson, AZ 85701, 792-1212.

YEAR-ROUND

* Gaslight Theatre	Gaslight Square
* Greyhound Racing	Greyhound Park
* Sunday Jazz	Westward Look Resort
* UA Dance, Music, Theatre	University of Arizona

JANUARY

Philatelic Exhibition	Tucson Convention Center
Pima County Sheriff's Posse—Horse Show	Pima County Fairgrounds
• Senior Olympic Festival	Armory Park
• Southern Arizona Square and Round Dance Festival	Tucson Convention Center
* Trout Fishing Derby	Reid Park
Tucson Coin Show	Tucson Convention Center

FEBRUARY

Friends of Tucson Public Library Annual Book Sale	Tucson
O'odham Tash (Casa Grande's Indian Days)	Casa Grande, AZ
Taste of Scotland	UA
* Tubac Festival of the Arts	Tubac, AZ
• Tucson Balloon Festival	Tucson
• Tucson Gem & Mineral Show	Tucson Convention Center
Tucson Opera Dames Annual Home Tour	Tucson
Tucson Winter Classic Horse Show	Pima County Fairgrounds

FEBRUARY/MARCH

Designer's Showhouse Tucson Museum of Art League	Tucson
• La Fiesta de Los Vaqueros	Rodeo Grounds
• La Fiesta de Los Vaqueros Parade	Tucson

MARCH

A Taste of Chocolate	Tucson
Aerospace & Arizona Days	Davis Monthan AFB
* **Armory Park Homes Tour**	Armory Park
* **Cleveland Indians Training**	Hi Corbett Field
* **Primavera Jazz Fest**	Tucson
* **Tombstone Anniversary** (1st Friday weekend)	Tombstone
Tucson Poetry Festival	Tucson
* **Wa:k Powwow**	Mission San Xavier

MARCH/APRIL

Easter Pageant *(Simon Peter)*	TCC Music Hall
• **Fourth Avenue Street Fair**	Fourth Avenue
• **Pioneer Days**	Fort Lowell Park
• **San Xavier Pageant & Fiesta**	Mission San Xavier
• **Silver & Turquoise Ball**	Tucson
Taste of Tucson	Tucson Convention Center
• **Tucson Festival**	Tucson
• **Tucson Int. Mariachi Conference**	Tucson Convention Center
• **Yaqui Easter Ceremonials** (During Holy Week)	Pasqua Villages

MARCH—JUNE

* **UA Baseball**	UA Wildcat Field

APRIL

Baile de las Flores	Tucson
* **Cleveland Indians Training**	Hi Corbett Field
* **Jazz Sundae**	Reid Park
Kiwanis Annual Barbecue	Reid Park
* **La Vuelta de Bisbee Bike Races** (last weekend)	Bisbee, AZ
• **Pima County Fair**	Pima County Fairgrounds
• **Spring Fling**	UA Campus

APRIL—SEPTEMBER

* **Toros Baseball**	Hi Corbett Field

179

MAY

* **Cinco de Mayo** — Kennedy Park, Tucson
  (May 5th) — and Nogales, AZ

* **Festival de Jazz at Puerto Penasco** — Mexico

  Medieval Fair — St. Phillips in the
  Hills Church

* **Patagonia Arts & Music Festival** — Patagonia, AZ

  Summer Mud Puddle Party — Freedom Park, AZ

  Tucson Press Club Gridiron Show — Tucson Convention Center

* **Wyatt Earp Days** — Tombstone, AZ
  (Memorial Weekend)

* **Kentucky Derby Day** — Sonoita, AZ
  Santa Cruz County Fairgrounds

MAY—JUNE

* **Music Under the Stars** — Reid Park
  DeMeester Outdoor Performance
  Center

MAY—AUGUST

* **Annual Summerset Suite** — Tucson Museum of Art

* **Tucson Summer Arts Festival** — Tucson

JUNE

* **Coronado Music Festival** — Tucson & Mount Lemmon

  Flagstaff Music Festival — Flagstaff, AZ

• **Juneteenth** — Tucson

  Quarter Horse Show — Sonoita
  Santa Cruz County Fairgrounds

JULY

  Frontier Days — Prescott, AZ

  Flagstaff Festival of the Arts — Flagstaff, AZ

AUGUST

* **Bisbee Poetry Festival** — Bisbee, AZ

  Chili Cookoff — Mount Lemmon
  Alpine Lodge

• **La Fiesta de San Agustín** — Arizona Historical
  Society

  Prescott Smoki Ceremonials — Prescott, AZ

AUGUST/SEPTEMBER

Arizona Junior Rodeo   Pima County Fairgrounds

SEPTEMBER

* **Annual Greek Festival**   St. Demetrios Greek
                                    Orthodox Church

  Annual Navajo Nation Fair   Window Rock, AZ

* **Brewery Gulch Days**   Bisbee, AZ
  (Labor Day)

* **Diez y Seis de Septiembre**   Kennedy Park, Tucson
  Mexican Independence Day   and Nogales, AZ
  (September 16th)

  Junior League Rummage Sale   Tucson Convention Center

* **Music Under the Stars**   Reid Park
  Demeester Outdoor Performance
  Center

  Old Pueblo Horseshow   Tucson

* **Wild West Days**   Tombstone, AZ
  (Labor Day)

SEPTEMBER—NOVEMBER

* **UA Football**   Arizona Stadium

OCTOBER

  Annual Air Show   Ryan Field

  Annual Fall Gem & Mineral Show Tucson Convention Center

• **Arizona Wine Festival**   Sonoita, AZ

  Bisbee Mineral Show   Bisbee, AZ

  De Anza Fall Festival of the Arts Tubac, AZ

  Green Valley Country Fair   Green Valley, AZ

  Heldorado Days   Tombstone, AZ

  London Bridge Days   Lake Havasu City, AZ

* **Michelob—Continental Rugby**
  Classic   Tucson

  Mountain Bike Race &
  Convention   Peppersauce Canyon

  Oktoberfest   Mount Lemmon Ski Valley

  Palo Verde Kiwanis   Reid Park
  Annual Pancake Feed

  Rex Allen Days   Wilcox, AZ

* **St. Francis of Assisi**   Mission San Xavier
   Celebration (Oct 3 and 4)

• **Tucson Meet Yourself**   El Presidio Park

   UA Homecoming   University of Arizona

OCTOBER/NOVEMBER

Tohono O'odham Rodeo & Fair   Sells, AZ
NOVEMBER

Arizona State Fair   Phoenix, AZ

Copper State Horse Show   Pima County Fairgrounds

• **Desert Harvest Bazarr**   Desert Museum

   El Tour de Tucson/Bike Race   Tucson

   UA Intercollegite Rodeo   Old Tucson
NOVEMBER/DECEMBER

• **Arizona Daily Star Book &**   Tucson Convention Center
   and Author Event
DECEMBER

• **Angel Ball**   Tucson

   Christmas Eve Festival of   Tumacacori, AZ
   the Luminarias (December 24)

• **El Nacimiento**   Tucson Museum of Art

* **Feast Day of San Francisco Xavier**   Mission San Xavier
   (December 3)

• **Fourth Avenue Street Fair**   Fourth Avenue

• **Holiday in Lights Festival**   El Presidio

* **Holiday Revelry**   Tucson Museum of Art
   Plaza of the Pioneers

   Indian Arts Show   Tucson Convention Center

   Tucson Botanical Gardens   Tucson Botanical Gardens
   Luminaria Ceremony

* **Tumacacori Fiesta**   Tumacacori, AZ
   1st Sunday

• **Winterhaven Festival of Lights**   Winterhaven
DECEMBER/JANUARY

Tucson Writers' Conference   Tucson
(Tucson Public Library)
DECEMBER—MARCH

* **UA Basketball**   McKale Center

WINTER

SENIOR OLYMPIC FESTIVAL
El Presidio
791-4865

$3 general fee
$1—$3.50 per event
January

It's never to late to be an olympic star, even if you're in that category known as "senior." Over 1,000 seniors joined in Tucson's 1988 Olympic Festival and some qualified for and participated in the National Senior Olympics in St. Louis.

Headquarters for the four-day event is Armory Park, however the events themselves are held at various locations around town. Sports included are: croquet, horseshoes, table tennis, softball throw, shuffleboard, badminton, handball, raquetball, bowling, running and dance.

Gala opening ceremonies include visiting dignitaries, a parade of athletes and the lighting of the olympic torch. Previous to the festival, Tucson Parks and Recreation sponsors a number of workshops.

SOUTHERN ARIZONA SQUARE
AND ROUND DANCERS ASSOCIATION
Tucson Convention Center

El Presidio
Admission charge
January

The 40th Annual Tucson Southern Arizona Square and Round Dance Festival was presented in 1988. Over 200 squares, 1,600 people, from all over the U.S. and Canada join together each year for workshops, clinics and dancing. It's a colorful and fun-filled gathering and spectators are invited for a small fee.

As one of the largest associations in town, the **Old Pueblo Square Dancers Association** perform in the festival and provide opportunities for anyone to join in both square and round dancing here in Tucson, with beginner's classes offered. Contact Old Pueblo Square Dancers Association, P.O. Box 41314, Tucson, AZ 85717, phone 293-4110 or 886-0866.

TUCSON GEM & MINERAL SHOW
El Presidio
Tucson Convention Center

Admission charge
February

From a small show first held in 1954, the Tucson Gem and Mineral Show has burgeoned into an international event drawing gem and mineral enthusiasts from around the world. Museum quality pieces are featured with collections from such museums as the Smithsonian

Institution, The Sorbonne, Geological Museum of China and the American Museum of Natural History. Each year a different mineral is featured to encourage mineral competition. Educational talks and lectures are ongoing by visiting museum curators and professional and amateur mineralogists.

Retail and wholesale dealers from over 40 countries and 50 states offer the widest possible selections from fifty-cent beginner's specimens to those priced at several thousands of dollars. Although there is a charge for the convention center show, many dealers open their hotel room doors and visitors are free to wander in and out of the rooms enjoying the exquisite crystalline jewels, gems and fossils.

Bob Jones, a contributor to Rock and Gem Magazine, has said: "It is, simply stated, the greatest single gem and mineral event of the year in this country, and probably the world." In fact, one of Europe's most prestigious gem and mineral shows now bills itself as "The Tucson of Europe."

For further information, dates and times, contact the Tucson Gem and Mineral Committee, P.O. Box 42543, Tucson, AZ 85733 or the Chamber of Commerce.

TUCSON BALLOON FESTIVAL   Marana
Continental Ranch   Admission free
884-9952   February

Albuquerque still has the largest balloon display, but we're rapidly catching up and Tucsonans come out in droves to participate in one of the most colorful events in town. The show starts early (gates open at 5:30am), and over 90 air-filled balloons are expected to take off around 7am in 1989. Admission is free, however a minimum $4 parking charge benefits local charities. (Included with that $4 is an elegant festival magazine with loads of info on ballooning.)

If you're a real early bird, get there before 6am for the "Dawn Patrol" launch. Even more exciting than daylight flights, light from the burners of the balloons glowing through seemingly gossamer fabrics creates "oohing and ahhing" time.

Visitors may walk right to the field, but you are requested not to smoke (the balloons are fueled by propane, a highly volatile gas), not to walk on the balloons (they can be punctured), and as dogs are frightened by the size and sounds of the balloons to leave them at home. AND DON'T FORGET YOUR CAMERA WITH PLENTY OF FILM!

Take I-10 north and drive west at Cortaro Road exit. There will probably be direction signs. For further information, write 738 North 5th Avenue, Suite 214, Tucson, AZ 85705.

Budweiser Clydesdales

LA FIESTA DE LOS VAQUEROS

Rodeo Grounds
4801 South 6th Avenue
792-1212

San Xavier
February/March
Tickets/Chamber
of Commerce

La Fiesta de Los Vaqueros (The Festival of the Cowboys), America's largest outdoor midwinter rodeo and the oldest in the Southwest, has been an outstanding part of Tucson's culture since 1925, when the first rodeo was held in the ten acres owned by an eastern industrialist, Leighton Kramer, across the street from the present location of the Arizona Inn.

The rodeo draws top cowboys and cowgirls from all over the nation displaying their talents in calf roping, bareback riding, steer wrestling and team roping, while the antics of fearless clowns complete the events. The Quadrille de Mujeres (Ladies Quadrille) also performs their fast and furious precision riding.

The four-day rodeo comprises only one of several celebrations held during rodeo week in Tucson. School is let out the Thursday before rodeo, and everyone heads downtown for the world's longest non-mechanized parade. **La Fiesta de Los Vaqueros Parade** has more horses than you've probably seen before (and possibly including the Budweiser Clydesdales); cowgirls and cowboys, decked out in western duds; and, bands, bands and more bands. The parade starts at 9am. Be downtown by 8am to get a good curbside seat.

An outstanding part of the parade is the antique equipment pulled by those horses. Stored during the year at the Rodeo Parade Museum and maintained by the Rodeo Parade Committee, you will see two-wheeled buggies, stage coaches, buck boards, surries and all the necessary additional paraphernalia. The **Rodeo Parade Museum,** located at 4825 South 6th Street, is open infrequently before and during rodeo times; there you can see the famous Maximilian Coach, donated to the committee in 1932 by the governor of Sonora, Mexico. For hours, call the Rodeo Parade Office, 792-2250.

Everyone gets together the night before the parade at the Arizona Historical Society (*see also* LA CIUDAD DE LOS MUSEOS) for the official **Rodeo Romance Dance** and if you don't dance too late, you might enjoy a robust cowboy breakfast the next morning at the **Kiwanis Cowboy Breakfast.**

A **Burro Derby, Fiddler's Contest** and other western activities follow during the week. To join in any or all of these events, call the Chamber of Commerce for specific dates and times.

SPRING

4th AVENUE STREET FAIR
4th Avenue near 6th Street

University
March/April

You've never really shopped until you've attended the 4th Avenue Street Fair. Beginning on Friday, this three-day event brings out most of Tucson, with the 1988 fair drawing over 250,000 visitors! Fourth Avenue is closed for several blocks with booths lined up and down the center of the street. Over 300 artists and craftspeople from throughout the United States display their crafts while numerous food booths and entertainment will allow you to stay and shop for hours. (The fair is also a happening in December of every year.)

TUCSON FESTIVAL

Easter Season
March/April

The **Tucson Festival Society** annually presents the Tucson Festival, a month-long celebration of Tucson's multi-cultural heritage. The numerous events reflect centuries-old traditions of the Indian, Spanish, Mexican, and Pioneer-American phases of our city's development.

Known as one of the ten most outstanding festivals in the United States, the events include: the **Fiesta de los Ninos,** a costumed children's parade for all children through the 8th grade; the **Fiesta de la Placita,** a traditional Mexican Fiesta with mariachis, refreshments, games and the presentation of the Fiesta Queen; **Pioneer Days,** which takes place at Old Fort Lowell, where family entertainment includes a chuckwagon barbecue, pioneer crafts and **Military Field Day,** with cavalry, artillery and infantry in full regalia.

The bonfire-lit **San Xavier Pageant and Fiesta** commemorates the founding of the mission. Tohono O'odham and Yaqui dancing enhances the occasion, along with Indian crafts and foods. A narrator interprets the events while mounted Spanish Lancers, robed monks, and costumed pilgrims wind down a hillside to the mission's plaza amid music, bells and fireworks.

The grand finale of the festival and one of Tucson's glamour spectacles, is the **Silver and Turquoise Ball.** Many women wear gowns in theme colors, and you will see a king's ransom in silver and turquoise jewelry on both men and women. Luminarios set along the roof line of the Arizona Inn impart a distinct southwestern touch to this gala.

TUCSON INTERNATIONAL
MARIACHI CONFERENCE
Tucson Convention Center

    El Presidio
    March/April

Introduced in 1983, the phenominal growth of this event rapidly made it a permanent part of the **Tucson Festival.** Tucsonans consider mariachi music as much a part of the Anglo society as the Hispanic and quickly gather 'round to enjoy the sounds of those beautiful brass trumpets, the mainstay of any mariachi group.

The conference includes study workshops with the world-famous Mariachi Vargas de Tecalitlan, widely regarded as the world's best. However, when not studying, the groups provide music-loving Tucsonans with sensational melodies.

Friday night opens the festival with **Garibaldi Night,** a re-creation of Mexico City's famed Plaza de Garibaldi. The free event includes strolling mariachis, dancers and Mexican refreshments in the TCC plaza. Saturday afternoon is the **Mariachi Fiesta** with the registered groups playing in concert. There is a small charge for this event.

Mariachi Espectacular, the Saturday night finale, includes concerts by the best groups, ending in a friendly musical duel. Tickets sell out rapidly. (During the past two or three years Tucson's own Linda Ronstadt has appeared and tickets disappeared like magic.) For further information, contact the Chamber of Commerce.

YAQUI EASTER CEREMONIALS
Old Pascua Village, Barrio Libre
and New Pascua   Easter Week

The Yaqui Indians' religious interpretation of the events leading to the
crucifixion and resurrection of Christ yields a solemn and impressive
ceremony. The passion play is a combination of Catholic ritual and
tribal traditions with the forces of good triumphing over the forces of
evil. As a social time for the Yaquis, many friends and relatives attend
the numerous rites.

Visitors are welcome, however it is requested that no photographs
be taken. Old Pascua Village is located one block south of Grant Road
and four blocks west of Miracle Mile at 2265 North Calle Central.
Barrio Libre is at 418 West 39th Street, between 10th and 12th Avenues
and New Pascua is at 4821 West Calle Vicam (go west on Valencia and
turn south on Calle del Oeste).

PIMA COUNTY FAIR
Pima County Fairgrounds   Admission charge
Houghton Road, south of I-10   April

The Pima County Fair lasts from seven to ten days. Livestock shows
include poultry, pigeons, rabbits, goats, beef, sheep and swine.
Showmanship and market classes are professionally judged and many
ideal market and breeding animals are exhibited. One of the highlights
of the animal section is the livestock auction.

The Open Division includes 4-H homemaking arts, science and
engineering projects and fine arts displays of photography, sculpture,
paintings and crafts.

Local and national names provide entertainment. You'll hear
choruses, barbershop quartets, children's ensembles, and bands of all
types, from army and high school to jazz and mariachi. Yo-yo
exhibitions, skateboard challenges and bubble gum blowing contests
will also entertain you.

Dancing includes everything from square, to belly and folk. And
what's a fair without a bright, sparkling midway, dazzling rides and
carnival atmosphere? Plenty of free parking and picnic areas available.
Call the Chamber of Commerce for specific dates.

Take I-10 east to exit 275 (Houghton Road). Turn right on
Houghton and go south for one mile to the fairgrounds.

SPRING FLING
UA Campus

April

The largest student-run carnival in the nation takes place on the UA campus. Over twenty-five carnival rides include ferris wheels, merry-go-rounds, special kiddy rides, haunted houses and the Super Loop.

Along the midway you can try your skills at basketball, darts and the dunking of football players. Although not necessarily nutritious, loads of food booths provide sustenance for all. It's a great place to take the kids. For dates, call the *Arizona Daily Wildcat,* 621-3551.

SUMMER

TUCSON SUMMER ARTS FESTIVAL
621-1162

May—Aug

Twenty, or only ten years ago, Tucson's summer art scene faded into the sun's glare from May to October. The only available theatre was at The Old Globe in San Diego and not everyone could make it to that city by the sea. Well, that all changed in 1983 when the University of Arizona and the Metropolitan Tucson Convention and Visitors Bureau got together to produce a Summer Arts Festival, sponsored in 1988 by Hotel Park Tucson and America West Airlines. We now have a planned summer arts season with music, theatre, dance, exhibitions and lectures.

Included in 1988 was the Invisible Theatre's *Jacques Brel is Alive and Well and Living in Paris,* the University's *The Lion in Winter* and *Don Giovanni* and the Tucson Jazz Society's **Summerset Suite 88.**

Tickets are available at the Festival Box Office, Dillard's and TCC Outlets. (*See also* A CULTURED COMMUNITY.)

JUNETEENTH
Vista Del Pueblo Park
1800 West San Marcos Blvd.

Santa Cruz
Middle of June

Juneteenth is Tucson's celebration of the Emancipation Proclamation when black slaves learned they were free. The celebration, observed in Texas for more than a century, began in Tucson in 1970. The actual date is unknown, but the celebration is generally around the 19th of June. Events include picnics, games and live music and entertainment.

Events are held in various locations about town, with the major celebration at Vista del Pueblo Park, located on the south side of "A" Mountain. Call the Chamber of Commerce or Convention Bureau for further information.

LA FIESTA DE SAN AGUSTIN

Arizona Historical Society
628-5774

University
Late August

It may be hot but we still gather 'round to celebrate Tucson's birthday and Tucson's patron saint, San Agustín. The tradition began over 200 years ago as Tucson's first celebration. Later the fiesta was the "big wingding" of the 1800s. Through the years the spirit of celebration faded until 1983, when the tradition was revived by the Arizona Historical Society.

Second Street, in front of the Society, is blocked to traffic, food booths are set up, there's entertainment and dancing and artifacts from Tucson's earlier years are displayed in the museum.

FALL

ARIZONA WINE FESTIVAL

Santa Cruz County Fairgrounds
Sonoita, AZ

October*
Sunday

Arizona Indians were making wine before the Spanish arrived and in 1912 at least three Arizona wineries were in operation, but in 1913 Arizona law eliminated the wine industry for some time. Ideal growing conditions and prospects for future excellent wine production has seen the beginning of three vineyards in southern Arizona in recent years: Arizona Vineyards, R.W. Webb Winery and Sonoita Vineyards, all of whom are participants at the wine festival (see also PLACES TO GO AND THINGS TO DO.) Since its inception in 1984, the participants, the Arizona wineries and the Arizona Wine Festival has grown immensely.

Besides wine tasting, attractions included a demonstration of home wine-making techniques, grape stomping, a wine auction and arts and crafts.

Santa Cruz County fair grounds are just south of the junction of Arizona routes 82 and 83. Take I-10 east and turn south at exit 281 onto highway 83. Festivites run from 10am—6pm. (See also A DAY AWAY.)

*Problems with new legislation may put a crimp in the wine festival dates. Call the Chamber of Commerce or Convention Bureau to verify.

Tucson Meet Yourself

TUCSON MEET YOURSELF
El Presidio Park   October

Originated by Jim Griffith, Director of the University of Arizona's
Southwest Folklore Center and his wife, Loma, this unique cultural
fiesta began in 1974. Sponsors include the Folklore Center, the
Cultural Exchange Council of Tucson, Pima Community College and
the City of Tucson. Tucson Meet Yourself is, as Jim Griffith says, *the*
place to "enjoy a taste of the real Tucson—people from a wide variety
of cultural traditions, united by shared ideas and mutual respect."

The festival celebrates the cultural traditions of Tucson's talented,
creative people and is dedicated to preserving our ethnic heritages.
Continuous entertainment includes such delights as Laotian dancers,
Japanese koto music, Tohono O'odham polkas and Scots piping.

At the workshop stage you may learn Armenian dancing, or hear
oldtime fiddlers compare their methods of playing. Crafts demonstrations might include Yaqui paper flower makers, a Thai seamstress,
Mormon women quilting or a Jewish calligrapher.

Friday evening begins the festivities, which continue through
Saturday and into Sunday. A piñata party on Saturday will thrill the kids
and they participate in children's games on Sunday.

In 1984 more than forty ethnic groups prepared their culinary specialties, including Brazilian, Greek, German, Norwegian, Afghan, Swedish, Irish and Soul food, contributing to a nickname for the festival of Tucson Eat Yourself.

The O'odham close Sunday's performances with the ceremonial closing of the festival, the O'odham Circle Dance.

DESERT HARVEST BAZAAR
Arizona-Sonora Desert Museum

Tucson Mountains
November

Tohono O'odham dancing adds to the celebration of our desert abundance, including its gems, minerals, cacti and foods. Papago fry bread, prickly pear cactus jelly and punch, tepary beans and mesquite bean flour is available, along with native wildflower seeds.

Demonstrations in pottery and Tohono O'odham basket making are also scheduled. The bazaar is free, admission charge for the museum. (*See also* PLACES TO GO AND THINGS TO TO DO.) Phone 883-2702 for dates.

ARIZONA DAILY STAR
BOOK & AUTHOR EVENT
Tucson Convention Center

El Presidio
Admission charge
November

If you list being a bibliophile on your resumé and are lucky enough to be in Tucson in late November or early December, make plans to attend the *Arizona Daily Star's* increasingly popular Book and Author Event.

Launched in 1980, the Star brings in three or four popular authors who speak and present their most recent books. The event has grown in attendance every year with such authors as Jean M. Auel, *The Clan of the Cave Bear, Valley of the Horses* and *The Mammoth Hunters;* Gerry Spence, *Gunning for Justice;* and Abigail Van Buren, *The Best of Dear Abby.* You'll have a chance to meet the authors, and obtain their autographs, and they are, invariably, entertaining speakers.

For exact date and location, call the *Arizona Daily Star,* 294-4400.

4th AVENUE STREET FAIR
4th Avenue near 6th Street

You've never really shopped until you've attended the 4th Avenue Street Fair. Beginning on Friday, this three-day event brings out most of Tucson, with the 1988 fair drawing over 250,000 visitors!. Fourth Avenue is closed for several blocks and you'll find booths lined up and down the center of the street with over 300 artists and craftspeople from throughout the United States. Food booths and entertainment will allow you to stay and shop for hours. (The fair is also a happening in March/April of every year.)

HOLIDAY ACTIVITIES

Tucson's **Holiday In Lights Festival** opens the downtown season with the lighting of a "high-tech" Christmas tree. Past festivities have included buggy rides, gallery tours and special dining events.

El Nacimiento, a Mexican-styled Nativity scene makes its appearance every year at La Casa Cordova, adjacent to the Tucson Museum of Art, 140 North Main Avenue. Admission is free and the scene can usually be viewed through January.

The **Festival of Lights,** in Winterhaven subdivision, is a treat for young and old alike. Winterhaven has been decorating its homes and huge pine trees since 1949. You may drive through in your car or catch a bus at shopping centers for the tour (no charge for seeing Winterhaven, but a small charge for the bus ride). Gridlock is common, so don't plan on rushing. Winterhaven is just north of East Fort Lowell between North Tucson Boulevard and North Country Club Road.

Carrillo Intermediate School at 440 South Main Avenue holds its **Las Posadas** every year. This traditional Mexican event celebrates the traveling of Mary and Joseph through Bethlehem trying to find an inn.

Numerous social activities also occur during the holidays. The Tucson Symphony Women's Association **Cotillion,** the **Angel Ball** (a major fund-raising force in the community) and the **Assistance League** dance are just a few of numerous sparkling events.

Brewery Gulch—Bisbee, Arizona

A DAY AWAY

Several areas within a day's drive from Tucson are well worth visiting and can be combined for a full day's exploring.

The jaunt west to **Kitt Peak National Observatory** will not take a full day, unless you plan a drive into Sells for some purchases of Indian crafts. You might consider combining that drive with a visit to **Mission San Xavier Del Bac**. (*See also* PLACES TO GO AND THINGS TO DO.)

Mission San Xavier del Bac, Tubac, Tumacacori, Nogales, and **Patagonia** are directly south of Tucson and it is possible to visit them all in one lo-n-n-g day. If you prefer to make two days of it, hotels in Nogales, Arizona and a bed and breakfast and hotel in Patagonia are quite enjoyable. The visit to the **Fred Lawrence Whipple and Multiple Mirror Telescope Observatories** on Mt. Hopkins will take you a full day, due to the scheduled tour up to the observatory. **NOTE: HIGHWAY DISTANCES ON I-19 ARE GIVEN IN KILOME-TERS. MULTIPLY BY .6 TO CONVERT TO MILES.**

The **Amerind Foundation, Bisbee** and **Tombstone,** located southeast of Tucson, each require nearly a full day of visiting, considering the length of the drive. It is possible, if you begin at dawn and return quite late, to catch all three in one day, but that won't do any of them justice. You might consider a stopover in Bisbee or Tombstone for a night, which would allow ample time to take in all three.

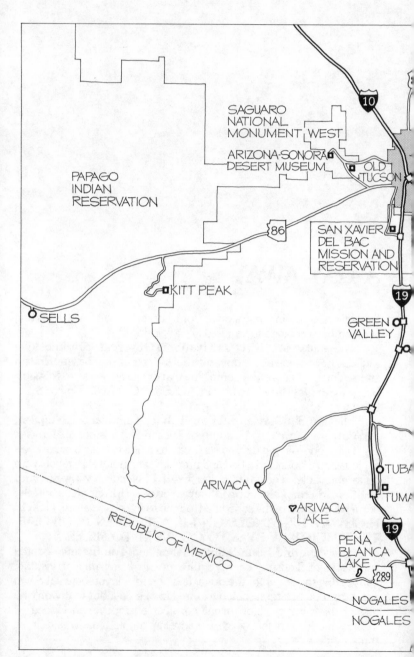

SUMMERHAVEN

OUNT
MMON

ROSE
CANYON
LAKE

SAGUARO
NATIONAL
MONUMENT
EAST

COLOSSAL
CAVE

AMERIND
FOUNDATION

BENSON

TAL

83

90

80

ADERA
ANYON

SONOITA

82

TOMBSTONE

VATORY

PATAGONIA

SIERRA
VISTA

PATAGONIA
AKE

83

PARKER
CANYON
LAKE

RAMSEY
CANYON

BISBEE

92

RA

10

REPUBLIC OF MEXICO

KITT PEAK
NATIONAL OBSERVATORY

56 miles southwest of Tucson
Elevation 6,882 feet

Admission free
Daily 10am—4pm
Films 10:30am & 1:30pm
Closed Dec 24 & Dec 25

Known as the Astronomy Capital of the World, Southern Arizona has, within a fifty-mile radius, more astronomical observatories than anywhere else on our planet.

One of the most famous is the National Optical Astronomy Observatories (NOAO), on Kitt Peak in the Quinlan Mountains. This site, located on the 2.7 million-acre reservation of the Tohono O'odham Indians, was selected after a three-year survey covering more than 150 mountain ranges and employing all types of media, from rocket photographs to horseback travel. The nearly 7,000-foot mountain is ideal due to its location below the rare clouds, but above the dust and haze.

Long before you arrive at Kitt Peak National Observatory, you will see the gleaming white domes of the telescopes reflecting in the distance, looking a great deal like something out of *Close Encounters of the Third Kind*.

Over a dozen different telescopes are here, several of which have visitor galleries to provide close-up views of the telescopes and explanations of their operation. Three of the more spectacular ones are:

THE MCMATH SOLAR TELESCOPE. The largest solar telescope in the world, the McMath uses a system of mirrors to take the solar beam hundreds of feet into the earth, where it is reflected back through an optical train to instruments at the base of the huge, triangle-shaped observatory. The end product is a unique, high-resolution, thirty-inch-diameter solar image for solar astronomers and their battery of modern instruments to scrutinize in their search for further understanding of our nearest star.

THE 158" MAYALL TELESCOPE. One of the four largest in the country, this telescope has light gathering power equivalent to a million human eyes and has an accuracy of one to two-millionths of an inch. The interior is maintained at night-time temperatures to prevent optical distortion caused by warm or cold air currents. An elevator takes visitors to an observation gallery encircling the huge dome. Visitors can see Mexico, the scattered villages of the O'odham and the city of Tucson. A short set of stairs takes you to the telescope itself, with its fifteen-ton quartz mirror.

The 84" TELESCOPE. This telescope, housed also in a large white dome, has enough power to "see" a candle flame at 3,000 miles.

Kitt Peak is operated by the Association of Universities for Research in Astronomy Inc. (AURA), under contract to the National Science Foundation. AURA, a non-profit consortium of universities with strong programs in astronomy, includes seventeen member institutions across the U.S.

At the headquarters building in Tucson, adjacent to the University of Arizona, complete engineering support capabilities are maintained. Most of the sky research is done by computers and electronics have replaced a great deal of the slower more cumbersome methods, even in picture taking. A scientist at a computer in Tucson tells a telescope on Kitt Peak to lock onto a certain star. The telescope will stay fixed on the star, as the earth rotates, while the computer prints out data on the composition of gases, the star's temperature, spectroscopic analysis of its makeup, etc.

Visiting astronomers from around the world apply for a specific viewing date a year or so ahead. Annually over 600 stargazers hope they will be blessed with a clear Arizona sky. If not, their names go back to the end of the list and their research may be postponed a long while.

As Kitt Peak is the center of U.S. astronomy, it is sometimes forgotten that the selection of the site did not meet well with the elders of the O'odham tribe and many conferences were necessary before the go-ahead was given to locate on Kitt Peak.

The O'odham realized many years ago the uniqueness of Kitt Peak and it is the site of sacred caves where they have also searched the heavens in their studies of the stars. The mountain is also the second home of I'itoi, the O'odham god whose chief abode is "at the center of the universe," on the crest of spectacular Baboquivari Peak, twelve miles south of Kitt Peak.

After first being turned down, the astronomers invited the elders to the UA where they were given a tour of Steward Observatory, along with the opportunity of viewing the moon through a 36" telescope. Although awed by the clearness of the lunar landscape, the elders stated, (quite truthfully) "It really doesn't look much different than the land on the reservation!"

The tour helped convince them, however, of the benefits of the proposal and on Oct. 24, 1958, a 99-year renewable lease was signed, with the reservation that the sacred caves would remain off-limits to all but the O'odham. At the dedication ceremonies early in 1960, Dr. Alan Waterman, Director of the National Science Foundation, said, "It seems appropriate that we should have as landlords the Papago Indians who were watching the stars from these mountains long before our forefathers crossed the seas."

Incidentally, Tucson has adopted legislation requiring all outdoor illumination to be shielded from above in an effort to eliminate excess light reflection in the night-time skies. This also assists us ordinary stargazers in observing our clear desert skies more distinctly.

The facilities include a visitor center and museum, with exhibits, models and daily film showings at 10:30am and 1:30pm. Simple graphic displays allow a glimpse of some of the mysteries of the universe.

Brochures are available for self-guided walking tours. Guided tours (of about 1 1/2 hours) are conducted on Sat, Sun and holidays (except Christmas). In addition to the weekend tours, special arrangements can be made for weekday tours for fifteen or more. Night tours are offered several times a year. The ticket price covers round-trip transportation from NAOA headquarters in Tucson to Kitt Peak. (If you do join a night-time tour, especially in the fall to spring months, dress for a very cold evening.)

A small gift shop in the visitor center features O'odham handicrafts and booklets and posters about the observatory. All profits from sales go to the Tohono O'odham Tribe.

No food, other than candy and soft drinks, is available on the mountain, but a lovely picnic area with cooking grills, tables and benches is located a mile and a half before the top of the mountain. As the temperature is usually 15—20° cooler than Tucson, it is wise to take along a sweater.

Take highway 86 (Ajo Way) west toward Gila Bend, watching for the turnoff south (Arizona 386) to Kitt Peak. The trip is approximately fifty-six miles. As the road can be impassable in the winter, it is best to call for road conditions.

Kitt Peak National Observatory   Tour Information
Public Information Office   623-5796 ext 250
P.O. Box 26732   Road Information
Tucson, AZ 85726   623-5796 ext 250

A SIDE TRIP TO SELLS

If you are especially interested in O'odham baskets or pottery, you may wish to take a short side trip further into the O'odham reservation while going to or returning from Kitt Peak. It is but a short drive (eighteen miles) from the turnoff on highway 86 to continue west to Sells, the capital and largest village of the O'odham nation.

Several trading posts and shops are in town, including the Santa Rosa Trading Post and Margaret's Arts and Crafts. You will probably be able to find both new and old baskets, along with other gift items.

If you drive on to Sells, and then drive onto the reservation for further sightseeing, be sure to make inquiries into road conditions, as many roads are not passable following severe weather conditions. Also, some roads are restricted. Non-O'odham need permits to drive within the southern districts of the Tohono O'odham Indian Reservation.

FRED LAWRENCE WHIPPLE and MULTIPLE MIRROR TELESCOPE OBSERVATORIES

41 miles south of Tucson

Adults $5
6—12 $2.50
Apr 1—Thanksgiving
Mon Wed Fri

As part of Tucson's seemingly star-filled destiny, one of the most outstanding of the more than thirty telescopes girding the Old Pueblo is located on Mount Hopkins in the Santa Rita Mountains.

The Multiple Mirror Telescope (MMT), a prototype for future telescopes, is a joint research facility of the Smithsonian Institution and the UA (where the mirrors were ground and polished at the Optical Sciences Center), and is operated by the Multiple Mirror Telescope Observatory. The third largest telescope in the world in light-gathering capacity, the MMT consists of six separate mirrors, each 72″ in diameter, which equal a single larger mirror 176″ in diameter.

One of the major technical problems of large telescopes is their sizable housing and mountings. The multiple mirror concept overcomes high costs, not only in production of the mirrors, but also in land coverage and the tall buildings required for larger telescopes. The MMT rests in a simple altitude-azimuth mount built and tested in northern Italy by a firm specializing in cable car manufacturing. The mount was then disassembled, shipped to Tucson and reassembled on the mountain, before the building was built. Structural support needed for the mount was much simpler than the usual cumbersome mounts of other telescopes, also resulting in high savings.

The designers, knowing the top half of the building had to turn with the telescope, suggested that possibly the entire building could rotate, which would satisfy the engineers' desires to place the necessary electronics equipment near the instrument. (The telescope itself is completely separate from the building and thus rotates separately, in synchronization with the building.) As the six telescopes are extremely compact, the space needed (in front of the telescope) was no more than that for any one of the MMT'S six telescopes.

Multiple Mirror Telescope—Mount Hopkins

Jane Hanson Weinzapfel, UA College of Architecture alumna, had project responsibility for the four-story, 500-ton building—offices, laboratories, workshops and telescope. The "sugar cube," as it is known, stands 55-feet high, is 44-feet wide and 64-feet long. Its 90° movement, in sixty seconds, is so smooth that it is imperceptible to those working within the building until they note the changing mountain views through the windows. Huge L-shaped doors slide open from the sides and the top to reveal the MMT in operation.

The MMT's electronic light detectors are so sensitive that care must be exercised when focusing on bright, nearby stars, so the detectors are not damaged by too much light. Instead, it focuses deep into space, seeing light that was generated seven billion light years ago, or twice the age of earth. It was the first instrument to see the coma of Halley's Comet in April, 1984.

The applications of the MMT are unlimited. It is a powerful scientific instrument with the goal of understanding the nature of the universe. Most observations are done automatically; in fact, an astronomer need not even be present for research, as the telescope can respond to preprogrammed instructions. On-line computers also receive instructions from the Smithsonian Astrophysical Observatory in Cambridge, Massachusetts.

Volunteer tour guides provide a miniature astronomy course during the tour. You'll understand a lot more about the telescopes, why and what they are doing and what their future possibilities are.

Tours of the Fred Lawrence Whipple Observatory are conducted from approximately April 1 through Thanksgiving, depending upon weather and flood conditions in southern Arizona. Tours begin at 9am with a videotape presentation and the bus leaves at 9:30am. Visitors should bring a lunch. Picnic tables, water and soft drinks are available on the mountain. It usually is fifteen degrees cooler on the summit, so a sweater or wrap is recommended, along with casual clothes and walking shoes.

As the elevation of Mount Hopkins is 8,550 feet, those persons affected by high altitude or with health problems should consult their doctors first. The eighteen-mile road up the mountain is unpaved, oneway, very rough and with few guard rails. If you are uncomfortable with narrow, mountain roads you might reconsider the trip.

If the above details don't bother you, and the day is clear, you will enjoy unsurpassed, breathtaking views at every turn. Five mountain ranges into Mexico are visible, along with Tucson and the telescopes at Kitt Peak, forty-six miles away.

Reservations must be made and can be made up to a month in advance. Visitors are asked not to bring children under the age of six. Call the number below for reservations and further information.

To reach the Amado office, drive south on I-19 and take exit 48, east to the frontage road. Drive south 1 1/2 miles, then turn east. The office is a short distance further on. (The trip is forty-one miles and fifty minutes from Speedway and Stone.)

Fred Lawrence Whipple Observatory
P.O. Box 97
Amado, AZ 85645-0097
(1) 398-2432

TUBAC, ARIZONA
45 miles south of Tucson

Tubac, the town "Where Art and History Meet," is a growing retirement community picturesquely situated in the verdant Santa Cruz Valley. Populated by many artisans and craftspersons, the **Tubac Center of the Arts** and numerous other studios and galleries in town offer handscreened prints, batiks, pottery, contemporary jewelry, antiques, wood carvings and paintings. At last count over fifty shops provide browsing and shopping, although summer visitors won't find all those shops open as many Tubacans retreat to cooler climes from May to October.

Students of history will enjoy **Tubac Presidio State Historic Park** (1-398-2252) and its museum. The museum (for which there is a small admission charge) includes artifacts over two centuries old, along with some of the original printing equipment from Arizona's first newspaper. (The press was brought around the horn to Guaymas, Mexico and then carried by pack cart to Tubac.) Excavations in 1974 by UA archeologists identified the original foundations and plaza of the old presidio. These can be viewed in an archeological display enclosure which also shows the cultural levels representing much of Tubac's colorful history, and whose origins began with the arrival of the Hohokam in about 300 A.D.

The Old Tubac School House, built in 1885, is a short walk from the museum. You may visit the ancient building where classes were held on and off until 1964, and check out the graffiti on the original old desks. Across from the schoolhouse is St. Ann's Church, built in 1920 on the site where several churches dating back to 1700 have stood.

Like so many other Arizona towns, the population of Tubac has had more ups and downs than an elevator. Maurading Apache caused the abandonment of Tubac eight times and the town was left to crumble in the dust when its populace heard the cry of gold from San Francisco.

At one time the home of Hohokam Indians, written history of Tubac begins with the establishment in 1752 of a Spanish fort, Presidio de San Ygnacio del Tubac, as a protection from Indian raids for the settlers and the surrounding missions (such as San Jose de Tumacacori).

Tubac was the jumping-off place for those who discovered and established the city of San Francisco. Juan Bautista de Anza, the second commander of the presidio, dreamed of finding an overland route to California. De Anza and Fray Francisco Garcés (a principal founder of Tucson) explored the route in 1774, with Garcés going as far as Yuma and de Anza leading the colonists on to found the city by the bay.

In 1776 the garrison of the presidio was moved to Tucson, once again leaving Tubac prey to Apache attacks. The unprotected settlers refused to leave their lands, however, and ultimately, in 1787, a garrison of Pima soldiers arrived. The relative quiet of this period resulted in a Spanish land grant in 1789 and the first Arizona school was established.

Following Mexican independence in 1821, the presidio, along with San Jose de Tumacacori, was left to wither in neglect. The maurading

Apache once again took advantage and when the California gold strikes began in 1849, the settlers needed no further encouragement to move on.

As part of the Gadsen Purchase of 1853, Tubac was but a ghost town. But in 1860, tales of the discoveries of ancient mines and minerals in the Santa Cruz Valley abounded and prospectors, mining companies, storekeepers, journalists and travelers quickly moved in. Tubac became the largest town in Arizona, publishing Arizona's first newspaper, the *Weekly Arizonan*. Numerous other Arizona "firsts" include: the first European settlement, the first school and more recently, the first state park.

The advent of the Civil War drained Tubac of its troups once again and with many of the town's leading citizens joining the Confederacy, Tubac once again was undefended and the Apache returned. Those few Tubacans left fled either to Tucson or to Sonora in Mexico. After the war, Tubac became part of Arizona Territory and some Tubacans returned home, but she never regained her stature and importance.

The colorful **Tubac Festival of the Arts,** occurs each February, De Anza Days are held in October, and **Fiesta Navidad,** with luminarios and caroling welcomes the Christmas holidays in December; all great times to visit Tubac. Check with the Tubac Chamber of Commerce or the Tucson Chamber of Commerce for dates.

Public restrooms are located near the museum on Presidio Drive between Calle Iglesia and Wilson Road.

To reach Tubac, drive south on I-19, taking exit 34 into Tubac Presidio State Park. The distances on highway I-19 are given in kilometers, multiply by .6 to convert to mileage.

Tubac Chamber of Commerce
P.O. Box 1866
Tubac, AZ 85646
(1) 398-2704

Tubac Presidio
State Historic Park
(1) 398-2252

The **Stables Restaurant** in nearby Tubac Valley Country Club is an excellent spot for breakfast, lunch or dinner. Large, arched windows overlooking the golf course and the Santa Rita Mountains provide a lovely setting. Prices are moderate to expensive and there is a bar (with bar stools made of horse saddles). To reach the restaurant, drive north (from Tubac) on the frontage road approximately .8 miles to the arched entrance of Tubac Valley Country Club. Follow Avenida de Otero and it will lead you right to The Stables.

Door—San José de Tumacacori

SAN JOSE DE TUMACACORI

48 miles south of Tucson
1-398-2341

$3/car load
Daily   8am—5pm
Closed Christmas

"The fruit has fallen and none to gather it. Corrals still standing—not a living thing seen. It has a melancholy appearance. The walls of the church still stand, no roof. . . . It looks desolate indeed. The dome over the altar covered with cement which shines white in the sun . . . rich and exquisite carving inside." So San Jose de Tumacacori was described by a Sonoran traveler in December of 1849.

Standing alone in the Santa Cruz Valley, the stately beauty of Tumacacori Mission still imparts a melancholy appearance. The roof has been replaced, along with some reconstruction. The dome still shines white in the sun, but the passing year have faded the colorful carvings.

Father Eusebio Francisco Kino visited the Pima village of Tumacacori, then located on the east bank of the Santa Cruz River, in January of 1691. After saying mass under a ramada constructed for him, he gave the village the patronage of San Cayetano and returned to northern Sonora.

In March of 1753, the village was moved to its present site and the patronage changed to San Jose. The Franciscan Order took over all Sonoran missions in 1767 when the Jesuits were expelled from the Spanish dominions, and in 1772 Tumacacori became the mission headquarters for the district.

When Father Narcisco Gutierrez, a Spanish Franciscan, arrived in 1794, he found a rapidly deteriorating church. Determined to build a church as magnificent as Mission San Xavier del Bac, he asked for and received official permission to plan a new one, employing an architect from the interior.

Construction began during the 1800s, with the local Indians doing much of the manual labor and artisans providing their talents for the more exquisite work. Father Guiterrez raised some of the necessary construction funds through the sale of 4,000 head of cattle from the Tumacacori herd. Although never completely finished, the church was in full use by 1822 just after Mexico's independence of 1821. Laws were passed that tended to weaken the churches, money for missionary aid was limited, and the new government could no longer provide adequate protection from hostile Indians resulting in the abandonment of the mission 26 years later.

Deserted by the Spanish settlers, soldiers and priests, frequent Apache raids soon made life in Tumacacori intolerable. Mexico sold the mission lands to a private citizen in 1844 and in 1848 the few remaining devout Indians transported themselves and the church furnishings to Mission San Xavier. Deserted, the church slowly fell into ruins, with only its massiveness keeping it from crumbling completely.

Administered by the National Park Service, the visitor center includes dioramas and relics of the area, depicting life in the early 1800s, and a model what it is believed the mission looked like. A tranquil patio garden invites relaxation.

As you walk toward the church, the ruins of Tumacacori village lie in the dirt beneath you. Note the structural elements of baroque architecture and inside, the original, but fading colors applied by the Indians. Also note how the entry arch was painted and grooved to make it resemble a European stone arch. The baptistry is to your right, with its nine-foot-thick walls supporting the three-story bell tower. A staircase winds upward to the choir loft entry and then to the bellfry; however, due to structural instability, it is closed. As all worshipers knelt or sat on the floor, there were no pews or seats.

As neglect and the ravages of the seasons had destroyed much of the nave, there has been some reconstruction of the mission, including the base of the pulpit. The roof had collapsed, along with the choir loft, and the beams were salvaged by local people. Treasure hunters looking for non-existent gold in the latter part of the nineteenth and early twentieth centuries destroyed the original floor.

Window placement allows for the best use of natural lighting in the rather dimly-lit space with windows below the dome creating a softly lighted nave. The side altars, used by worshipers for prayer and meditation, receive light from the small windows high above and opposite them. Morning and afternoon light would have illuminated the statues and decorations placed in the niches.

Look back toward the front door and up to where the choir loft would have been and you can see on the left, the loft entry, and on the right, a groove where the loft floor fitted.

North of the church is the Campo Santo or mission cemetery. After abandonment of the church, cattlemen used the grounds as a round-up corral and later, treasure hunters looking for Padres' Gold, robbed what remaining bodies were left. The graves you see are all less than a century old and are those of settlers who returned to the valley after the Apache wars.

Around the cemetery wall are deep niches which once held statues representing the Stations of the Cross. The circular structure, which was never completed, was a chapel. A common feature of church complexes, last rites were administered here and the bodies prepared for burial.

The convento grounds are on the east side of the church. Located here were the missionary's domicile, dwellings for his assistants and visitors, kitchens, corrals and the other outbuildings and storage rooms necessary for a successful mission. Beyond the walls, along the Santa Cruz, irrigated fields supplied the Indians and missionaries with needed foods and pastures and rangelands for cattle and sheep.

Wheelchairs and strollers are available. There are picnic tables, but no campgrounds.

Craft demonstrations are frequently presented on weekends from 9am to 3pm. On the first Sunday in December the mission hosts its **Annual Tumacacori Fiesta**. Originated in 1970, the day features music, Native American crafts and dances, food and other events.

To reach Tumacacori, drive south on I-19 and take exit 29. The distances on highway I-19 are given in kilometers; multiply by .6 to convert to miles.

You may also wish to stop at the **Santa Cruz Chile Factory**, across the road from the mission. Spices are for sale at quite reasonable prices.

San Jose de Tumacacori
Box 67
Tumacacori, AZ 85640

NOGALES, SONORA
MEXICO

66 miles south of Tucson

To reach Nogales (Spanish for walnuts), drive south on I-19. (Note the distances on I-19 are given in kilometers; multiply by .6 to convert to mileage, otherwise you will think it is much further than it is.) You will pass **Mission San Xavier del Bac**, **Tubac Presidio State Historic Park** and **Tumacacori Mission** and may wish to stop and visit these sights also. (*See also* PLACES TO GO AND THINGS TO DO.)

Just 100 years ago, this route was known as El Camino de Los Muertos, The Deadmen's Highway. Apache raiders rode through here until Geronimo's capture in 1886, leaving death and destruction everywhere. Torn-down fences and burned-out houses filled the valley and anyone traveling the road was on constant guard for Indian arrows. Murder was the common subject of conversation and artist and writer of the day, John Ross Browne, wrote in his book, *Adventures in the Apache Country,* that in traveling forty miles of the highway he saw as many graves.

But now a little over a peaceful hour's drive brings you to Ambos Nogales, the junction of two nations and two cultures. You'll drive through the verdant Santa Cruz River Valley, where flatlands, cactus and creosote give way to rolling, grassy foothills, pecan groves, cattle lands and usually cooler weather, as Nogales is nearly 1500 feet higher than Tucson.

An American citizen does not need a visa or passport to spend the day in Nogales. If you plan on going into the interior or staying in Mexico longer than seventy-two hours, you must have a tourist permit (visa) and an automobile permit, both obtainable with proper identification (birth certificate, passport, notarized affidavit of proof of U.S. citizenship), at the Nogales border crossing, or at the Mexican Consulate in Tucson. If you are *not* an American citizen, check U.S. regulations before entering Mexico.

Many U.S. auto insurance companies cover driving several miles into Mexico. If yours does, be sure to have proof of coverage with you. If you do not know whether your car insurance is good in Mexico, I advise that you park at one of the several locations available on the Arizona side and walk across. Most shopping and restaurants are just a short distance across the border.

Of course, the main reason for going to Nogales is TO SHOP. Bargains include rugs, embroidered dresses, woven shawls, hand-carved wooden furniture, colorful hand-blown glassware, tooled leather goods, tinwear, and unique paper maché items, all from Mexico; French silks and perfumes; cameras, toys and porcelain from Germany; and cameras and optics from Japan. And, of course, the inevitable liquor stores. Liquor prices are not all that good anymore, due to the peso devaluation. Savings can be made, however, on Kaluha and tequila and some liqueurs. U.S. currency is accepted at all shops in border areas and most shops also accept major credit cards or personal checks.

Everyone speaks English, so don't worry about communication problems. And if you know some Spanish, use it. Mexicans are very helpful when you try to speak their language.

Most tourist shops are along either Avenida Obregon or Calle Elias. These stores handle the more inexpensive items and will usually bargain on prices; however, not all items are bargains and caution is recommended. **Maya de Mexico** #150 offers lovely women's clothing with a traditional Mexican look. Fashions include shawls, embroidered dresses and blouses and some modern-style dresses.

Several newly built and quite attractive pedestrian malls have changed the shopping style in Nogales. The first is **Centro Comercial Juarez** with over 50 shops selling in the typical Nogales manner. It is

located just south of Calle Campillo, the first street you will walk to. You'll find many leather goods, glassware, jewelry and embroidered clothing and public rest rooms are available here.

As you walk south on Avenida Obregon, you'll find several more malls, some with elegant high-quality items. Several blocks south are **La Casa Del Sol** and **Plaza Nogales** on the same side of the street as the school and **Plaza San Miguel** across the street. All have particularly nice shops and Plaza Nogales has public restrooms.

A few unique shops offer antique furniture, stone carvings, folk art, tin and brass ware, paintings, rugs and colorful woven fabrics. The prices are not inexpensive, and are usually fixed, but compared to state-side import shops, they are bargains. Regarding "fixed prices:" numerous shops will have signs so stating, however, depending upon the time of the year and the sales for that day, you may be able to bargain.

The most fascinating of these shops is **El Changarro,** located at Calle Elias #93, phone 2-03-45. (Note: La Roca Restaurant is upstairs.) Wandering through the several rooms and courtyards filled with rugs, hand-carved and antique furniture, stone statues, fountains and flowers, brass and silver-plated chandeliers and mirrors, hand-blown glass ornaments and hand-woven cotton and wool fabrics is a joy in itself. It is as though you have been transported back in time to a nineteenth-century Mexican ranchero. It's well worth the visit, just to look. The shop is closed on Sundays.

While on Calle Elias, check out **Casa Espana** and **La Hacienda,** where you will find wood carvings, mirrors, Oaxaca pottery, custom-made furniture, wrought-iron chandeliers, hand-painted sinks and carved doors.

Approximately three-quarters of a mile south, at Avenida Ruiz #427 (across the railroad tracks), is **Antigua de Mexico.** Not quite as fine as El Changarro, but still with lovely items, you will find religious art, glassware, rugs, artificial flowers, pottery, furniture and mirrors and you can order custom-made furniture.

La Roca, one of the better-known restaurants, is located at Calle Elias #92, phone 2-07-60. (They're right above El Changarro.) You will find excellent cuisine in elegant surroundings of art and antiques. The building itself is quite unusual with several separate dining areas overlooking a courtyard. A varied selection of authentic dishes from inland Colonial towns is offered, along with seafoods and beefsteak. Dancing, with music by the best of Latin-American musicians, takes place in the evening.

Another restaurant with excellent meals is **El Cid,** located on Avenida Obregon #24, phone 2-64-44. Owned by the folks who made the Caverna famous, you'll find the same high-quality food, including delicious Green Turtle Soup. (Hamburgers and sandwiches are also available, for the less adventurous.) You can dine on the balcony and watch the streetside activity. (The Caverna is a restaurant that burned in 1984 which has not yet been rebuilt. As they say in Mexico: mañana, mañana.)

One of the most exciting and emotional elements associated with Mexico and Spain is bullfighting. Nogales bullfighting occurs on summer Sundays, at the Plaza de Toros, approximately three miles south of the border. For complete information on schedules check with the people at CARTEL, the *Newsletter of Mexican Torero,* P.O. Box 318, Cortaro, AZ 85652.

Upon returning to the U.S., you must declare your purchases, with a $400 duty-free personal exemption. One person may make a joint declaration for all family members residing in the same household and returning together to the U.S. That is, a family of three may bring in articles valued up to $1,200 retail value free of duty, on one declaration. Infants and children are entitled to the same exemptions

NOGALES

as adults (except for alcoholic beverages). Many items, such as wooden furniture (for personal, not business use), leather goods, jewelry and perfume are duty-free, no matter what their cost. If you have specific questions, check with U.S. Customs officials before you cross the border.

One liter (33.8 fl. oz.) of alcoholic beverage per month may be included in your $400 exemption if you are twenty-one years of age or older and it is purchased for your own use or as a gift. Fireworks and switchblade knives are prohibited in the U.S.

DO NOT BUY MEXICAN VANILLA. Although cheap, many brands contain a highly toxic substance called coumarin. As it is impossible to know which brands contain coumarin, the safest course is not to buy any. Several foodstuffs are also prohibited, particularly fresh foods. Animals and birds may require a several week quarantine, if they can be entered into the U.S. at all. If you plan to purchase such unusual items, check with customs beforehand.

I highly recommend you not have that certain canaibis plant in your possession, either in Mexico or upon your return. Our custom authorities are very critical about the importation and possession of same while Mexican officials are known to be even more critical. Also, with the recent "Zero Tolerance" implemented by the U.S. Government, one small marijuana cigarette could cost you your automobile. For good.

If traveling with a cat or dog, rabies vaccination papers are required upon your return. Check with customs before crossing the border for additional requirements. Otherwise, you may find that your animal must go into quarantine for up to three months.

If carrying valuable foreign-made items (e.g. cameras, watches, binoculars) you may wish to check with customs before you leave the states or have with you proof of prior purchase, otherwise you may have to pay duty charges upon your return.

If not "shopped out" additional "goodies" are available at **Garrett Wray Curios,** 492 Grand Avenue in Sonora, AZ, (1) 287-2115. They carry Mexican imports, including furniture, tinware, baskets, pottery, and a tremendous selection of glassware. They're open Tue—Sat, and closed the month of August.

The Mexican Consulate, 553 South Stone Avenue, 882-5595 is open 9am—4pm to obtain visas. Persons not American citizens must obtain passports and hours for this service are 9am—3pm. The consulate is also available to assist Mexican citizens with problems in this country.

PATAGONIA, ARIZONA
9 miles northeast of Nogales.

When leaving Nogales, an alternate route to Tucson, beginning on highway 89, takes you through some of Arizona's richest horse and cattle country. Numerous Hollywood productions have been filmed in this part of the country, including portions of *A Star is Born*.

(This route will also take you past **Zulas,** a favorite of Tucsonans who drove to "Nogy" long before the new highway was built. Zulas was the "must" stop before heading home. It still is for those of us who know about it. Zulaburgers are mouth-watering and inexpensive—as is the Mexican food—and the pies—and about anything else you might wish to order. And if you aren't going on to Patagonia, keep driving north and you'll get back to I-19.)

Take highway 89 north to highway 82 and go east. This will lead you past **Lake Patagonia** (*see also* FISHING AND BOATING) and the **Patagonia-Sonoita Creek Sanctuary.** The sanctuary, a 312-acre strip extending more than a mile along Sonoita Creek, contains a flourishing area abounding in sycamores, cottonwoods, willows, oaks and ash, year-round water, more than 200 species of birds and a wide variety of aquatic and terrestrial animals. If you stop to enjoy this wildlife refuge, please remain on marked trails and do not take your pets. Picnicking and camping are not allowed. Several other rest areas and creeks nearby provide ideal locations for picnics.

The **Museum of the Horse** (1-394-2264) is the only U.S. museum dedicated to the horse. Collected by Ann Stradling, the six rooms of items from all over the world have an estimated value of $4 million. Included are a collection of ladies side saddles, horse brasses from England, prints and paintings, horse-drawn carriages, a Greek chariot bit, a Roman horse comb, items from archaeological digs and Indian traders and Stradling family furniture dating from 1855. There is an admission fee.

Several ghost towns are found to the south and east, in the Patagonia Mountains. An unpaved mountain road climbs southeast out of Patagonia, making a forty-five mile loop, taking in the no-longer towns of Harshaw, Mowry, Washington Camp and Duquesne. The **Stage Stop Inn** (1-394-2211) offers a motor tour of much of the area. If you plan on driving, be sure it hasn't been raining, as the roads rapidly become impassable. *Arizona's Best Ghost Towns,* by Philip Varney, is an excellent guide to this area and many other spots in the state.

Be sure to stop at **The Ovens of Patagonia**. Two Tucsonans fell in love with Patagonia a few years ago and in an effort to live there and make a livelihood, they opened a bakery. You'll find fresh breads and sweets and some sandwich choices (if they're not sold out). A great place for an afternoon snack.

If you decide Patagonia warrants more time and you want to stay over, Don and Doris Wenig have a wonderful bed and breakfast, called **Little House**, P.O. Box 461, Patagonia, AZ (1-394-2493). Each of two adobe guest rooms has a sitting area with a corner fireplace, patio and private bath. Don is a gourmet cook who'll prepare a wonderful breakfast for you and you'll find the conversation stimulating. The surroundings and the Wenigs are wonderful additions to a favorite area.

When leaving Patagonia, continue north through rolling grass-lands, and go through nationally-known Sonoita, where quarter horse and thoroughbred racing meets have been held since the 1950s. (*See also* SEASONAL EVENTS AND SPORTS.) Sonoita is also the location of the Santa Cruz County Fairgrounds. At Sonoita, take highway 83 north to I-10 and back into Tucson from the east.

AMERIND FOUNDATION

64 miles east of Tucson

Adults $3   Seniors $2
12—18 $2   Under 12 free
Daily 10am—4pm
Closed major holidays

Those interested in the archeological and ethnological aspects of the Pimeria Alta region will enjoy the Amerind Foundation, which has one of the most extensive collections of archeological activities in the Southwest. The Amerind (a contraction of American Indian) Foundation was established in 1937 by William S. Fulton to house and systamize the expanding scope of his extensive archeological activities in the Southwest. It is a non-profit archeological research facility, museum, and library which recently won accreditation by the American Association of Museums, the highest honor a U.S. museum can receive.

Since Mr. Fulton's 1915 discovery of an olla (an Indian-made ceramic vessel) and his subsequent interest in archeology, the foundation has continued to be involved in archeological research and has grown to include a magnificent collection of pottery, jewelry, toys, musical instruments, crafts, baskets, hunting and cooking instruments and clothing from numerous New World tribes.

Major displays may stay in place a year or longer, while smaller displays are changed once a year or so. The museum's collection incorporates many times as many relics in storage as are exhibited.

Displays in 1988 include *Hopi Works of Art on Paper, Navajo Ways* and *Dance in Ceremony*. One of the most outstanding collections, particularly for students of Apache lore, is the White Mountain Apache basket collection. These baskets are of particularly refined craftsmanship and design.

Numerous artifacts were recovered from a dig on the eighteen acres of land surrounding San Cayetano del Tumacacori, the mission site south of Tucson.

The Amerind collection of bultos (hand-carved religious statues) is considered to be one of the best. As the travel north from Mexico was quite arduous, Franciscan Fathers left behind many of their religious items. Upon reaching their destination in the Rio Grande Valley of New Mexico, they made new statues, but soon turned the carving over to the local parishioners of the area. These items, carved between 100 and 200 years ago, have a stylized serenity unique to that area.

Since the early 1960s, scientists from the foundation have been working with Mexican officials at the excavation site of Casas Grandes (no relation to Arizona's Casa Grande ruins), 130 miles southwest of El Paso, Texas. Inhabited during the years A.D. 1060—1340, it is estimated that Casas Grandes was one of the most advanced and affluent North American cultures of its time. Artifacts from this excavation are on display throughout the museum.

Besides these and other outstanding artifacts, the museum offers a 20,000 volume library containing a vast selection of books and articles on the history, anthropology and archeology of the Southwest and Mexico. Use of the library is limited to scholars and researchers.

An art gallery open to the public and a gift shop provide Western-related art.

An attractive picnic area provides shade and tables. No food is available at the foundation, however the Triangle T Guest Ranch next door serves breakfast, lunch and dinner.

If arrangements are made ahead of time, special group rates are available at $2/person for ten or more.

The pink stucco Spanish-style building is near Texas Canyon, overlooking the Dragoon Mountains. Texas Canyon itself is worth the drive, just to see its dramatic, unbelievable rock formations. Take I-10 east from Tucson and exit at marker 318. Follow the Dragoon road south for a mile, then turn at the left-turn sign.

The Amerind Foundation
Dragoon, AZ 85609
(1) 586-3666

Yucca

TOMBSTONE, ARIZONA
80 miles southeast of Tucson

"The Town Too Tough to Die," one of our most famous western towns, was immortalized in 1881 by that famous "Gunfight at the O.K. Corral" and was dedicated in 1962 as a Registered National Historic Landmark. The history you are probably most familiar with is that of a rip-roaring, shoot-em-up town with frequent killings in the streets, occasional robberies, two known lynchings and that one infamous battle.

It's difficult to reconcile the fact that Tombstone's historical significance was established by the most famous gun battle in the West, when she was, at one time, the epitome of elegance and sophistication.

Her heyday began in 1878 when a prospector named Ed Schieffelin filed five mining claims in Tucson for property in the San Pedro Valley, a vast, empty expanse of land lying between the Dragoon, Whetstone and Huachuca mountains. When told by a friend he would only find his tombstone there, the prospector chose that name for his claim. Schieffelin's discovery quickly brought other miners, and a year later 600 people were living in a tent city clustered around Tombstone's only and very unglamorous saloon.

Within another year, 10,000 more souls had arrived and Tombstone became the largest and most important city between El Paso and San Francisco. When news of the silver strike reached the east, big-time operators arrived (as they seem to do in all booming cities—then and now), methodically buying up the properties of the independent prospectors. By 1881, the holdings had been consolidated in several large companies from New York, Philadelphia, Los Angeles and San Francisco.

A dozen lavishly decorated establishments replaced that original saloon, with white-jacketed bartenders serving drinks in stemmed glasses from behind mahogany bars. Although two out of three buildings were saloons or gambling halls, millinery shops featured $500.00 gowns. The social set entertained lavishly with grand masked balls and elegant weddings. The hotels were urbane hostelries with thick carpets, crystal chandeliers and costly oil paintings. The rooms had the newest of furnishings, including spring mattresses and china toilet fixtures of the latest design. Imported wines were served, menus were printed in French, and the best seafood served between New Orleans and San Francisco arrived by stage from California.

The luxuriousness, if not the notoriousness, changed rapidly when water began filtering into the silver mines and Tombstone began its descent. Over a million dollars in silver ore came out of the mines before the subterranean waters flooded the underground tunnels, ending mining operations. Over six million gallons of water pumped daily failed to lower the water level. Within a few years the richest mines had closed and mining was down fifty percent. Strikes and the American silver crisis of 1893-94 created more problems; the declining price of silver chased all away and by 1910 the mines had closed for good, leaving Tombstone not much more than a legend in the valley.

In the early 1960s several persons interested in the uproarious and exciting past of old Tombstone began restoring some of the more historic sites. Be prepared for some commercialization however and admission charges. The following are some you might find interesting,

BOOTHILL CEMETERY
Highway 80 west of town

This, the most photographed of Tombstone's landmarks, is located just outside of town on highway 80 and contains the graves of those killed in that famous gunfight, lynched outlaws, and others who "died with their boots on." Of course, you must stop here, if only to read some of the inscriptions on the tombstones. One of the shortest and saddest reads: "George Johnson—hanged by mistake."

O.K. CORRAL
Corner of 3rd Street and Fremont

It was October 26, 1881, when the feud between the Earps and Clantons was settled in dust, bullets and death. At that time, Wyatt Earp rode shotgun for Wells Fargo and owned twenty-five percent of the Oriental Saloon. Bat Masterson and Luke Short dealt faro there and Wyatt's old friend, Doc Holliday, was a frequent visitor, as were most of the notorious gamblers and gunmen of that period. You can visit the O.K. Corral where lifelike statues are positioned to recreate the famous scene.

THE ORIENTAL
Corner of 5th and Allen

This gambling hall, built in 1880 and partially owned by Wyatt Earp, was the haunt of numerous notorious characters in its time.

THE BIRD CAGE THEATRE
On Allen Street near 6th

Now a museum, the Bird Cage had a reputation in its heyday of being the bawdiest night spot in the West. The song, "Only a Bird in a Gilded Cage," was supposedly inspired by this combination theatre-dancehall-gambling casino.

CRYSTAL PALACE
Corner of 5th and Allen

The showplace of the Southwest during Tombstone's brief and violent history, the Palace, with its massive mahogany back bar, has been completely restored to its original nineteenth-century magnificence.

FLY'S PHOTOGRAPHY GALLERY
On Fremont near 3rd Street

Tombstone had its resident photographer in the person of Camillas S. Fly. A collection of his work is on display at the gallery, including his photos of Geronimo's surrender and life in the Indian camps.

ROSE TREE INN MUSEUM
On 4th Street, near Toughnut

Tombstone's first adobe structure was built on this site, although it was nowhere near as large as the present one, as each owner has made additions. Within this museum is reputedly the largest rose tree in the world. The Lady Banksia rose spreads over 8,000 square feet of supports, blooms its white blossoms every April, and grows larger every year. The rose grew from a slip sent from her homeland to Mary Gee, the Scottish bride of a mine official. The museum exhibits also include antique furnishings brought to Tombstone by covered wagon in 1880.

SCHIEFFELIN HALL
On 4th Street, near Fremont Street

Touring stock companies from the New York, Chicago, Denver and San Francisco theatre circuit played here, often providing a cultural contrast to the town's rough, primitive mining-camp lifestyle. Historama, a 45-minute program combining film and lifelike figures on a revolving stage depicts the colorful history of Tombstone.

TOMBSTONE COURTHOUSE
Corner of 3rd Street and Toughnut

Tombstone was the first county seat of Cochise County (named after the famous Apache chief, Cochise) and remained that until 1929, when the county seat was transferred to Bisbee. The old courthouse, now part of Tombstone Courthouse State Historic Park, was built in 1882, and is the oldest standing territorial courthouse in Arizona. The scene of famous trials and hangings, it now functions as a museum, displaying historic objects and documents from the boomtown times of the turn of the century. Restrooms, picnic tables and drinking water are available. For further information, call (1) 457-3311.

Every Sunday throughout the year, beginning at 2pm, historic Allen Street is blocked to vehicular traffic and parking and there are re-enactments of historic gunfights and other events. No charge, but contributions are accepted.

On the first and third Sundays, "The Wild Bunch" performs inside the O.K. Corral. There is no increase in the normal O.K. Corral admission for this event.

Wyatt Earp Days are held on Memorial Day weekend and **Wild West Days** on Labor Day, while the first Friday weekend in March is Tombstone's anniversary.

Stop and pick up a copy of the Tombstone Epitaph, the West's most famous newspaper. The Epitaph has chronicled western history for over 100 years now, having been founded in 1880 by John P. Clum. Mr. Clum named the paper when he stated, "Every Tombstone has its Epitaph."

Public restrooms are located at City Park, 3rd and Allen, and at Edna Landin Park, east of the city.

To reach Tombstone, drive east on I-10 to Benson (exit 303) and take highway 80 south.

BISBEE, ARIZONA
95 miles southeast of Tucson

Nestled a mile high in the Mule Mountains, "The Climate Capitol of the World," with its sunny days and cool nights, is a perfect year-round vacation spot. The city's scenic beauty and nineteenth-century architecture combine with a fascinating historical heritage that offers lots to see and do, while an impressive selection of arts and crafts are available from the city's talented artisans.

Ancient, weathered buildings and homes, many being authentically restored, are a photographer's paradise. Clustered on steep hillsides, these lovely homes are reached by streets so narrow that Bisbee's thirty-year old fire engine was specifically designed with an extra-narrow chassis to navigate the extreme turns.

A typical frontier mining town in the 1930s, Bisbee combined the bawdy coarseness of the miners, known as "iron men," with the elegance of turn-of-the-century homes. Victorian charm abounded, along with the questionable "charm" of Brewery Gulch. Known as the finest watering hole between San Francisco and New Orleans, the Gulch sported over fifty saloons. An equal number of bordellos provided needed diversions for men spending lonely, dangerous hours in the over 2,000 miles of tunnels located under the city.

The Copper Queen mine paid over $300 million in profits and dividends at the turn of the century and gave the world over two billion pounds of copper. The Queen and the Lavender Pit, from whence comes Bisbee's famous turquoise, created a population of over 20,000 people in 1900, making Bisbee Arizona's largest, wealthiest and liveliest town. The boom hit its height in 1910, with mining operations continuing spasmodically until 1975 when Phelps Dodge Corp. closed both mines.

Determined their city would not become another Arizona ghost town, Bisbee residents began a resurrection of the city. That spirit, combined with considerable hard work, has helped Bisbee prosper once again. Besides walking and driving around this picturesque town, you'll find mine tours, museums, unique shopping opportunities and several special events.

LAVENDER PIT MINE

This narrated bus tour covers thirteen miles along the perimeter of the 300-acre Lavender Open Pit Mine. The total production from this mine and the Copper Queen approached the $2 billion mark in the ninety-year history of Bisbee. Incidentally, "Lavender" refers not to the color of the pit, but to Harrison Lavender, a Phelps Dodge executive who developed the open pit mine.

COPPER QUEEN MINE

Phelps Dodge has leased the "Queen" to the City of Bisbee for $1.00 per year and veteran miners guide you deep into the mine through

6,000 feet of solid rock. Donning a miner's equipment of heavy yellow slicker and hard hat with miner's lamp, you will experience some of the awe and excitement, and possibly a bit of the fear that those long-ago miners felt every day of their lives in their subterranean world.

You will ride into and out of the tunnel on a "man car," the same narrow, knee-hugging mine train the miners used. Exhibits explain blasting and drilling techniques and steel ore cars capable of hauling a ton of crushed rock and ore to the surface are displayed, along with an elevator and level station which has been reconstructed to enable you to visualize the complete operations of mining underground.

Many Bisbee school children ran for the safety of the mines during Apache raids in the 1800s. Geronimo's campaigns created an ongoing fear and the children were instructed to head directly for the nearest mine shaft when the town whistle blew four times (two shorts, a long, and a short).

Bring warm clothing. Although you'll be partially protected by the slicker, the temperature within the tunnel stays at forty-seven degrees winter and summer. The tour is on level ground, not an underground shaft, except for a visit into one stope that requires walking up some wooden steps. Tours are daily at 10:30am, noon, 2pm and 3:30pm and there is an admission fee.

COPPER QUEEN HOTEL

I've made it a practice to not recommend hotels, but one exception must be the historic Copper Queen Hotel. Built by the Copper Queen Mining Company in 1902, the hotel has played host to territorial governors, executives, and some of the most flamboyant names of the past, including Teddy Roosevelt and "Black Jack" Pershing, who stopped over on his way to search out Pancho Villa in the Mexican hills.

The Queen's turn-of-the-century charm and grandeur invite a visit to her dining room or saloon, or an overnight stay in her lovely old rooms where you might well imagine participating in those uproarious mining days when Bisbee was the Queen of the mining camps. If weather permits, enjoy lunch or dinner on the terrace. (Phone: 1-800-247-5829.)

BISBEE MINING AND HISTORICAL MUSEUM
At Queen Plaza

Built in 1895 as the General Office Building of the Phelps Dodge Corporation, this turn-of-the-century brick and oak structure also operates as Bisbee's Civic Center and is entered in the National

Register of Historic Places. Volunteers of Bisbee's Arts and Humanities Organization act as guides and inform visitors through realistic mining dioramas, micro-filmed archives, rare photo collections, oral history tapes, artifacts and many other momentos of Bisbee's colorful past.

A varied collection of mining, geological, historical, cultural, genealogical, and research data on Bisbee can be found in the **Shattuck Memorial Archival Library,** also located in the museum.

COCHISE COUNTY COURTHOUSE

Cochise County was named after the famous Chiricahua Apache Chieftan, and the stately Cochise County courthouse is another historic sight you shouldn't miss. Designed by Tucson architect Roy Place, the early 1930s courthouse is an outstanding example of the art-deco style.

Standing at the gateway of the county buildings is a Bisbee landmark, the *Iron Man,* with his hammer and muscles accentuating his role as a hard-rock miner. The statue is not made of iron, but represents the hardy copper miners who were known as "iron men" because of their strength and stamina.

RESTORATION MUSEUM
37 Main Street

Four floors of memorabilia, in the historic Fair Store Building, are devoted to recapturing some of Bisbee's fascinating history and to preserving the possessions of adventurers who came to this area in the late 1800s and early 1900s. Articles range from a blackjack table and tall dealer's chair from the notorious Brewery Gulch to a cache of antique furniture and clothing in use during Bisbee's magnificent past.

MUHEIM HOUSE
207 Youngblood Hill

In 1979 this elegant ten-room dwelling overlooking Brewery Gulch was the first Bisbee home to be listed in the National Register of Historic Sites, and it, along with its Queen Anne decorations, has been opened as a Living Museum.

Originally a four-room home constructed 1898—1902, the home was enlarged to its present ten rooms in 1915. The home was the residence of the saloonkeeper, mining entrepreneur, and co-founder of Miners and Merchants Bank, Joseph M. Muheim, Sr.

SHOPPING

A number of artists reside in Bisbee, renovating some of the picturesque homes located there and contributing to Bisbee's reputation as an art center. Collections of their work are available at the several art galleries and crafts and gift shops throughout the city. Numerous workshops, theatrical productions, film programs, studio classes, and a broad range of community events occur throughout the year.

HISTORIC HOME TOURS

Bisbee's 5th annual Historic Home Tour will be held in the fall of 1988. Tours include both Old Bisbee and a section of town known as Warren, just south of the Lavender Pit. Many elegant Old World homes once owned by mining operation's bosses are located there. Usually a dozen or so homes are on the tour and several are open to the public. Check with the Bisbee Chamber of Commerce for exact dates.

Several other events occur annually, one of which is especially unique, the **Vuelta de Bisbee Bicycle Race.** Once you see the hills and vales in and out of this city, you will more than appreciate the efforts made by those who participate in this race. In 1980, when Bisbee hosted the U.S. Cycling Federation's National Championships, it was stated that Bisbee offers, "The most demanding multi-stage race on the American continent." Bisbee residents agreed and instituted their own annual race, occurring during the fourth weekend in April.

One wonders if there are wages on the bicycle races as bold as one made in 1880 by George Warren of Bisbee, who bet his share of the Copper Queen mine on a foot race and lost. That share later turned out to be worth $12 million, making it one of the most expensive races in history!

Other events include a **Rodeo** in March, **a Renaissance Festival** in June, a **Fourth of July** celebration, a **Poetry Festival** in August, the **Cochise Art Festival** in September, a **Mineral Show** in October, and in December, **Santa's Workshop Festival.** Check with the Bisbee Chamber of Commerce for dates.

To arrive at this lovely historic gem, drive east on I-10 to Benson (exit 303), travel south on U.S. 80 through the "time tunnel," and before you will be the City of Yesteryear.

Greater Bisbee Chamber of Commerce
P.O. Drawer BA
Bisbee, AZ 85603
(1) 432-2141

THE MILE HI/RAMSEY CANYON PRESERVE

If you are at all interested in "birding" and are returning from Bisbee between the hours of 8am and 5pm, you may want to take a different route back to Tucson and visit The Mile Hi/Ramsey Canyon Preserve, just outside of Sierra Vista.

The Mile Hi/Ramsey Canyon Preserve is owned by **The Nature Conservancy,** a private conservation group that acquires biologically significant land through memberships and donations. This 280-acre preserve in the Huachuca Mountains offers an unusually moist, cool and stable environment. The major attraction is the number of hummingbirds that make their home in the canyon during the spring, summer and fall months. Over fourteen species having been seen and photographed, more than in any other place in the United States.

Picnicking is not permitted, but you may wander about the preserve. Parking is limited, so visits are suggested during the weekdays, rather than on weekends. Groups wishing to visit should obtain permission in advance. Pets are not allowed.

Rental cabins are available. Inquiries regarding the cabins or further use of the preserve should be made to The Mile Hi, R.R. 1, Box 84, Hereford, AZ 85615 phone (1) 378-2785.

To reach The Mile Hi from Bisbee, drive southwest on state route 92. Just past the road to Hereford, turn west on Ramsey Canyon Road. The Mile Hi is four miles into the canyon. (If coming from Sierra Vista, the turnoff is six miles south of town.) To return to Tucson, go back to highway 92, turn north and drive to highway 90 intersection, take 90 to I-10 and west into Tucson.

Trail Dust Town

TOMORROW WE DIET

As countless Tucson restaurants provide excellent dining, it is difficult to decide which to incorporate in *This is Tucson*. Criteria for inclusion is: consistent quality food and service and superiority of cuisine for the price. Also significant to dining enjoyment, the environment and decor have been taken into consideration.

Eighty-five restaurants are listed under the categories of: The Best in Town, Steaks and/or Seafood, Light Eating, This and That, Mexican (some of the best in the country), Chinese, Eastern/Near and Far, Greek, and Italian. Although dress in Tucson is generally casual, some restaurants require coats and ties for gentlemen. Check dress codes when you call for reservations.

Speaking of reservations; it's best to call for safety's sake. Wintertime especially finds a scarcity of space on Friday and Saturday nights.

The price guide is as follows: & inexpensive (dinner entrees under $8); && moderate ($8-$15); &&& expensive ($15-$25); &&&& very expensive ($25 and up).

All restaurants happily accept cash, however other acceptable forms of payment are also listed: AE—American Express, CB—Carte Blanch; D—Discovery; DC—Diners Club; MC—Mastercard; V—Visa; and CH—local checks with guarantee card and ID.

On pages 252-253 you will find a map of Tucson. The large free-form ovals, each with an identifying title, elucidate specific valley areas. Immediately under or opposite the name of each restaurant is the area in which that restaurant is located. The squares on the maps are locations of reviewed restaurants. The circles are the locations of shops mentioned in the next chapter. This clustering of restaurants and shops enables you to combine the two activities.

THE BEST IN TOWN

ARIZONA INN
University
2200 East Elm
Res. please 327-7646
A, MC, V, CH

B/L/D seven days
Cocktails
&&&
No-smoking section

This pink-stuccoed Tucson hotel, a landmark for over half a century, has welcomed such guests as the Duke and Duchess of Windsor and Burt Reynolds. Its luxuriant landscaping and romantic, old-world gardens afford sustenance for the soul as well as the body. Over fourteen shaded acres of lawn, flowers and fountains are frequently enjoyed by Tucsonans when "The Inn" is chosen for those very special events, such as weddings, graduations and the annual Silver and Turquoise Ball.

The elegant dining room, with its simple furnishings and table settings of silver and china on damask, evokes a graciousness of years past. The menu changes frequently, with veal one of the specialties, along with numerous American/Continental dishes and excellent, attractive salads. A "lighter-side" menu is offered also.

You may wish to visit the inn's gift shop which offers delightful handmade gifts, clothing and "grandma" type goodies.

CAPRICCIO
4825 North First Avenue
Res. please 887-2333
MC, V, CH

Rillito
D Mon—Sat
Cocktails
&&&

Reservations are a must at this small, elegant restaurant that serves sensational Italian food. The northern Italian cuisine includes some of the most exotic, distinct preparations imaginable, splendidly and quietly served.

Its coziness adds a romantic flavor, with low lights and soft background music. An excellent small wine list offers mostly Italian wines.

CHARLES
Pantano
6400 East El Dorado Circle
Res. please 296-7173
A, DC, D, MC, V, CH

D seven days
L Mon—Fri
Cocktails
&&&&
No-smoking section

As you drive through the cypress-lined driveway, you know, even before you reach the impressive cobblestone courtyard and fountain, that this old English manor home harbors an especially elegant restaurant, to which you can wear that formal or tux. Originally the home of Florence Ponds, the interior has been renovated to its original 1930s style and the grounds include terraced gardens and a waterfall.

Several small dining and sitting areas contain elegant furnishings and appointments that together with reserved, understated service and superlative food, provides one of the more memorable dining experiences in Tucson. In fact, Travel-Holiday singled out Charles as one of the finest restaurants in the West in 1984.

The continental cuisine, flavored to perfection, includes veal, seafood, lamb and excellent chicken dishes. All a la carte entrees include fresh vegetables and breads baked in their own bakery.

A little difficult to find, drive north on Wilmot from Speedway to the first street on your right marked El Dorado Circle. Turn right (east) and follow the road which angles to the left, through a row of cypress trees.

DANIEL'S
2930 North Swan
(Plaza Palomino)
Res. please 742-3200
A, CB, DC, MC, V, CH

Rillito
L/D Mon—Sat   D Sun
Beer and wine
&&
No smoking section

Dan Scordato has created a soft peach impressionistic atmosphere right out of Europe, with the sounds of classical music as background to excellent dining. Entrees are varied and include chicken, beef, seafood, duck, lamb, rabbit and "the most complete veal selection in Arizona." Homemade pasta dishes and minestrone and onion soup are wonderful additions to your meal. Desserts are served with cappuccino and espresso and an extensive wine list is available.

GOLD ROOM
WESTWARD LOOK RESORT
245 East Ina Road
Res. please 297-1151
A, CB, DC, MC, V, CH

Foothills
B/L/D seven days
Cocktails
&&&&

For those who distrust nouvelle cuisine and prefer classic dining, The Gold Room offers distinctive gourmet dining with exceptional service. As one of Tucson's favorite resorts, visitors from around the world will be found enjoying the superb cuisine.

Veal is the specialty of the house, with excellent choices also of beef, poultry, seafood and a delicious rack of lamb. Freshly-made soups, fresh vegetables and magnificent desserts provide further enjoyment. If you're not up to dessert, try the Spanish Coffee—a sinfully delicious concoction of brandy, kahlua, whipped cream, coffee and orange and sugar flavoring—prepared *a la flambe* at your table.

A recent addition is piano entertainment nightly and a wonderful Sunday Brunch.

JANOS
El Presidio
150 North Main Avenue
Tucson Museum of Art Plaza
Res. please 884-9426
A, MC, V

D Winter: Mon—Sat
D Summer: Tue—Sat
Cocktails
&&&&
No-smoking section

Located in what was the home of Hiram Stevens, one of Tucson's pioneer statesmen, a feeling of history permeates the atmosphere and it is easy to imagine Hiram and his wife, Petra, walking through the elegant old home. (*See also* WALKING THROUGH THE PAST.) The east porch, one of Petra's favorite spots, has been restored as an elegant diningroom, as have several other intimate, small rooms. The restoration by Noggle-McCarthy Architects and the interior design by Rory McCarthy is nothing but sublime.

Amid this luxurious ambience you will find extraordinary nouvelle American cuisine. The owner-chef, John Wilder, creates elegant, praise-worthy concoctions and presents them exquisitely. Fresh, seasonal vegetables and herbs, many grown by gardeners in the historic areas of town, are added to the entrees, which also are seasonal creations. They specialize in wine by the glass and patio dining is available.

JEROME'S
Pantano
6958 East Tanque Verde Road
Res. please 721-0311
A, DC, MC, V, CH

L/D Tue—Fri
D Sat—Sun
Cocktails
&&&
No-smoking section

One of the most cosmopolitan atmospheres in town, Jerome's presents a *deja vu* impression of San Francisco or Boston. The dress is informal, and the food is magnificent. Owner Jerome Soldevere, in creating one of Tucson's favorite restaurants, has given us an out-of-the-ordinary dining experience. As two of Tucson's restaurant reviewers have stated, "Everyone comes to Jerome's."

The appealingly unique menu includes not only authentic Creole and Cajun specialties, but gulf oysters and clams, shrimp, ceviche, veal, poultry and Cajun prime rib, all prepared in supremely tasteful concoctions. The blackened red fish is Jerome's Signature Dish (and what I always order). Save room for dessert, as the freshly-baked tarts, tortes, pies and cakes are pure ambrosia.

Jerome's also offers a great Sunday Brunch.

KATHERINE AND COMPANY
Pantano
6534 East Tanque Verde
Res. please, 298-6133
A, MC, V, CH

L/D Mon—Sat
Cocktails
&&&
No-smoking section

Surrounded by a chic burgundy, black and white color scheme and lush green plantings, you'll feel as though you're in the middle of an open patio. The charming ambiance of this eastside location is well matched by Katherine's excellent cuisine. Hand-written menus presented on an easel are changed daily. Lunch includes soups, salads, patés and fruits. Dinner might be Duck a l'Orange, seafoods, chicken, pork or veal.

Don't miss dessert! Willard Scott of *The Today Show* said: "We received the best dessert we've ever been sent by Katherine and Company in Tucson," and you'll agree after picking your selection from the revolving dessert carousel.

PALOMINO RESTAURANT
Rillito
2959 North Swan Road
Res. please 795-5561
A, CB, D, MC, V, CH

D Mon—Sat
Closed August
Cocktails
&&—&&&
No-smoking section

Owned and operated by the Gekas family, the Palomino has been offering continental, American and Greek cuisine since 1967.

The extensive menu includes thirty entrees, plus daily seasonal specialties and including excellent Greek cuisine. Be sure to try some of the desserts, such as Bananas Foster, Baked Alaska and the particularly wonderful Greek baklava. Following dinner, you may wish to enjoy coffee in the lounge, where local and international artists entertain on the grand piano.

PENELOPE'S
El Con
3619 East Speedway
Res. please 325-5080
MC, V, CH

L/D Tue—Fri
D Sat—Sun
Beer and wine
&&&
No-smoking section

This unimposing building hides a charming French country atmosphere, with friendly service and excellent food. The menu, though small, is well varied, according to whim and season. Please note that the price of the meal includes six-courses with appetizer, soup, entree, salad, cheeses and dessert. A wonderful place to linger over your meal.

RISTORANTE SAN REMO
2210 North Indian Ruins Road
Res. please 296-9378
MC, V, CH

Pantano
Cocktails
&&

A little difficult to find and quite unprepossessing on the outside, but inside a warm, cozy southwestern atmosphere, superlative food and the most cordial service in town. (We had a very young lady with us and the waiters were truly wonderful to her.)

The gracious inviting interior has white stuccoed walls and white linen cloths with accents in shades of mauve and burgundy. Three small dining areas include only twelve tables.

The menus change frequently and pasta dishes can be served as full or side orders. Portions are generous and entrees include smoked salmon, swordfish, shrimp, lamb, veal and chicken. Tremendous reasonably-priced desserts complete the meals.

SCORDATO'S
Tucson Mountains
4405 West Speedway
Res. please 624-8946
A, CB, D, DC, MC, V, CH

D seven days
Cocktails
&&&
No-smoking section

Italian dining with flair and elegance! A sunset drive toward the Tucson Mountains delivers you to an intimate atmosphere filled with crystal chandeliers and warm, dark woods. Scordato's, an excellent continental Italian restaurant, offers a myriad selection of excellent dishes.

Another family-owned and run restaurant, they specialize in veal, employing over a dozen different recipes. Other choices include an extensive selection of regional Italian specialties, superb pasta, and steak, chicken and seafood recipes. Many original selections and recipes are from the "old country."

An extensive selection of over 300 varieties of wine is offered.

THE TACK ROOM
Pantano
2800 North Sabino Canyon Road
Res. please 722-2800
CB, D, DC, MC, V, CH

D seven days
♿ Closed summer Mondays
Cocktails
&&&&
No-smoking section

Selected every year since 1976 by the Mobil Travel Guide for its Five-Star award and having received the Travel-Holiday award every year since 1978, Tucsonans consider an evening at The Tack Room as a noteworthy event where they are greeted by the third generation of owners.

The informal elegance of this lovely southwestern hacienda includes crystal and copper serving plates which blend well with the old adobe walls and the hand-hewn ceiling beams.

The continental a la carte menu includes distinctive gourmet selections, such as Tack Room Beef Wellington and Rack of Lamb Sonora. Breads and desserts are made on the premises and the fresh vegetables are incomparable. (I do believe, however, that tableclothes or place mats would be more appropriate than eating off of uncovered tables.)

TANQUE VERDE GUEST RANCH
End of east Speedway at the Rincons
Res. please 296-6275
A, MC, V, CH

Rincons
B/L/D seven days
Beer and wine
&&&

Located at the base of the Rincon Mountains and celebrated as one of the most famous and popular guest ranches in the country, you will find consistently outstanding food in this picturesque foothill setting.

Lunch is usually buffet style. Dinner may be served in the rustic western diningroom or in the cottonwood grove, where you'll have barbecued steak, beans, salad and spuds. All food is prepared at the ranch, including sumptious pastries.

The entrees change daily and three are offered each evening. Price includes a full dinner. Reservations are required, so call beforehand. Then you'll also know whether or not you should wear blue jeans for the barbecue.

STEAKS AND/OR SEAFOOD
See also THE BEST IN TOWN

BOBBY MCGEE'S CONGLOMERATION
Pantano
6464 East Tanque Verde Road
Res. please 886-5551
A, CB, D, MC, V

D seven days
Cocktails
&&&—&&&&
No-smoking section

Bobby McGee's Conglomeration includes waiters and waitresses dressed in the costumes of such characters as the Lone Ranger, Peter Pan, Little Bo Peep and Rudolph Valentino. The Hollywood soundstage setting makes for lively service with the appealing young servers enjoying the parts they play. A nostalgic atmosphere includes antiques, European stained glass, Tiffany lamps and packing crate booths.

The wide ranging selection of food includes steak and seafood as the main entrees, with daily additional choices. Don't stumble over the feet of the salad bar. It's a 9' long, beautifully ornate, ice-filled bathub.

EL CORRAL
Rillito
2201 East River Road
No res. 299-6092
MC, V, CH

D seven days
Cocktails
&&
No-smoking section

Located on River Road, just east of Campbell, you'll enjoy the casual western atmosphere of this old adobe ranch house. Prime rib is the house specialty, but you may also order BBQ ribs, steaks, chicken and seafood. Usually lots of action, so you may find the place just a bit noisy.

234

LIL ABNER'S STEAK HOUSE

Santa Cruz—North

8501 North Silverbell Road
Res. 744-2800
MC, V

D seven days
Cocktails
&&—&&&

Lil Abner's, a Tucson tradition for many years, prepares their steaks, chickens and beef ribs on large grills over a mesquite fire in the patio. You can eat in the patio or inside in a rather funky atmosphere of old license plates and paraphernalia. You'll be served ranch-style beans, a salad, salsa and toasted bread. Drive eleven miles north of Speedway on Silverbell Road.

PINNACLE PEAK
Pantano

6541 East Tanque Verde Road
Res. (large groups only) 296-0911
D, MC, V, CH

D seven days
Cocktails
&&
No-smoking section

Known as the home of the cowboy steak, Pinnacle Peak received special recognition in 1982 in the Salute to American Food Awards as representing the best in beef, beans and chili as enjoyed by the American cowboy. In 1987, *Tucson Lifestyle Magazine* awarded them their Culinary Academy Award for "Best Steaks."

T-bones, sirloins and BBQ pork ribs, all broiled over mesquite logs in the manner of the old "chuckwagon" days are on the menu, along with salads and the always-present pinto beans.

Don't wear a tie (unless it's one you're tired of), as it will be cut off. Take note of the thousands of ties hanging from the rafters from all those other well-dressed Eastern dudes! Jeans and cowboy shirts very appropriate.

SOLARIUM
Pantano

6444 Tanque Verde Road
Res. please 886-8186
A, CB, DC, MC, V, CH

L Mon—Fri
D seven nights
Cocktails
&&—&&&
No-smoking section

Set back amidst a forest of greenery, the Solarium is one of the most architecturally interesting restaurants in Tucson. Its ironwork, wood, tile mosaics, stained glass and wicker furniture, along with outstanding mountain views all make for an enjoyable repast.

The emphasis here is on seafood and they do it right. You'll find numerous seafood selections, along with some beef and chicken. They also offer numerous daily selections and a wide choice of desserts.

TRIPLE C RANCH
CHUCK WAGON SUPPERS

8900 West Bopp Road
Res. please 883-2333
MC, V, CH

Tucson Mountains
Dec—Apr D Tue—Sat
$15/meal and show
Kids 11 & under $10
Diningroom all no smoking

The Camp Family started their Chuckwagon suppers in 1971. Fashioned on the old chuckwagon suppers fed to working cowboys, the dinner includes BBQ beef, baked potatoes, chuckwagon beans, biscuits with honey and butter, fruit, cake and coffee or lemonade. The gate opens at 5:30 where you'll be given your seating (first come, first seated). Dinner is served at 7pm.

If you arrive early, the gift shop and snack bar are open. You may wish to bring a deck of cards to wile the time away. You may also wish to bring a cushion to place on those hard wooden benches!

After supper and you've bussed your cups and plates, the Camp Family Singers will entertain. Beginning shortly after Christmas, the Sons of the Pioneers join the Camp Family, providing tremendous entertainment every evening. Originated in 1933 by Roy Rogers, you're sure to have heard their Western singing style in such classics as "Tumbling Tumbleweeds" and "Cool Water." You'll find their talents also include big band sounds and all-round great musical entertainment.

Drive west on Ajo Way (highway 86) to Kinney Road. Turn right on Kinney Road and drive 1/2 mile to Bopp Road. Turn left on Bopp Road and drive 4 1/2 miles to the Ranch. You will see a windmill and gate at the parking lot entrance.

THE TUCSON CORK
Pantano
6320 East Tanque Verde Road
Res. 296-1631
A, CB, D, MC, V, CH

D seven days
Cocktails
&&—&&&
No-smoking section

Absolutely one of the best spots in town when the taste buds demand an excellent steak. You can also find a selection of fish and chicken and a prime rib specialty. The superior salad bar includes several lettuce selections and a variety of veggies, including broccoli, jicama and bean sprouts.

The cuisine is enhanced by the attractive southwestern atmosphere of cozy brick and stucco dining areas with beehive corner fireplaces. Casually-clad young men and women provide excellent, friendly service.

LIGHT EATING

See also MEXICAN and
THIS AND THAT

Numerous Tucson restaurants provide consistently attractive food for lunch or light dining at reasonable prices. The following are a very small sampling.

BLUE MOON
Pantano
1021 North Wilmot Road
Res. 790-0669
CH

L/D Tue—Sun
&—&&
No smoking allowed

Absolutely the best salad bar in town is found in this little gem. It's quite small, but full of creativity, both in decor and in cuisine. Blue shutters, blue tin plates and blue glasses contrast with white-white walls, while sugar-filled tins and individual-sized bread baskets (with a wide selection of breads) add their charm.

Another one of our favorite restaurants for its fresh home-cooked foods and unique flavor blends. The menu includes everything American: Italian, Oriental, Mexican, Greek, Cajun and vegetable. Daily specials are offered and they also serve a Sunday brunch. A place you shouldn't miss. Reservations suggested.

BLUE WILLOW RESTAURANT & POSTER GALLERY
2616 North Campbell Avenue
Res. Please 795-8736
CH

University
B/L/D seven days
Beer and wine
&
No-smoking section

Located in a renovated old house, this small, cozy restaurant is in the back of the poster gallery. Their specialties include omelettes and quiches, with great homemade soups, salads and desserts. Fresh ingredients are used in all dishes and everything is served on Blue Willow china, a pattern that appeared in England in the 18th century. An attractive, shaded patio is favored in good weather.

CAFE MAGRITTE
El Presidio
254 East Congress
884-8004
MC, V, CH

L Mon—Fri
D Tue—Sun
Beer and wine
&
No-smoking section

A true cafe in the old-European style with a charming, eclectic, surrealistic atmosphere (like the painter who is its namesake). A space worth visiting just to enjoy the art and architecture (and possibly some of the patrons). But don't stop with just a visit, unique cuisine with new and interesting flavors is here to be sampled. Everything is FRESH, to the degree that an item may be missing on the menu until new supplies are brought in.

You'll find a lot of arty types here and many stopping in either before or after the theatre. Don't worry about dress, anything is okay, but do try out this creative funky cafe. You'll want to return.

CAFE OLE
121 East Broadway
628-1841
MC, V, CH

El Presidio
B/L/D Mon—Sat
Beer and wine
&

With the atmosphere of a European coffee-house, you will find Viennese coffee and cappaccino, and a myriad choice of omelettes, soups, salads and sandwiches. They also have a Special of the Day. Many Tucson artists, intellectuals, and Bohemian-type individualists have called this their home. You'll find work of the Artist of the Month displayed on the walls. Stop in here for Sunday Brunch, too.

CAFE SWEETWATER
El Presidio
340 East Sixth Street
Res. 622-6464
A, D, MC, V, CH

L Mon—Fri
D Mon—Sat
Cocktails
&—&&
No-smoking section

Lots of different choices in the menu here with creative artistry using numerous herbs and spices. Blackened redfish and seafood brochette top seafood entrees, while veal and chicken are also available (my favorite is the Chicken Diablo, true to its name and hot but wonderful). Entrees include vegetables, french fries or pasta and choice of soup or salad. La Boulangerie bread completes a great meal. Fun to sit by the windows and watch the people on Fourth Avenue.

Lots of art on the walls and excellent service with style.

COFFEE, ETC. ON BROADWAY
Pantano
6121 East Broadway
Res. 790-9222
DC, MC, V, CH

B/L/D Mon—Sat
B/L Sun
Beer and wine
&
No-smoking section

A busy coffee shop located across from Park Mall. They have pastas, seafood, chicken and vegetarian dishes. Also great European gourmet desserts including white chocolate and Grand Marnier cakes. They also have great coffee beans ground to your specs, along with kitchen items. Entertainment on weekends.

THE COURTYARD CAFE
186 North Meyer
(Old Town Artisans Patio)
Res. 622-0351
CH

El Presidio
L Mon—Sat
Beer and wine
&
No-smoking section

One of the nicest, inexpensive locations downtown, with a lovely outdoor patio. Numerous trees and ramadas provide shade or you may also eat inside. Excellent, healthful and delicous soups, salads, sandwiches and quiches along with mesquite-broiled steak, fish and chicken.

Take time to wander through Old Town Artisans—you'll find lovely souvenir and gift items. (*See also* THE PAST IS STILL WITH US.)

DELECTABLES
University
533 North 4th Avenue
Res. 884-9289
A, MC, V, CH

L/D Mon—Sat
Beer and wine
&—&&
No-smoking section

Nostalgic old-time decor with simple wooden tables and chairs, ceiling fans and greenery. Note in particular the oaken cooler with its thick glass doors and the handsome brass cash register. You won't find plastics in this popular eatery serving Fourth Avenue patrons since 1973.

Deli-type offerings include a tremendous choice of imported cheeses, marinated roast beef, chef salads and great soups. Most items are served on breadboards with freshly-made breads.

Good-weather dining can be enjoyed on the European-style sidewalk patio. (P.S. They also do a magnificient job of catering.)

THE ECLECTIC CAFE
Pantano
7053 East Tanque Verde Road
No res. 885-2842
MC, V, CH

B/L/D seven days
Beer and wine
&
No-smoking section

An attractive, quiet atmosphere for breakfast, lunch or light dinner and inexpensive enough to take the whole family. The selection is, well, eclectic, with soups, crepes, quiches, sandwiches, vegetarian curry and a number of Mexican items. All dishes are freshly prepared. They also do catering for those special parties. If you see something on the wall that you like, ask, it may be for sale. They also do catering.

THE GOOD EARTH RESTAURANT
Pantano
6366 East Broadway (El Mercado)
745-6600
CH

   B/L/D seven days
   Beer and wine
   &—&&
   80% no smoking

Enticing aromas of spices and home-baked breads greet you as you enter this pleasant, plant-filled atmosphere. Fresh, delicious meals, attractively prepared and pleasantly served, include vegetarian specials, fluffy omelettes, great salads, homemade soups, and beef, chicken and seafood. The dressings, all made on the premises, offer perfect additions to the salads. If you like spices, be sure to try the Good Earth tea.

MI CASA
Pantano
6335 East Tanque Verde Road
Res. 885-5310
A, MC, V, CH

L Mon—Fri D Mon—Sat
Jan—May D seven nights
Cocktails
&&—&&&
No-smoking section

This attractive two-story restaurant is difficult to find. Easiest to drive north on Wilmot and enter from that street. The pleasant rooms include an indoor-outdoor patio.

    Mi Casa provides unique southwestern cuisine with the flavoring of special ingredients. The menu includes contemporary French-modern American cuisine with grilled meats, reduced sauces and wonderful vegetables. Entrees do not include salads, but several exotic combinations can be separately ordered. Several Mexican dishes are included, but prepared in novel ways. I particularly enjoy the quesadilla for lunch. Desserts, made in house, are outrageous. You might just wish to partake of coffee and . .

PRESIDIO GRILL
El Con
3352 East Speedway Blvd.
Res. 327-4667
A, MC, V, CH

B Sat—Sun
L/D Tue—Sun
Cocktails
&&
No-smoking section

Postmodern décor and sophisticated clientele complete the image of this midtown bistro. It's become the favorite of many for lunch and dinner and for weekend breakfasts. Numerous well-prepared appetizers are available, along with magnificent salads. Interesting entrees vary from duck and chicken to London Broil and Shrimp Linguine. As the menus change weekly, you'll always have a new variety.

    A wide selection of wines by the glass is offered along with one of the largest coffee choices in town. I'm told the espresso machine runs continually.

    This is also one of the few spots in town where you can get a late dinner on Friday and Saturday nights. They're open until midnight.

SILHOUETTES
University
2574 North Campbell Avenue
Res. please 327-3086
A, MC, V, CH

L/D Mon—Sat
Cocktails
&&
No-smoking section

Brightly colored awnings and lovely flowering plants impart a relaxing, garden atmosphere to this second restaurant of Katherine Hadley's. Well-prepared, inexpensive light meals include fresh fish, chicken and Cajun cooking. Lunch includes soups, salads, patés and fruits, with buttery, flaky croissants.

    Whatever you order, save room for a pastry, with the freshest of fruits and the richest of chocolates, you'll not be disappointed.

TOHONO CHUL TEA ROOM
Foothills
7366 North Paseo del Norte
(Tohono Chul Park)
797-1711
MC, V, CH

B/L Mon—Tue   9:30—5:00
B/L/D Wed—Sat   9:30—8:30
Brunch/D Sun   11:00—8:30
Beer and wine
&—&&
No-smoking section

Serenity personified in this wonderful desert retreat away from the hustle and bustle. A perfect place for a quiet breakfast, lunch or dinner or real old fashioned "tea." One small diningroom inside, while two lovely outdoor areas are available, one in the adobe courtyard with its covered arcade, flowers and fountain and one open to the desert, mountain views and animal life of the park.

Their sandwiches, soups, pastas and salads are tasty and appealingly served. A favorite dish is Torte Milanese, a luscious concoction of cheeses, prosciutto, bell pepper, black olives and pesto in a double crust. Desserts include Almond Torte with Raspberry Sauce, Chocolate Mousse Pie and Carrot Cake. Tea is served from 2:30—4:30 with "savories and sweets," all of which are elegantly presented.

Dinner entrees include Beef Tenderloin with Bernaise Sauce and wild rice, Vitello Tonnato (veal with tuna sauce, capers and orzo) and Grilled Shrimp with Toasted Garlic served on a bed of fettucini. All entrees include salad and rolls. You may also order from the luncheon specialties.

They also have a wonderful gift shop with many unique items, from wood crafts and jewelry to patio items. Be sure to stop and browse.

Drive east on Ina Road to the first stop light after Oracle (Paseo del Norte); turn north and drive in the second road on your right. You may also wish to spend some time walking through the park either before or after your repast.

THE VILLAGE AT COFFEE, ETC.
University
2830 North Campbell (Campbell Plaza)
881-8070
A, MC, V, CH

B/L/D seven days
Beer and wine
&
No-smoking section

From the croissants at breakfast to the various quiches, sandwiches, soups, teas, coffees and wines, this is a convivial spot for dining. An excellent selection of gourmet coffee items includes unique brewers and utensils and 80 coffees (including decaf), which can be ground to your request. Weekends includes entertainment by local groups. A $4 minimum purchase is required during performances.

The Walkabout Shop has clothing for camping, beaching and hiking and the Patagonia Annex sells Mexican items, cards and gifts.

MEXICAN

Although Tucson lost the First Annual Great American Mexican Food Championship Cook-off in December of 1987, many of us still say we are the Mexican Food Capital of the U.S. As stated in a local newspaper editorial, "Ordinary Mexican food in Tucson is excellent. The best is incredible." Of course, in order to creditably fill that category, we must include those wonderful restaurants in South Tucson. (These weren't included in that cook-off, which may be why we lost!) At the end of this section are listed those Mexican restaurants on South 4th Avenue, considered by many Tucsonans and visitors to be the best in the country.

My one complaint is a distinct lack of sopapillas. As a frequent traveler to New Mexico, my taste buds yearn for those wonderful honeyfilled concoctions. It is a shame they are not so freely available in Tucson.

We have so many excellent Mexican restaurants that it's difficult to pick out just a few. I'm including all of my favorites for you to choose from. Both the dress and the atmosphere are usually quite casual.

For those who know no Spanish, the following is a short guide to some of the Mexican food terminology you will run into. A pronunciation guide is in ETC., ETC., ETC.

Arroz	Rice	Maiz	Corn
Carne	Beef	Nieve	Ice cream
Carne Seca	Dried beef	Pollo	Chicken
Cerveza	Beer	Postre	Dessert
Crema	Sour cream	Queso	Cheese
Frijoles	Beans	Salsa	Sauce
Grande	Large	Sopa	Soup
Harina	Flour	Topopo	Volcano
Hueves	Eggs	Verde	Green
Leche	Milk	Vino	Wine

ARANETA'S INN
El Con
2640 East Speedway
327-1992
CH

L/D Tue—Fri
Cerveza y vino
&
No smoking allowed

More like a diner of the 50s the appeal of Araneta's is in its nostalgic charm and its frequently vegetarian Mexican food. No lard is used in cooking and no beef or chicken broth in the vegetable dishes. Be adventurous and try some of the numerous specials, all known by the names of the persons to whom they are dedicated. If you have a hearty appetite, you may find some dishes a bit sparse.

Alfonso and Rachelle Araneta are there at all times to be sure their customers receive the best possible food and concern. You'll feel like a member of the family. Note they are open only four days a week.

CASA MOLINA
Pantano
6225 East Speedway Blvd.
Res. 886-5468
A, CB, DC, MC, V, CH

L/D seven days
Cocktails
&—&&
No smoking section

Another Tucson favorite, they do their carne seca on premise and have great margaritas. All meals are a la carte and patio dining is available year round with heating and cooling.

CASA MOLINA DEL NORTE
3001 North Campbell Avenue
Res. 795-7593
A, DC, MC, V, CH

Rillito
L/D seven days
Cocktails
&—&&

Traditional Mexican food is served, including favorite Molina family recipes handed down for generations. A large selection of a la carte specialties on the menu, along with full dinners. Attractive Mexican decor with colorful paper flowers and pottery.

241

EL ADOBE MEXICAN RESTAURANT
El Presidio
40 West Broadway Blvd.
Res. 791-7458
A, MC, DC, V

L/D Mon—Sat
Cocktails
&—&&
No-smoking section

Located in the Charles O. Brown home, this original old adobe, built in the late 1860s, is one of the few remaining buildings from Arizona's territorial days and is listed on the National Register of Historic Places. (*See also* WALKING THROUGH THE PAST.)

The extensive menu includes the house specialty, El Adobe, a masterful concoction of charcoal broiled steak strips and veggies on three deep-fried *flour* tortillas, all topped with shredded cheese. For dessert, try their almendrado, with its green, red and white colors representing the Mexican flag. It's a light fluffy concoction that makes a perfect ending to a spicy meal.

If the weather permits, ask for a table on the patio. This delightful Mexican patio, resplendent with trees, colorful flowers and the melodies of birds, provides a taste of yesteryear. Close your eyes and you can imagine you are visiting an old Mexican hacienda during Territorial Days instead of sitting in the middle of busy, downtown Tucson.

EL CHARRO
El Presidio
311 North Court Avenue
Res. large groups 622-5465
A, MC, V

L/D seven days
Sunday brunch
Cerveza y vino
&—&&
No-smoking section

Serving Tucsonans since 1922, this family-owned restaurant is located in a nationally recognized El Presidio Historic Home, which was also the family home of the owners. (*See also* THE PAST IS STILL WITH US.) Note the elegant, stained glass window, known as Ventana Bonita (Pretty Window), in the west wall. The resplendent colors of a bouganvillea sparkle through 1666 pieces of glass, designed and set at the restaurant by Sandy Bernal.

El Charro prepares sun-dried carne seca (dried beef), makes their own chorizo and tamales and serves true Sonoran cuisine, including many dishes you'll not find elsewhere in town. Sunday brunch is served from 11am—2pm.

A small front porch provides outdoor dining, and the cellar includes gift shops where you may purchase china, pottery and home-made comestibles.

EL MARIACHI RESTAURANTE
Y CANTINA
106 West Drachman
791-7793
A, MC, V, CH

University
L Wed—Fri D Wed—Sun
Winter: L/D seven days
&—&&
No-smoking section

The specialty of El Mariachi is the nightly shows of the world-acclaimed International Mariachi America. This group also appears at our spring International Mariachi Conference. You'll enjoy their outstanding musical entertainment, along with great food. Enjoy Sunday Champagne Brunch and mariachi music at their all-you-can eat champagne brunch.

242

EL MINUTO CAFE
354 South Main Avenue
622-9534
CH

El Presidio
L/D seven days
Cerveza y vino
&—&&

Almost as much of a tradition as El Tiradito next door, the Shaar family at El Minuto have been serving Tucsonans since 1936. Long the favorite of old timers, it's the place to head when you get the late-night munchies for tacos and tamales 'cause they're open until 2am every morning.

EL PARADOR RESTAURANT & CANTINA
El Con
2744 East Broadway
Res. 881-2808
A, MC, V, CH

L/D Mon—Sat
D Sun
Cocktails
&&
No-smoking section

A lush, tropical garden greets you as you walk into El Parador. A pleasant spot to enjoy Mexican hospitality and flamenco guitar.

Native son John Jacob and his family feature Sonoran style cooking with everything, except the tortillas, made from scratch. Try the beef and chicken fajitas, charbroiled and served on a sizzling platter with guacamole, soft tortillas and fresh salsa.

KARICHIMAKA
San Xavier
5252 South Mission Road
Res. 883-0311
MC, V, CH

L/D Tue—Sun
Cerveza y vino
&
No-smoking section

If going to or coming from Mission San Xavier del Bac, stop at Karichimaka for a bite. They've been in this location since 1949 serving Mexican food, western-style steaks, hamburgers and fried chicken.

LA FUENTE
Santa Cruz
1749 North Oracle Road
Res. please 623-8659
A, MC, V, CH

L/D Tue—Sun
Cocktails
&—&&
No-smoking section

Tucsonans frequently take their out-of-town visitors to La Fuente where strolling mariachis entertain nightly. It is the largest, and probably the most attractive Mexican restaurant in town, with its adobe, red brick, fountains, plants, greenery, pinatas, mosaic tiles and Mexican artifacts.

An extensive menu specializing in toned-down Mexican cuisine is offered, including mole, an unsweetened Mexican cholocate chile sauce usually served with chicken. Where other restaurants serve pitchers of beer, La Fuente serves pitchers of Margaritas—ole! A little dressier than average.

243

LA PARILLA SUIZA
Pantano
5602 East Speedway Blvd.
No res. 747-4838
A, DC, CB, MC, V, CH

L/D seven days
Cocktails
&—&&
No-smoking section

Unless you've eaten in Mexico City, the Mexican food offered at La Parilla Suiza is different from what you may be used to. This northern-most location of a chain of Mexico City restaurants serves authentic Mexico City food.

Mostly charcoal grilled (parilla), you'll find a new "taste sensation," which has made this one of Tucson's favorite restaurants. An extensive menu provides numerous selections and several kinds of sauces accompany the chips.

LOS MAYAS
4280 North Campbell Avenue
(St. Phillips Plaza)
Res. please 577-8222
A, DC, MC, V, CH

Rillito
D Tue—Sat
Cocktails
&—&&
No-smoking section

What a great Mexican restaurant this is—and like nothing you've seen before, unless you eat regularly in Mexico. Spacious diningrooms, brick floors and arched doorways combine with white linens, fresh flowers and blue and white pottery dishes to create an intriguing setting.

Dishes include a wonderful selection of traditional recipes from Yucatán to Mexico City. The outstanding cuisine includes unique new flavors to excite your taste buds.

Along with several miniature loaves of their sourdough bread, I could make a meal out of the cilantro-flavored green rice and black beans alone. But that would be missing such yummies as Camarones al Queso (shrimp casserole with peppers, poblanos and melted cheese) or Pescado Nac Cam (Yucatan style fish steamed in banana leaves with achiote) or Puero con Piña (a stew of pork, pineapple, chiles and pimentos). They also have several mole dishes (a sauce blended of chiles and chocolate and very popular in Mexico).

This is one restaurant you don't want to miss.

MACAYO DEL NORTE
Foothills
7360 North Oracle Road (at Ina)
Res. please 742-2141
A, MC, V, CH

L/D seven days
Sun Brunch
Cocktails
&—&&
No-smoking section

A wide selection of unique dishes along with the old favorites are pleasantly served in this attractive northside location. Mariachis perform frequently.

MOLINA MIDWAY RESTAURANT
El Con
1138 North Belvedere Avenue
No res. 325-9957
A, MC, V, CH

L/D Tue—Sun
Cerveza y vino
&
No smoking section

Although you'll not find much atmosphere, this is a favorite of many Tucsonans (including me) and you may have to wait a bit for a table. You'll find consistently excellent food served in large quantities. Incidentally, "Midway" refers to a long-gone drive-in theatre that was a landmark just across Speeday for many years.

PAPAGAYO MEXICAN RESTAURANT
University
840 East Fort Lowell Road
Res. for 7 or more (602) 622-8233
MC, V

L/D seven days
Cocktails
&—&&

Run by the Perez family, 4th generation Tucsonans, you will find authentic Sonoran-style Mexican food. The extensive menu offers numerous selections, including huge chimichangas which I believe are the best in town.

Papagayo is Spanish for parrot and you'll see numerous papier maché parrots perched around the rooms, along with Mexican tile, paper flowers and piñatas. A patio allows for outdoor dining.

South 4th Avenue

Many fervent Mexican-food aficionados insist that only on South Fourth Avenue can you find *real* Mexican food. The decor isn't very fancy, but you won't be able to beat the food or the prices.

DOUBLE L
1830 South Fourth Avenue
Res. 792-1585
MC, V

B/L/D Mon—Sat
Cerveza y vino
&

A wide selection of Mexican food, pleasantly served. Spices aren't too hot, which is sometimes appreciated. Those who don't wish Mexican food can choose from an American menu that includes fried chicken, Guaymas shrimp and burgers. The fruit chimichangas are great for dessert.

EL TORERO RESTAURANT
231 East 26th Street
Res. for 6 or more 622-9534
CH

L/D Wed—Mon
Cerveza y vino
&—&&

This large, high-ceilinged room is usually full and noisy. Pictures of bullfighters and a sailfish on one wall gives the atmosphere of south of the border. Watch out for the salsa, it's fiery.

Just off 4th Avenue on 26th Street. The building sits back from the street, with parking in front.

MI NIDITO RESTAURANT
1813 South 4th Avenue
No res. 622-5081
MC, V

L/D Wed—Sun
Cerveza
&

Mi Nidito (My Little Nest) has been at this location since 1954. Might be a bit crowded and not much room inside to wait. Their numerous specialties include nopalitos (sliced prickly pear pads), chimichangas, topopos and flautas. An added specialty is white Mexican cheese.

245

MICHA'S
2908 South 4th Avenue
Res. 623-5307
A, MC, V, CH

B/L/D Mon—Sat
Cocktails
&

Very attractive, with pleasant service. If you're lucky, Mariachis will be playing. If there for lunch, try the cocido (Mexican vegetable soup), it is filling, tasty and like no vegetable soup you've had before.

ITALIAN

See also THE BEST IN TOWN

CARUSO'S
University
434 North 4th Avenue
Res. 6 or more 624-5765
V, MC

D seven days
Beer and wine
&—&&
No-smoking section

Specializing in southern Italian cooking, Caruso's has been a favorite since the 1930s. The atmosphere is homey-Italian and the homemade pasta and sauces are excellent. Try the eggplant parmigiana, chicken cacciatore or the house favorite, lasagna al forno. If weather permits, enjoy dining under the stars and twinkling lights in the "old world patio."

DA VINCI
3535 East Fort Lowell Road
No res. 881-0947
CH

  Rillito
L/D Mon—Sat
Cocktails
&—&&&

You'll probably have to wait for a table, but the relaxed, attractive atmosphere makes the wait tolerable. The extensive menu includes daily blackboard specials, along with regional specialties, including manicotti, cannelloni, tortellini, and fettucine. You'll also find veal, chicken and innumerable seafood dishes. Your greatest problem probably will be making up your mind.

    Dinner includes salad or soup (the minestrone is delicious) and warm breads. Service is friendly and you'll not go away hungry; in fact, you may ask for a doggy bag.

FREDACHINI'S *Pasta Italiano*
University
1927 East Speedway
327-3744
MC, V

L Mon—Fri
D Tue—Sun
Beer and wine
&—&&
No-smoking section

One of our favorite urban locations, with it's second story diningroom overlooking a tree that you'll have to touch to believe it's not real. A la carte dinners include great Italian bread and herb butter and you can order such treats as Eggplant Rollatini, Sausage & Peppers, Rigatoni Parmigiana or veal, chicken or the fish of the day. Good service and nice uptown atmosphere.

246

LOCASTRO'S
El Con
4010 East Grant Road
Res. please 795-4400
MC, V, CH

D Mon—Sat
Cocktails
&&
No smoking section

The sign says pizza, but they serve a lot more and all of it well-prepared. Appetizers include antipasto, mussels and baked clams. Traditional pasta dinners are available at inexpensive prices, and entrees include veal, seafood and chicken. Desserts include espresso and cappucino.

MAMA LOUISA'S CAMPBELL PLAZA
University
2960 North Campbell Avenue
Res. 795-1779
A, MC, V, D, DC, CH

L/D seven days
Cocktails
&—&&
No-smoking section

The second location of Mama Louisa's (the other is Mama Louisa's La Cantina at 2041 South Craycroft Road), this spot has been jumping since it opened. An old-fashioned southern Italian restaurant, they offer every pasta you might wish and it's all homemade and fresh. Fancier dishes include Chicken Francese and Veal Marsala, but the pasta is the standout.

SCORDATO'S ON BROADWAY
El Con
3048 East Broadway
Res. please 323-3701
A, MC, D, DC, V

L/D Mon—Sat
Cocktails
&—&&
No-smoking section

Located in one of Tucson's special architectural spaces, designed by Josias T. Joseler, this is another one of our favorite restaurants where an excellent filling meal is available for reasonable prices. The Scordato family continues providing excellent food for Tucsonans with special touches on potatoes and veggies and wonderful sauces. Sometimes seems to be a bit noisy and crowded, but when not too busy it is a special spot. Patio dining is fun when it's not too warm or windy.

My one complaint would be that the luncheon menu is the same as for dinner and I would appreciate a lighter menu for lunch. Hearty eaters, however, have no problem with this situation.

GREEK

See also THE BEST IN TOWN

If you're in town late September—early October, check with St. Demetrios Church and Hellenic Center for the dates of their annual Greek Festival. This event offers some of the best Greek food in town. The women start preparations months ahead of time. You'll find dolmathes (stuffed grape leaves), spanakopita (lamb), souvlaki (meat shish kebab) and moussaka (eggplant casserole) along with baklava (flaky pastry and honey), diples (honey curls) and loukoumades (drop biscuits). The food is inexpensive and wonderful. You'll also find handicrafts and import items for sale, along with music and entertainment.

MARATHON RESTAURANT
1134 East 6th Street
623-1020
CH

University
L/D Mon—Sat
&-&&
No-smoking section

Here is some of the best and most inexpensive Greek food in town. And for those new to Greek food, the menu explains the content of the dishes.

OLIVE TREE RESTAURANT
Pantano
7000 East Tanque Verde Road
Res. please 298-1845
A, MC, V, CH

L/D Mon—Sun
Cocktails
&&—&&&
No-smoking section

Greek-American cuisine meticulously prepared from fresh ingredients, using old family recipes. The decor is luxurious and intimate, with comfortable booths, soft hues and candle light. Pleasant dining is also found in the patio area; with Greek melodies wafting through the air, you might imagine you are in Athens.

The appetizers are especially delectable, as are the distinctive crisp salads. Entrees include classic moussaka, shrimp and pasta dishes, spinach-and-cheese pie, fish and chicken dishes and a bountiful selection of lamb preparations. You will also find an ample choice of excellent Greek wines.

(*See also* THE PALOMINO in THE BEST IN TOWN.)

CHINESE

Songwriter and lyricist, Billy Joel, appearing on the *Today* show, said "Creativity comes from eating Chinese food . . . it may be all that MSG going through the body, but the takes are different after Chinese food!" Not all will agree, but many believe a certain hunger will only be placated by the devouring of Chinese food.

ALI SHAN
4373 East 22nd Street
745-1818
MC, V, CH

El Con
L/D seven days
Cocktails
&—&&&

Cantonese style. Not too attractive outside, but pleasant inside. Friendly, efficient service. A large choice of meals.

CHINA WALL
2547 East Broadway
323-2024
A, MC, V, CH

El Con
L/D seven days
&

Small, but mighty, this is one of Tucson's favorite stops. They have luncheon specials for $3.25 served Mon—Fri 11:30am—2:30pm which include tea, soup, egg roll, steamed or fried rice and a fortune cookie. They also have free delivery on a $10 minimum Mon—Fri 4:30pm—9:30pm and Sat—Sun noon—9:30pm.

248

HUNAN'S RESTAURANT
4689 East Speedway Blvd.
323-3737
MC, V, CH

El Con
L/D seven days
Cocktails
&

Northern, Szechuan, Hunan, Shanghai and Canton cuisines in what is the most attractive Chinese restaurant in town. Watch for the starred dishes, they are the fiery ones (who says Mexican food is hot?). This and the New Peking on North Oracle are owned by Willing and Phung Cheng.

PANDA VILLAGE CHINESE RESTAURANT
Pantano
6546 East Tanque Verde Road
(602) 296-6159
MC, V, CH

 L/D seven days
Beer and wine
&
No-smoking section

Located in La Plaza Shoppes, they serve Mandarin, Szechuan and Cantonese cuisine, prepared by the former head chef of a Chinese embassy. You may order your food without MSG.

NEW PEKING RESTAURANT
7963 North Oracle Road
297-8000
MC, V, CH

 Foothills
L/D Seven days
Cocktails
&

Very attractive, owned and operated by the Chengs, who also own and operate Hunan's on East Speedway. Same choice of cuisine. Excellent food, pleasantly served. Peking Duck available if ordered a day in advance—expensive.

EASTERN/NEAR AND FAR

Three restaurants have received good reviews for their **Thai** food. All provide good service and prices for what has become to some a supplement to Chinese food. A caveat: if you haven't tried Thai food, be VERY cautious of the chiles and spices. When they say hot, it is HOT.

CHAR'S THAI RESTAURANT
5039 East Fifth Street
Res. 795-1715
A, MC, V

El Con
L/D Mon—Sat   D Sun
Beer and wine
&—&&

MINA'S THAI RESTAURANT
6061 East Broadway
Res. 790-0438
MC, V

El Con
L/D Mon—Sat
Beer and wine
No-smoking section

THAI THANI
El Con
4537 East Speedway Blvd.
795-1421
MC, V, CH

L/D Mon—Sun
Cocktails
&
No-smoking section

249

SELAMAT MAKAN
El Con
3502 East Grant Road
Res. 325-6755
MC, V, CH

D Mon—Sat
Beer and wine
&-&&
No-smoking section

One of the most popular restaurants in town for **Malaysian** and **Indian** cuisine. A family-owned spot, many Tucsonans appreciate the warmth and friendship of the owners. The egg rolls are especially good and the chicken satay is a favorite. Most of the foods include curry and some can be quite hot.

THE SHEIK
6350 East Broadway
(In El Mercado)
790-5481
A, MC, D, DC, V, CH

Pantano
L/D Mon—Sat
Cocktails
&—&&
No-smoking section

Middle Eastern/Lebanese food and also the friendly American hamburger. Entrees include baked chicken and several lamb dishes. The Sheik's Combination offers an opportunity to sample them all. You can also order pita bread sandwiches.

Appetizers include baba ghanoojh (a cool dish of baked eggplant whipped in sesame oil, garlic and lemon) or hummos (chickpeas mixed in the same manner) both great for scooping up with pita bread.

For dessert, try the knafi—it's fantastic. Belly dancing every Friday and Saturday night. If Kathryn Ferguson, of Xanadu Studio, performs, be prepared for a special treat. She is a true artist.

THIS AND THAT

Looking for **JUST A SNACK, HAMBURGERS** or a **COFFEE HOUSE**?

Austin's, 2920 East Broadway, 327-3892. A favorite location in town for many years, they have great hamburgers, homemade soups and a large selection of ice cream. Mon—Thu 11am—10pm; Fri—Sat 11am—11pm. No credit cards.

Big A Restaurant, 1818 East Speedway Blvd., 326-1818. A favorite spot for many years for unique hamburgers and desserts. Variety of choices, flame-broiled, not fried, all made to order. Mon—Sat 11am— 9pm. No credit cards.

Bob Dobb's Grill, 2501 East 6th Street, 325-3767. Basically a neighborhood bar, but some of the best hamburgers in town can be found here. Daily dinner specials include chicken ($3.50) and rib-eye steak dinners ($5.25). Busy, noisy, lots of yuppy traffic. Also have quiches and cheesecake. Mon—Sat, 11am—1am. No credit cards.

Bum Steer, 1910 North Stone Avenue, 884-7377. Unique atmosphere, numerous paraphernalia, airplanes, junk and stuff hanging from ceiling. College age singles bar. Great hamburgers, hot dogs and excellent quality spirits for house liquors. Seven days till 1am. MC, V.

Kippy's Hamburgers & Things, 831 North Park Avenue, 622-9357. Near UA. Lite meals, including grilled halibut and chicken, salads in numerous sizes, sandwiches, homemade desserts and a dozen types of fantastic hamburgers. Mon—Sat 7:30am— 9pm. Closed Sunday. No credit cards.

Wildcat House, 1801 North Stone Avenue, 622-1302. UA hangout. If school is in session, probably very noisy. Teriyaki chicken and huge hamburgers and accoutrements for reasonable prices. Mon—Sat 11am—1am. MC, V.

Bentley's House of Coffee & Tea, 810 East University (The Geronimo) 795-0338. Would you believe like the coffee houses of the 60s? Patrons are encouraged to enjoy, converse, listen to folk music, whatever. Sometimes crowded, people will share their tables. Great coffees, desserts, croissants, soups, specials. Also lovely fountain and patio outside to enjoy the recent renovation of this old hotel.

How about BARBEQUED RIBS?

Jack's Original Bar-B-Que, 5250 East 22nd Street, 750-1280, is where those in the know go for great ribs, chicken, sloppy Joes, tacos and some of the best beans in town. I told Laura Banks they should bottle their great sauce and found out they already have! You will want to pick some up.

HIGH TEA in the desert? Why not?

Tohono Chul Tea Room, 7366 North Pasea del Norte, 797-1711 serves tea from 2:30—4:30pm daily. (*See also* LIGHT EATING.) **Loew's Ventana Canyon** serves High Tea from 3pm—5pm Mon—Sat from the 1st of Sep—Jun and 3pm—5pm Fri and Sat during the summer months. Reservations are a good idea.

Try sinfully-delicious CINNAMON ROLLS:

Seems like a silly heading, right? Wrong. These are the greatest cinnamon rolls you'll ever taste. But you'll probably have to wait in line to try them. **Robert's Restaurant,** 1101 North Alvernon Way, 7951436, looks like a drive-in restaurant of the '50s, but behind those walls are many regulars who make this their morning stop. You won't be sorry if you join them to enjoy this great home-cooked food. Mon—Sat 6:30am—3pm serving breakfast and lunch.

Looking for BAGELS?

Try **Hot Bagel Bakeries,** 1110 South Park Avenue, 624-3616 (University); 2829 East Speedway Blvd., 795-0742 (El Con); and 7114 East Broadway, 296-4164 (Pantano). You can enjoy lunches and lite dinners at all three bakeries. Seven days 6am—6pm.

Fantastic SUNDAY BRUNCHES:

Extravaganzas to end, or begin, your week. Bountiful tables laden with blintzes, pastries, seafoods, fruits, omelettes and all manner of other delicacies to entice you. The **Cactus Rose** at the Doubletree, 445 South Alvernon, 381-4200. **Victoria's Lounge** at the **Sheraton Tucson El Conquistador,** 10000 North Oracle Road, 742-7000. **Loews Ventana Canyon,** 7000 North Resort Drive, 299-2020. **Blue Moon,** 1021 North Wilmot Road, 790-0669. **Westward Look's Gold Room,** 245 East Ina Road, 297-1151. **Jerome's,** 6958 East Tanque Verde Road, 721-0311. And **El Mariachi Restaurant y Cantina,** 106 West Drachman, 791-7793 where you can get an all-you-can-eat champagne brunch of tamales, menudo, enchiladas, taquitas and bacon and eggs along with music by International Mariachi America.

251

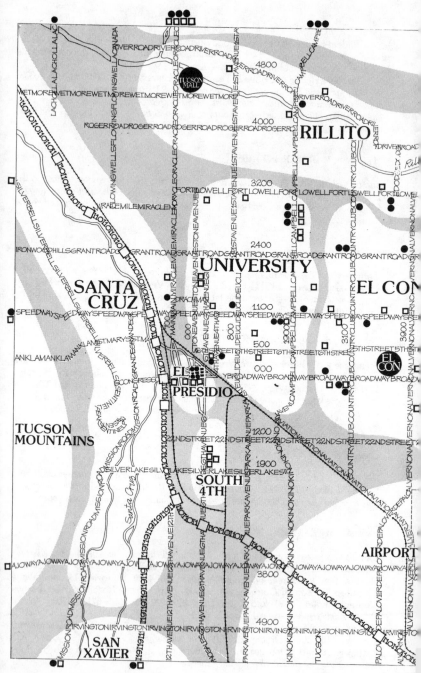

The large free-form ovals, each with an identifying title, delineate specific valley areas to which each subject in the text is referred.

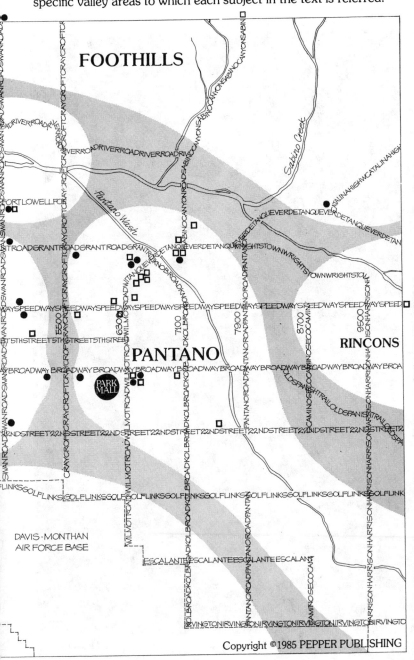

FOOTHILLS

PANTANO

RINCONS

PARK MALL

DAVIS-MONTHAN
AIR FORCE BASE

253

The Museum Shop

IMPROVING
TUCSON'S ECONOMY

Shopping in Tucson is limited only by the gas in your car and the money in your pocket. From fine arts galleries and elegant hidden-away boutiques to extravagant, large malls, you'll have a grand and glorious time improving Tucson's economy.

On pages 252-253 you will find a map of Tucson. The small circles shown are locations of shops and shopping areas mentioned in this chapter. The squares on the map are locations of restaurants mentioned in the preceding chapter. This clustering of shops and restaurants enables you to combine the two activities if you wish.

The larger free-form circles, each with an identifying title, elucidate specific valley areas. Immediately under or opposite the name of each shop is listed the area in which that shop is located.

PEDESTRIAN SHOPPING

Numerous small shopping areas provide enjoyable browsing away from mall hustle and bustle. Many shops are locally-owned and nearly all offer unique specialty items not found in the larger malls. Check throughout this chapter for numerous other shops and more complete descriptions of some of these shops.

BROADWAY VILLAGE
El Con

Southwest corner of Broadway
and Country Club Road

A favorite Tucson architect, Josias Joesler, designed this charming group of buildings, one of Tucson's first shopping centers.

Two shops geared to the young set are **Grandma's Treasures** and **Mrs. Tiggy-Winkle's** (who has an exceptional selection of children's books and a special reading spot). **Rochelle K** offers designer's fashions and **French Bred** is a delightful French country boutique. **Primitive Arts** provides American Indian and pre-Columbian arts, great natural-fabric fashions can be found at **Zona Boutique** and **The Bag Company** has a tremendous selection of handbags, belts and jewelry.

The **Broadway Village Market** will probably have those gourmet items you can't find elsewhere and **Table Talk** has any and all kitchen accessories. If you're a devotee of the mystery genre, stop at **The Footprints of a Gigantic hound** and art and books on the Southwest are available at **Coyote's Voice Books.**

CROSS ROADS FESTIVAL
El Con

Northeast corner of Grant
and Swan Roads

Architecturally, this shopping center is the sorriest in town, but ignoring that, several unique, wonderful shops can be found here.

Intercontinental Imports has marble and travertine furniture and accessories; the collection of dolls and stuffed animals at the **Doll Cottage** is wonderful; **Wineworks** provides not only an excellent collection of wine and accoutrements, but musicales; the **Wooden Apple** has sophisticated country items and a tremendous supply of dried flowers; Indian jewelry, blankets and southwestern items are at **Riding Horse Gallery**; and **Settings** is one of the most elegant crystal/linen/gift shops in town.

Your sweet tooth can be fed by **T. J. Cinnamons Bakery** and **Ethel M Chocolates** or if you're on a diet, try **"TCBY" Yogurt.**

You'll also find a six-theatre complex here, **Cineplex Odeon.**

EL MERCADO DE BOUTIQUES
Pantano

Southeast corner of Broadway
and Wilmot

Mexican decor provides a pleasant shopping atmosphere. You will find leather items, fine gems, excellent art galleries and several restaurants. If you are a chocoholic, you'll find sweets to die for at **Truffles by James** with handcrafted truffles in such exotic flavors as Baileys Irish Cream and Grand Marnier, all elegantly wrapped, if desired.

West Fine Leather invites you to discover unique designs and superb craftsmanship by their creators of fine leather goods. The **Maya Palace** has handcrafted clothing from around the world, including fashions from Josefa and tapestries from Teotitlan. **Abbott Taylor Jewelers** provides unusual handmade jewelry creations. One of Tucson's favorate restaurants, **The Good Earth**, is here.

4TH AVENUE SHOPS

4th Avenue, from 4th Street
south to Seventh Street

Fourth Avenue, with a large selection of unique craftshops, ethnic stores and boutiques offers almost any handicraft you might wish, along with restaurants, antiques, stained glass, books, jewelry and fashions. The bright wall mural on the southeast side of 4th Avenue and 6th Street was commissioned by the 4th Avenue Merchants Association and done by members of the Tucson High School Commercial Arts Club.

The **Food Conspiracy Co-op**, Tucson's food co-op, is *the* place to buy spices and herbs. **Antigone Books** specializes in feminist literature and non-sexist children's books, along with cards and periodicals. **Piney Hollow** probably has the largest selection of beads in town, along with cards, gifts and a good selection of silver and gold works. **Paint Rags**, known as an "art boutique" includes handpainted clothing, accessories, jewelry, gifts and home furnishings.

Creations has a wide selection of clothing and **Arroyo Design** has a tremendous collection of American arts and Mexican furniture and accessories. **Goodbooks** has fine, rare, new and old books. **Metal Man** provides gift items and several stores offer "previously worn" clothing. **Futons Etc.** has a wide selection of—futons, of course. Several excellent small restaurants offer healthy, attractively prepared repasts. (*See also* TOMORROW WE DIET.)

In late April and early December, the **4TH AVENUE STREET FAIR** draws thousands for browsing, shopping and entertainment. Fourth Avenue is closed to traffic from University boulevard south to 9th Street and artisans from all over the Southwest bring their juried wares to sell. Bands, jugglers, and violinists are but a few of the entertainers. Food booths sell a variety of ethnic foods, including pita sandwiches and Indian fry bread. It's loads of fun, if only to take part in some serious people watching. Check the newspapers or call the Chamber of Commerce for exact dates.

OLD TOWN ARTISANS
186 North Meyer Avenue
623-6024

Located in the middle of historic El Presidio, Old Town Artisans covers an entire city block and includes renovated old adobe townhouse buildings from the 1860—1870s era with their original high saguaro-rib ceilings.

Over 150 local craftspersons are represented, plus American Indian and Latin folk art. You'll find a continually changing collection of quality, hand-made gifts including pottery, jewelry, fashions, stained glass and paintings.

A delightful, tree-shaded patio invites retrospection, and, if hungry, you can order a wide selection of homemade soups, sandwiches and individually prepared salads at **The Courtyard Cafe.**

At 15 West Telles Street you'll find **Old Town Bake Shop**, a great spot to pick up taste-tempting sweets, including cheesecakes, strudel and quiches. **El Rapido** at 77 West Washington (on the other side of the block), is *the* stop for tortillas, bean burros, chimichangas, tacos, quesadillas and tamales.

THE PLAZA AT WILLIAMS CENTER

Southwest Corner of Broadway
and Craycroft Road

Firenze Boutique sells men's and women's European fashions; **Silverberg and Sons**, a Tucson jeweler for nearly 50 years provides jewelry and gifts, **Pierini Design** offers unique custom-designed jewelry, **Creative Creations** has fine southwestern crafts, gifts and accessories and original art is available from **Mary Peachin's Art Company**.

If you're hungry, stop in **Fancy Dancy Foods** for sandwiches, soups and salads. With black, white and deep red decor and lots of mirrors, this is one of the most attractive delis in town. You'll find exquisite items to take home for that next party or just for yourself.

Directly across Broadway, in the Embassy Suites Hotel, you'll find **GIFTS . . . at the Embassy**, a tiny, but mighty gem. Patti Frederick has created a charming, relaxed setting where you will find Victorian antiques, REAL pawn jewelry, whimsical cards from Tubac's Virginia Hall, books, magazines and a videotape on the Arizona-Sonora Desert Museum.

PLAZA PALOMINO   Rillito
Southeast corner of Swan
and Fort Lowell Roads

Far too many wonderful shops to list, but a few include: **Maya de Mexico** for Mexican furnishings and accessories; **The Scarabee**, where you may purchase custom designed exotic beads and jewelry; **Changes Boutique**, for the ultimate and unusual in style; **The Crystal Carver**, for fine crystal gift items; **Impressions II Gallery** and **Art Visions**, art galleries; a wonderful children's shop, **Piccolo Bambino**; **Maya Palace** for Mexican fashions; and to feed your sweet tooth, relax on the patio at **Ilsa's Konditorei & Cafe** and partake of traditional European tortes and pastries.

ST. PHILLIPS PLAZA   Rillito
Southeast corner of North Campbell
Avenue and East River Road

One of the most inviting shopping areas in town is located at the southeast corner of Campbell and River Road. With its attractive architecture, landscaping, plazas and fountains, it is a favorite.

Galleries include the **Obsidian Gallery**, and **Beth O'Donnell Gallery**. **Maricopa Design Jewelers** has elegant jewelry and will do custom designs for you; **Bahti Indian Arts and Rivas Bahti Gallery** provides excellent art work; and **Cele Peterson's** and **Limited Editions** have elegant women's fashions. You'll find silk floral designs, including trees and plants, at **The Great Southwestern Floral Co.**; **Design West Interiors** offers a little bit of Santa Fe in Tucson and **Pine Crossing Ltd.** has primitive antiques from the European countryside.

St. Phillips also provides free concerts during various times of the years. (*See also* MUSIC.)

THE VILLAGE   El Con
2900 East Broadway

Brand new and not all spaces are rented, but you'll want to stop and visit **Changes** for their unique fashion styles for women; **Desert Son** to see books, Indian jewelry, pottery and leather work, **Carats**, for jewelry by Susanna and **The Departure** for ethnic fashions and accessories.

258

ANTIQUES

ANTIQUE JEWELRY EXCHANGE
4730 East Speedway

El Con
881-6525

Exceptionally unique antique jewelry. Estate sales include beauitiful pieces created in the slower, quiet days of the past. Appraisals, redesigning, pearl stringing and watch repair. Mon—Fri 10am—5:30pm, Sat 10am—4pm.

BUFFALO EXCHANGE
803 East Helen at Euclid (884-9978)
6544 East Tanque Verde Road (885-8392)

University
Pantano

As one of the most popular "previously worn" clothing stores in town, you'll find an excellent selection here. The "campus" shop on Euclid is frequented by UA students. This and numerous other used clothing stores in town have given Tucson the title of "Used Clothing Capital of the U.S." East Helen open Mon—Sat 11am—6pm. Tanque Verde open Mon—Sat 10am—6pm, Sun noon—5pm. (Tanque Verde has some new clothing and accessories.)

CHRISTINE'S ANTIQUES
4940 East Speedway

El Con
323-0018

Established in the 1950s, this is one of Tucson's oldest antique stores. Christine Olson prides herself on having the largest selection of antiques in the Southwest, with a specialty in dolls, Hummels, furniture, cut glass, silver and china. Her doll museum houses over 4,000 antique dolls. Mon—Sat 10am—5:30pm.

GOLDEN EAGLE
ANTIQUES & GIFTS
2320 North Swan Road (Main shop)
4758 East Grant Road (Show room)

El Con
790-3333
326-5797

Ginger Jackson-Carter says her Main shop is a "little bit of Nantucket in the desert" where she has a wide selection of silver, period furniture and Americana. She carries over 100 eastern gift lines (not southwestern), 90% of which no one else in Tucson carries and she specializes in silver.

Around the corner in the same center is the Show room where you'll find antiques, fine used furniture and decorative accessories. She averages a half dozen estate sales a year and will be happy to put your name on her mailing list. If you notice some lovely antiques in Goldwaters, they're from Ginger's stores also. Mon—Sat 9:30am—5pm.

HOW SWEET IT WAS
636 North Fourth Avenue

University
623-9854

Shades of yesteryear, the clothing you're looking for from that vintage year can be found here, from the turn of the century to the more recent 1950s. Clothing, jewelry and accessories include many purchased from estate sales. Mon—Sat 11am—6pm

KAY MALLEK
3859 East Grant Road

El Con
327-6118

A highly respected dealer who established her decorative tile and commemorative plate business in 1947, Kay continues with that business at 2013 North Swan (323-7841), while her Grant Road shop offers antiques and top-of-the-line contemporary used furnishings.

259

Antiques include china, crystal and silver, jewelry (including old Indian turquoise and silver), fireplace tools and irons, Persian rugs, canopy beds, old toys and Victorian sofas and chairs. Empire and early American furniture is available in pine, walnut, cherry, tiger maple, mahogany and oak. Her stock includes the largest collection of antique silver in the state. Mon—Sat 9am—6pm.

TREASURE EXCHANGE   **El Presidio**
24 East 15th Street   622-5070

Operated by the Tucson Symphony Women's Association, the Treasure Exchange is located in the Amado House, a Victorian treasure in itself. The shop carries antique items on consignment, including jewelry, silver, crystal, small furniture items and small oriental rugs. Note: Consignment day is Friday. Open approximately Sept—May, Tue—Sat 10am—3pm. (See also THE PAST IS STILL WITH US.)

ART IN TUCSON

(See also MUSEUM SHOPS, INDIAN ARTS,
PEDESTRIAN SHOPPING, MEXICAN CRAFTS AND IMPORTS)

Tucson's future Downtown Arts District will present an excellent selection of galleries and works from our abundance of artists. The district will include the Convention Center, Main Library, historic areas, and theatres. As the district is only now in the planning stage I can't include specifics. Check with the Chamber of Commerce or the Convention Bureau for further information.

I can't possibly list all of our exceptional galleries and recommend you pick up a free copy of the Southern Arizona edition of *Art Life*. Published twice a year, it is an extensive guide to arts of the Southwest. Most galleries have copies, however if you're unable to find one, write Yoakum Publishing Company, P.O. Box 42228, Tucson, AZ 85716, 323-6889.

AMERICA WEST PRIMITIVE &
MODERN ART GALLERY   **El Presidio**
363 South Meyer Avenue   623-4091

This lovely old building, with its original mesquite and pine beams and saguaro-ribbed ceilings is an ideal setting for the pre-Columbian, African, Oceanic, Asiatic and American Indian art you will find here. Not open all the time, call for an appointment.

CABAT STUDIO   **University**
627 North 4th Avenue   622-6362

Erni Cabat's rich, radiant paintings of the Southwest, Sonoran missions, and numerous locations around the world illuminate any space with a *joie de vivre*. His work has been likened to the French Impressionists, though Erni feels his approach is colorfully and joyfully his own.

Rose Cabat's whimsical, fantastic "feelies" (you'll have to pick one up to understand that nick-name), are also featured. These extraordinary pieces of art were chosen to be on display at the Smithsonian for over two years and were exhibited at the Renwick Gallery for a year, along with a two-year tour around the country.

In 1987, these two wonderful people were honored by the Tucson Museum of Art with a two-month retrospective of their work.

June Cabat's beautiful handmade jewelry is also on display in the shop, along with Erni's pottery, books and notecards made from his paintings. (*See also* SOME OTHER GOOD BOOKS.)

The studio is not open all the time. Give them a call; Erni says, "We'll fit our schedule to yours."

CENTRAL ARTS COLLECTIVE
250 East Congress

El Presidio
623-5883

Presently, from embryonic art to the more mature works, Tucson's avant-garde art is found in this gallery, Dinnerware and others along downtown's Congress Street.

CREATIVE CREATIONS
5420 East Broadway
(The Plaza at Williams Centre)

Pantano
790-1888

Ellen Reiner has put together a varied array of unique southwestern gifts and accessories. Fine hand-crafted items such as ceramics, weavings, painted folkart furniture, pottery, wood carvings, wearable art and unusual jewelry abound. Truly a shopper's delight with a wide price range.

Ellen also has a "Wish Box." Drop a card in it stating your desires for the gift you wish and ask your special someone to stop in. Ellen will pull the card from the box and voila! easy shopping for your friend and you get your wished-for item. Mon—Fri 10am—5:30pm, Sat 10am—5pm, Sun by appointment.

DINNERWARE ARTISTS' CO-OPERATIVE GALLERY
135 East Congress Street

El Presidio
792-4503

Founded in 1979, this gallery is the grand-daddy of Nuevo Centro in the art district of downtown Tucson. National, regional and international shows are presented two or three times a year. An eclectic collection of new, different and unique art in all medias.

EL PRESIDIO GALLERY
182 North Court Avenue, and
201 North Court Avenue

El Presidio
884-7379

You'll find two El Presidio Art Galleries on Court Avenue, one just across from the other, and just around the corner from the Tucson Museum of Art. The focus is on southwestern art, with some contemporary. Both prominent and emerging artists are shown in a wide diversification of styles and media. Paintings are their major artwork, but they also have a choice selection of pottery and sculpture. Mon—Sat 10am—5pm, Sun 1pm—4pm.

ELEANOR JECK GALLERIES
6336 East Broadway
(El Mercado de Boutiques)

Pantano
790-8333

An excellent contemporary art, sculpture and ceramic gallery, featuring oils, acrylics, pastels, water colors, graphics and posters. Artists include local, national and internationally-known persons, such as: Zuñiga, Tobiasse, Papart, Rizzi and Coignard. Tue—Sat 11am—4pm or by appointment.

ETHERTON/STERN GALLERY
135 South 6th Avenue

El Presidio
624-7370

Photography as an art form is well assembled by Director Terry Etherton. Works by Todd Walker, Ansel Adams, Dick Arentz, Judith Golden, Linda Connor, Louis Bernal, Timothy O'Sullivan and many others contribute to an excellent collection of vintage and contemporary fine art photography.

The gallery also presents a select group of paintings and sculptures by local artists, including works by Gail Marcus-Orlen, James G. Davis and Barbara Grygutis. Also available are books, posters and limited editon portfolios of original prints. Wed—Sat noon—5pm, Thu noon—7pm.

GALERIA ANITA
825 North Anita

El Presidio
792-0777

Anna Franklin's home is also her gallery and here you'll find her wonderful handcrafted dolls and marionettes, numerous unique Mexican imports, and paintings, sculptures and carved doors by Frank Franklin. The works of both Anna and Frank are known by many of their aficionados in Tucson. Anna's old adobe home and its enchanting patio are located in Barrio Anita, one of Tucson's oldest barrios. Please call for an appointment.

IMPRESSIONS II, LTD.
2990 North Swan Road
(Palomino Plaza)

Rillito
323-3320

Impressions II features excellent contemporary and southwestern art by locally and internally-known artists. Included are the works of R.C. Gorman, Lawrence L. Lee, John Nieto and Clifford Beck. Mon—Sat 10am— 5:30pm. Thu eve by appointment.

MARY PEACHIN'S ART COMPANY
3955 East Speedway Blvd. (881-1311)
5350 East Broadway (747-1345)
(The Plaza at Williams Centre)

El Con

Pantano

Mary's galleries carry excellent selections of contemporary and southwestern lithographs, posters and original art, sculptures and bronzes. And if your psyche is at all whimsical, stop in the Williams Center gallery to see her "wooden critters" from Oaxaca. These hand carved and hand painted beings will walk right into your heart along with coyote carvings by Alvarez and Elizondo. Mary also provides award-winning custom framing. Mon—Sat 10am—5:30pm.

OBSIDIAN GALLERY
North Campbell Avenue and
East River Road
(St. Phillips Plaza)

Rillito
577-3598

The Obsidian presents handcrafted objects by regionally prominent and national known artists in clay, glass, metal, fiber and wood, with an emphasis on one-of-a-kind, high-quality art. Mon—Sat 10am—5:30pm.

ROSEQUIST GALLERIES
1615 East Fort Lowell Road

Rillito
327-5729

The art of western America, both past and present, is presented in oils and watercolors, bronze, wood and stone sculptures, batiks, pottery, Indian weavings, etchings and prints. Custom framing and restorations also available. Tue—Sat 10am—5pm and by appointment.

THE WEST
4759 East Sunrise Drive
Northeast corner of Swan and Sunrise

Foothills
299-1044

All moneys raised through sales at The West aid local charities. Staffed by volunteer members of the Brewster Home, they sell an exceptionally unique selection of gifts, toys and handcrafted items. Their selection of needlework supplies, including books, kits and yarns, is one of the largest in the Southwest. They offer needlework classes and custom designs. Mon—Sat 10am—5pm.

In the **Foothills** area, just north of the intersection of Campbell Avenue and Skyline Road (6420 North Campbell) a tranquil, tree-shaded patio welcomes you to browse through four superb galleries.

BLACKHAWK GALLERIES	577-7647
SANDERS GALLERIES	299-1763
SETTLERS WEST GALLERIES	299-2607
WOLFE GALLERIES	299-5655

Blackhawk Galleries features contemporary western and Indian art, wildlife art and bronzes. They also have an outstanding collection of contemporary western jewelry. Mon—Sat 1am—5pm, Sun noon—4pm.

Sanders Galleries features traditional western and contemporary southwestern paintings, and bronze sculpture and alabaster sculpture by such nationally known artists as: Bob Scriver, Ron Stewart, Richard Iams, Don Jaramillo, Jim Norton and Gayle Nason. Also presented is fine arts jewelry by such creative artists as Dee Williams, Eleanor Caldwell and Yell Newman. Mon—Sat 10am—5pm.
Sanders Galleries has a second location at Westin La Paloma, 3800 East Sunrise, 577-5820. Hours are Mon—Sat 10am—7pm, Sun 10am—6pm.

Settlers West, considered nationally to be one of the premier galleries of western and wildlife art, includes work by Howard Terpning, Morris Rippel, Tom Hill, Harley Brown, Michael Coleman, James Reynolds, William Acheff and Richard Schmidd. Works of past masters also available. Mon—Sat 10am—5pm, Sun noon—4pm.

Wolfe Galleries exhibits representational and impressionistic works of art, regional as well as non-regional. You will find oils, acrylics and watercolors, crystal, etchings, woodcarvings and porcelain pottery. Tue—Sat 11am—4pm.

TUBAC CENTER OF THE ARTS
Tubac, Arizona

Oct through May
398-2371

The works of numerous contemporary artists in a variety of media are shown at the center. Countless other galleries, include **Steigers**, selling Harwood Steiger's handprinted silk screen fabrics; **La Paloma Boutique**, Mexican designer clothing, Guatemalan cotton sportswear and items from Spain; **Hugh Cabot Gallery**, art for the discriminating collector; **The Potted Owl** a studio and gallery with pottery and fine art; the **Peck Gallery** which shows Navajo rugs, paintings, jewelry, basketry, antiques and woodcarvings; and the **Windsong Gallery**, where Marjorie Nichols, who specializes in batiks, jewelry, watercolors and oils, has created a haven for over thirty different varieties of birds in her delightful shaded yard which has been designated a National Wildlife Federation Backyard Habitat. (*See also* TUBAC.)

One of the best bookstores in Southern Arizona is the **Tortuga Bookshop** in Tubac's Mercado de Baca at 190 Tubac Road. The warm, inviting space includes art on the walls, a fireplace flanked by chairs and a great view of the Santa Rita Mountains. They encourage loitering and you'll have time to peruse many outstanding publications.

BOOKSTORES

(*See also* ART IN TUCSON and
PEDESTRIAN SHOPPING)

The Old Pueblo is blessed with a superb selection of outstanding privately-owned bookstores, along with B. Dalton Booksellers in our four major shopping centers and Waldenbooks in three shopping centers. If you are that genus of homo sapien that can't walk by a bookstore without wandering in, Tucson is your kind of town. It's impossible to list all of our bookshops, but the following are some of my favorites.

THE BOOK MARK
4765 East Speedway Blvd.

El Con
881-6350

Any bibliophile in Tucson knows that if they can't find a particular book The Book Mark will probably have it. And if they don't, they'll order it.

Established in Tucson in 1958, and listed as one of the 100 Best Bookstores in the U.S., this family-owned store is ably managed by Ed Eggers. The store is an outstanding "general" bookstore carrying the latest publications of all major publishers. Mon—Thu 9am—6pm, Fri 9am—9pm, Sat 9am—5pm.(They're open December Sundays 9am—5pm.)

BOOKMAN'S USED BOOKS
1930 East Grant
325-5055

El Con
325-5055

This huge bookstore (it used to be a major grocery store) has a tremendous selection of books and is the "largest newsstand in the Southwest" with over 3500 new magazines and national and international newspapers.

They advertise over 500,000 hardbacks, paperbacks, records and magazines. Selections include best sellers, novels, westerns, romance, science fiction, gothic and mysteries. Mon—Sat 9am—10pm, Sun 11am— 6pm.

BOOKS BROTHERS, LTD.
3242 East Speedway

El Con
326-3332

Mitchell Bunting and Michael Heimbuch present a wide collection of paperback and selected hard cover bestsellers, and an extensive selection of periodicals, with over 365 feet of magazines; some of which are unattainable elsewhere. Check here for unusual magazines, either foreign or American.

They also carry an excellent selection of books and magazines on design, graphic arts, commercial arts, architecture and interiors. I've found several very unusual and beautiful architecture and art books here. Mon—Fri 9am—9pm, Sat 9am—6pm, Sun 11am—5pm.

THE BOOKSHOP
SOUTHWEST PARKS & MONUMENTS ASSN.
223 North Court at Council

El Presidio
792-0239

Located in historic El Presidio, this charming adobe building predates 1887 and at one time was known as The Stork's Nest, Tucson's first maternity ward.

Dedicated to all aspects of the Southwest, you'll find books on natural history and national parks, Native American arts, botany, fiction, cooking, children's literature and hiking guides. Native American jewelry and music is available along with educational videos on the Southwest. A limited selection of American arts and crafts and southwest travel information is also available. Tue—Fri 11am—5:30pm, Sat 10am—3pm.

COYOTE'S VOICE BOOKS
South Eastbourne Avenue
(at Broadway and Country Club)

El Con
327-6560

Tania and John Messina specialize in books on the Southwest, architecture, art, photography, children, cooking and travel. You'll find a special selection of books on far-away places. They also have a selection of cards. Mon—Sat 10am—5:30pm.

FOOTPRINTS OF A
GIGANTIC HOUND
123 South Eastbourne
(at Broadway and Country Club)

El Con
326-8533

Martha, the "gigantic hound" greets you as you enter this unique bookstore. She's the Labrador-Newfoundland mixture who owns the bookstore owners, Elaine and Joseph Livermore and from whom (along with Sir Arthur Conan Doyle's *Hound of the Baskervilles*) the name suggestion came.

As Arizona's only mystery bookstore, and with over 5,000 volumes on the shelves, this is where to find the latest whodunit. Their stock includes first editions and a large range of paperbacks. About 200 out-of-print first editions are also available. Mon—Sat 10am—5pm.

GOODBOOKS
431 North 4th Avenue

University
792-9551

The space is small, but the selection is outstanding. Conrad Goeringer has a fascinating collection of QUALITY new, used and rare books that will keep you browsing for hours.

265

He specializes in art, first editions, cookbooks and the Southwest. Located near the UA, the used books cover a multitude of technical fields rarely found in bookstores dealing with used books. A "search service" is also provided. Mon—Sat 10am—10pm, Sun noon—10pm.

THE HAUNTED BOOKSHOP
Foothills
7211 North Northern Avenue
297-4843

Here you will find not only stacks of excellent books with a toy train running on an overhead track, special "hidey holes" for the kids and a pleasurable welcome feeling, but also a captivating nature preserve right outside the front door. (See also PARKS AND RECREATION.)

Their stock includes fiction, non-fiction and science fiction, crafts, health and reference books, an extensive selection of books on the Southwest, and maps, kites and a winning zoo of stuffed animals. Mon—Sat 9:30am—5:30pm, Sun noon-5pm.

Specialist Joan Robles will assist you in finding a rare edition or appraise volumes for you. She is available Tuesdays and Fridays 1pm—4pm or call for an appointment.

Drive north on Oracle; turn west on Ina Road, go one short block to Northern and turn north. The entrance is just north of the bookstore.

PLACES & PEOPLE
University
2623 North Campbell Avenue
322-6211

A one-of-a-kind store with everything you'll want or need for your travels. Calling itself A Travel Bookstore, you'll find books, maps, foreign periodicals, globes and travel accessories for near and far. Mon—Fri 9am—6pm, Sat 10am—5pm, Sun noon—4pm. (See also IMPORTS.)

RAINBOW MOODS
Rillito
3322 North Country Club Road
326-9643

Here you'll find new age and metaphysical books, along with a large selection on the world's religions. You'll also find books on sociology, psychology and wholistic health. Meditation tapes, crystals, cards, videos, posters, oils and incenses are also available.

CONTEMPORARY GIFTS AND FURNISHINGS

CONTENTS
El Con
4380 East Grant Road
881-6900

Contemporary and southwestern furnishings which complement a variety of decors. Many of the furnishings are imported from Italy and Latin America. You'll also find a large selection of the very popular Southwestern folk art and saguaro rib furniture. Accessories include lighting fixtures, pillows, Indian weavings, baskets, pottery, paintings and brass from Morocco. Interior designers are available to assist customers. Mon—Fri 10am—6pm, Sat 10am—5:30pm, Sun Noon—5pm.

266

COPENHAGEN

Rillito

3660 East Fort Lowell Road
(Tucson Interior Design Center)

795-0316

Along with an outstanding view of Tucson's mountains, Copenhagen offers fine Scandinavian furniture of natural teak, oak or rosewood. Cookery, a diverse selection of lamps, and exquisite gifts of crystal, glassware, china, ceramics and jewelry are also available.

They also have an exceptionally large selection of patio furniture and accessories. If contemporary items are your cup of tea, Copenhagen is unrivaled. Mon—Sat 9am—6pm, Sun Noon—5pm.

DENMARKET INTERNATIONAL HOME FURNISHINGS

Rillito

3660 East Fort Lowell Road
(Tucson Interior Design Center)

881-7815

International home furnishings, lamps and gifts in inexpensive lines, to be carried home. A number of items in white enamel and light, natural woods, such as oak and ash. A pleasant place for the price-conscious buyer to purchase good design. Mon—Sat 9am—6pm, Sun noon—5pm.

HOUSE N' GARDEN FURNITURE CO.

El Con

4310 East Broadway

327-5675

Part of Tucson's design scene for many years, this is *the* place to find patio furniture and accessories, and rattan, wicker and indoor furnishings. Also, a tempting array of gift items, from clocks and glassware, to wall hangings, rugs and chess sets. Mon—Fri 9am—5:30pm. Mar— June: Sat 10am—4pm.

SETTINGS

El Con

Northeast corner of Swan and
Grant Roads (Crossroads Festival)

One of the most exciting, posh gift shops in town, and a perfect place to treat yourself also. If you're looking for that extraordinary wedding gift, you'll find it here in an unlimited selection of sparkling crystal, china, silver and luxurious linens. So many elegant items to choose from you'll have difficulty deciding.

TABLE TALK

2936 East Broadway Blvd.	(881-3322)	**El Con**
6843 East Tanque Verde Road	(886-8433)	**Pantano**
Tucson Mall	(293-7140)	**Rillito**
Foothills Center	(742-1777)	**Foothills**

You are bound to find what you are looking for in kitchenware at these four great shops. Everything for the kitchen or dining room in stoneware, copperware, cookware, glassware, wood, pottery, cutlery, gadgets, tables, chairs, coffeemakers (including espresso and cappuccino) and gourmet vinegars and jellies. Broadway and Tanque Verde locations: Mon—Fri 10am—6pm; Sat 9:30am—5:30pm; Sun Noon—5pm. Mall hours at other locations.

267

IMPORTS

(*See also* PEDESTRIAN SHOPPING,
MEXICAN CRAFTS and IMPORTS)

AFRICAN ARTS, LTD.
Country Club and Grant Roads — **El Con**
(Decorator Square) — 795-1997

This unique gallery, run by Phil and Margie Matter, carries fine arts and crafts personally collected from virtually all parts of Africa. Included are paintings and prints, handwoven rugs, traditional sculpture in wood and stone, baskets, musical instruments, unusual jewelry, clothing and fabrics. Silk batiks depicting the peoples and animals in East Africa by Robin A are extra special. The practical and attractive Safekeeper vests are a real boon to the traveler. As an agent specializing in African trips, Margie can even assist with travel arrangements. Mon—Fri 10am—5:30pm, Sat 10am—5pm. Open by appointment only during July.

BERTA WRIGHT DESIGNS
1736 East Speedway — **University** 325-2591
7401 North La Cholla Blvd. — **Foothills**
(Foothills Center) — 742-4134

A Tucson tradition since 1950, "Berta's" has long been the shop in which to buy those rare, exotic fashions that she calls "wearable art." Materials purchased from the distant lands of Guatemala, Thailand, El Salvador, Mexico, Panama and Afghanistan are fashioned into elegant designs by Berta and her daughter, Casonti, for those creative individuals who wish to wear something different.

Other elegant items include primitive art for collectors, ancient beads stunningly asembled into lovely jewelry, Paolo Soleri wind-bells, sculptures and Berta's own handscreened designs. Speedway hours Tue—Sat 9:30am—5:30pm. Foothills hours are those of the Center.

NOTE: The university store will be moving to 260 East Congress, 882-7043 at a "far-opening" date.

THE DEPARTURE
2900 East Broadway — **University** 327-5721

This unique shop has a little bit of everything, with its collection of contemporary and ethnic fashions, jewelry, clothing, folk art and hundreds of gift items and collectibles. One of the largest collections of earrings in town, all very reasonably priced. Mon—Sat 10am—6pm.

PLACES & PEOPLE
2623 North Campbell Avenue — **University** 322-6211

A one-of-a-kind store with everything you'll want or need for your travels. Calling itself A Travel Bookstore, you'll find books, maps, foreign periodicals, globes and language aids. This is the place at which to begin your trip, as they will help you find those travel accessories you'll need. Gifts include native arts and crafts from around the world, while their selection of travel books is outstanding. They also have videos to rent for a preview of your next exotic vacation. Mon—Fri 9am—6pam, Sat 10am—5pm, Sun noon-4pm.

268

PIER 1 IMPORTS
5636 East Broadway
and
4343 North Oracle Road

Pantano
747-3896
Rillito
888-7758

An uncommon shop with loads of imports from the world over. You'll find white porcelain from Japan, brass items and cotton clothing from India, cotton fashions from Greece and Turkey, sea shells, candles, cards, kitchenware, posters, colorful cushions and pillows, hundreds of baskets and lots of wicker furniture. Mon—Sat 10am—9pm, Sun 11am—6pm.

UNITED NATIONS CENTER
Country Club and Grant Road
(Decorator Square)

El Con
881-7060

The UN Center has one of Tucson's largest selections of imports and folk art from around the world, all of which are reasonably priced. Included is unique antique jewelry and brassware, decorative accessories, natural fibre clothing, wood carvings, assorted baskets, a wide selection of woven wall hangings and rugs, UNICEF cards and U.N. literature.

They maintain a free lending library on international affairs and provide a speakers bureau free to schools and organizations. Mon—Fri 10am—5:30pm, Sat 10am—5pm; closed Mon from Memorial Day to Labor Day; open Dec Sundays noon—3pm.

INDIAN ARTS

(*See also* MUSEUM SHOPS and
PEDESTRIAN SHOPPING)

Like our art galleries, a myriad number of businesses provide excellent Indian art and it is impossible to list them all. The following is just a sampling.

ALBERTO CONTRERAS AND SIX SONS
146 West Drachman

Santa Cruz
624-1594

Known as the "Cellini of the Southwest," Alberto Contreras has been designing distinct silverwork in Tucson since 1949. His sons have joined him in the demanding craft and their silversmithing and goldsmithing is nationally known.

The shop on West Drachman Street sells their custom creations, along with Indian crafts and jewelry from tribes throughout Arizona. The shop also has a museum with numerous memorabilia from the 1800s on display. Mon—Sat 9am—5pm.

**BAHTI INDIAN ARTS and
RIVAS BAHTI GALLERY**
4300 North Campbell
(St. Phillips Plaza)

Rillito
577-0290

Mark and Dolores Bahti offer fine authentic Indian arts, including superior jewelry, paintings, kachinas, pottery and contemporary art work of many Tucsonans. Mon—Sat 10am—6pm, Sun Noon—4pm.

DESERT HOUSE
2837 North Campbell Avenue

University
323-2132

A distinctive place in the desert since 1945, you will find authentic southwest Indian arts and crafts, such as Seri Indian carvings, top-of-the-line pottery (including storytellers), Navajo rugs, basketry and fetishes. Their elegant contemporary silver and gold jewelry includes exotic stones and designs.

They also have an exceptional collection of kachinas, specializing in "one-piece" kachina carvings with natural finishes. Mon—Sat 9:30am—5:30pm.

KAIBAB SHOPS
2841 North Campbell
(In the Rear Courtyard)

University
795-6905

One of the Southwest's finest specialty shops for over thirty-three years, you will find original Kaibab moccasins and natural-fibre Kaibab clothing along with an excellent collection of ethnic fashions from Central America. A wide selection of Indian pieces, all chosen for their uniqueness and individuality, includes jewelry, pottery, O'odham and Seri baskets, Hopi kachinas and Navajo weavings. Their extraordinary collection of Mexican folk art includes unique dance masks and their selection of Nambeware is the largest outside of Santa Fe.

In their second building you will find a significant furniture selection including pine pieces from Santa Fe with a northern New Mexico look, and handcarved furniture from Mexico, which, although appearing quite ancient, is new. They also will be happy to build to your specifications. Mon—Sat 9:30—5:30pm

MANY GOATS INDIAN GALLERY
Tucson Mall—Second Floor

Rillito
887-0814

Unusual and distinct items, a large number of which were created by local artists. Included are extraordinary jewelry, prints, sculptures and a superior selection of kachinas. Their art gallery includes a significant number of prints and rugs, but their most impressive art is their oustanding handmade jewelry.

MORNING STAR TRADERS
2020 East Speedway Blvd.

University
881-2112

Specializing in authentic American Indian Art, you will find an exceptional collection of antique baskets and pre-historic and pre-Columbian pottery. They also carry western and Indian art. Mon—Sat 9am—6pm.

PRIMITIVE ARTS
3026 East Broadway
(Broadway Village, Upstairs)

El Con
326-4852

Michael Higgins, a collector of Indian art, specializes in nineteenth century and early twentieth century American Indian art, including Navajo textiles from the 1940s and earlier.

Paul Shepard's specialty is pre-Columbian art, with extraordinary examples of feather work, textiles, ceramics, wools and gold. Tue—Sat 10am—4pm. (They say they "may doze, but never close" and are happy to make appointments at other than business hours.) Call the number above.

THUNDERBIRD SHOP
40 East Broadway   **El Presidio**
(El Adobe Mexican Restaurant)   623-1371

In business for over fifty years, original jewelry designs by Frank Patania and authentic Indian arts and crafts, along with primitive art from New Guinea, are available.

THE HOPI KACHINAS

The more than 300 kachinas are not worshipped as gods, but represent the spirits of all things in the universe. Their home is the San Francisco Peaks, north of Flagstaff. (If you ever drive to the Hopi mesas and look south to the San Francisco Peaks, you will understand why the kachinas have picked that location as their home.)

As the spirits of nature, they are believed to have control over the weather, visiting the Hopi mesas beginning on the winter solstice and acting as intermediaries between the Hopi and the "rain people" and other spirits. They dance in the plazas, frequently bringing gifts to the children when they visit. They spend about six months on the Hopi mesas and then return in July to San Francisco Peaks.

MEXICAN CRAFTS

(*See also* PEDESTRIAN SHOPPING,
IMPORTS, MUSEUM SHOPS AND INDIAN ARTS)

ANTIGUA DE MEXICO   **Foothills**
7037 North Oracle Road   742-7114
(Casas Adobes Shopping)
10,000 North Oracle Road   629-2830
(Sheraton El Conquistador)

The northern branch of a Mexican company that also has a store in Nogales, they have Mexican colonial antiques and custom-made Mexican colonial furniture, along with clay and ceramic pottery, folk art, tinware, glassware, stone sculpture, fountains and loads of colorful paper flowers. You'll also find Mexican dinnerware and equipale (pigskin) furniture. Casas Adobes open Mon—Sat 9am—5pm. Sheraton open Mon—Sat 8am—5pm, Sun 9am—3pm. Summer hours may vary.

CASA JOAQUIN   **El Con**
3132 North Country Club Road   881-JACK

Jack Dickson offers an eclectic selection of furniture, accessories and classic treasures from Mexico and the Southwest. If you don't find what you want, Jack will look for it on his buying trips to Mexico. Tue—Sat 11am—4pm.

EL BANDITO IMPORTS
40 West Broadway Blvd.   **El Presidio**
(El Adobe Mexican Restaurant)   624-6666

Fine, quality pottery and handicrafts from Mexico and South America; everything from paper flowers to leather huaraches and loads of bright colorful piñatas to choose from.

271

EL CHANGARRO
3063 Alvernon Way

Rillito
795-8980

What fun to have El Changarro in Tucson. Their Nogales store has an outstanding collection of art and furniture from Mexico and now you can see some of these items in town. They have a wonderful collection of handcarved furniture, oil paintings, beveled mirrors, wall hangings, pottery and decorative stonework from Mexico. Tue—Sat 9am—5pm.

MAYA DE MEXICO
Southeast corner of
Fort Lowell and Swan Roads
(Plaza Palomino)

Rillito
323-2256

An excellent selection of merchandise from the interior of Mexico. A number of South American and Latin treasures include glass, pottery, straw, carvings and paper flowers in home furnishings and accessories. Design services are provided.

SEIS, INC.
424 North 4th Avenue

El Presidio
622-1146

Primarily a wholesaler to designers, Seis, Inc. also has a large retail show room featuring the finest and most innovative custom and imported southwest and salsa style furnishings, decorative accessories and functional art. Besides striking, unique furnishings (a large amount of which is by local artists), you'll find masks, rugs, chandeliers, pottery and extraordinary collectible folk art. Mon—Sat 10am—5pm or by appointment.

MUSEUM SHOPS

ARIZONA HISTORICAL SOCIETY
949 East Second Street

University
623-8915

Walking into the **Territorial Mercantile Company** is like walking into a general store during Tucson's territorial days. Volunteers, dressed in clothing of that era, will be happy to show you glass and china antiques, Mexican rebozos, pottery and glassware, Hopi baskets, and an excellent collection of books, both old and new, on the Southwest.

ARIZONA-SONORA DESERT MUSEUM
Kinney Road—West of Tucson

Tucson Mountains
883-1380

Here you will find an excellent selection of gift items, including Indian jewelry and basketry and a large collection of books on Sonoran desert life. You'll also find unique inexpensive tourist items, including cactus jellies and elegant posters done by some of the museum's own artists.

ARIZONA STATE MUSEUM
UA University Drive
east of Park Avenue

University
621-6302

Located in the South Building, the work of local craftspersons includes Navajo rugs, Pueblo pottery, turquoise and silver jewelry, and baskets made by Pima, Tohono O'odham, Hopi and Tarahumara Indians. A good selection of regional books are available.

Gifts concurrent with special exhibits are for sale. Items in the past have included Mexican and Guatemalan masks, looms, Huichol yarn weavings and Tarahumara dolls.

DE GRAZIA GALLERY IN THE SUN
6300 North Swan Road

Foothills
299-9191

Prints, note cards, books and collectibles of De Grazia. His original art work is not for sale.

FLANDRAU PLANETARIUM
UA Northeast corner of Cherry
and East Third Street

University
621-4515

The Astronomy Store contains unique gifts with a definite astronomical persuasion, including an exciting variety of star charts, astronomical posters and slides, literature, science kits, games and minerals.

MISSION SAN XAVIER DEL BAC
294-2624

San Xavier

Along with the newly opened museum at San Xavier, you will find a gift shop selling southwestern art gifts of pottery and wood, religious items, Tohono O'ohdam baskets and numerous interesting regional book selections. **San Xavier Plaza**, across the square, has Indian jewelry and crafts and, once-in-awhile, O'ohdam refreshments.

TUCSON MUSEUM OF ART
At the corner of Meyer and
Alameda Streets

El Presidio
624-2333

John McNulty, local potter and manager of **The Museum Shop**, has created an elegantly-displayed art gallery of his own. The diverse selections presented are all by members of Tucson's Craft Guild and the shop is, without a doubt, incomparable. Hand-woven shawls, dresses and blouses, leatherwork and carvings, some of the southwest's finest pottery, lovely glassware and exquisite hand-crafted jewelry, all by Tucson's leading artists, will be found here.

If you're in town in late November, plan to attend the **Holiday Revelry**, a fiesta held by the Tucson Craft Guild and the Arizona Designer Craftsmen in the Plaza of the Pioneers. The event includes food, entertainment and elegant gift items created by Arizona's top craftspeople.

273

THE MALLS

America's malls have replaced the parks and promenades of earlier years as the place to see and be seen and Tucson's malls are no different. If you don't wish to shop, you can people watch, go to a museum, attend the movies or just walk. In fact, there are structured walking sessions at all four of our malls. Tucson's major malls include several large department stores and an extensive variety of specialty shops and restaurants. All four malls are completely enclosed and air-conditioned.

El Con

Tucson's first shopping mall, **El Con**, was established in 1960 on the site of the famous old El Conquistador Hotel, located on Broadway between Country Club and Alvernon. Major department stores include Goldwaters, Foleys, J.C. Penney and Montgomery Ward, along with 130 specialty stores. El Con Six Theaters, with first run features, is located on the north side.

El Con's walking program is offered between 8am and 10am, Mon, Wed and Fri.

Foothills—West

Architecturally, **Foothills Center**, in the 7400 block of North La Cholla Blvd at West Ina Road, is by far the most attractive of our malls. Goldwaters, Foleys and many other shops are located here including **Berta Wright Designs** and **Table Talk.** (*See also* PEDESTRIAN AREAS.) Several quick-food shops provide snacks; if you want a full meal, try **Keaton's** (297-1999).

The major difference between Foothills Center and the other three malls is **The Old Pueblo Museum**. This excellent museum provides a change of pace from the standard mall. (*See also* LA CIUDAD DE LOS MUSEOS.)

Movies are available at Foothills Cinemas—Cineplex Odeon.

Organized walks begin at 10am, Mon and Wed. Doors open at 9:30am, Mon—Sat and at noon Sun for shopping or walking.

Pantano

Park Mall, at Broadway and Wilmot, has Dillards, Broadway and Sears as the major retailers, along with 110 other stores.

Walking can be done anytime the mall is open for business. Doors open at 9am weekdays.

Rillito

Tucson Mall, at 4500 North Oracle Road (just north of Wetmore Road), is our only two-story mall. Several fountains, numerous plants and trees adorned with twinkle lights provide pleasant shopping. You'll find Dillards, Broadway, Mervyns, Sears, J.C. Penney and 175 other shops.

Tucson Mall's Picnic Place has a large number of eateries offering burgers, chicken, crepes, cookies, pizza, chocolate and ice cream.

Walkers meet at the McDonald's Restaurant and walking is from 7—10am.

ETC., ETC., ETC.

FACTS & FIGURES

Spread throughout the desert valley, Tucson's city limits cover over 125 square miles and the metropolitan area spreads over 450 square miles. Our metropolitan population in 1987 was 645,000 with nearly 2,000 arrivals each month (and a corresponding increase every time there's a blizzard back east).

Tucson is the county seat of Pima County, one of the first four counties established by the First Territorial Legislature in 1864. Pima County covers nearly 9,240 square miles, almost half of which is occupied by the San Xavier and Tohono O'odham Indian Reservations, the second largest in the nation. Known by the Spaniards as Pimeria Alta (the "upper land of the Pimas"), the area was named after those Indians who settled here long before the Spaniards arrived in the sixteenth century. The Pima Indians are still a large segment of the Indian population, including the O'odham as members of their family.

Elevations range from 1,200 feet at the lowest part of the desert floor to the 9,157 foot peak of Mount Lemmon, in the Santa Catalina Mountains. Tucson, itself, has an elevation of 2,390 feet.

Originally, the traditional four "C's"—Climate, Cotton, Copper and Cattle made up Pima County's economy. But all things change and the only "C" left is Climate, while diversification has made our economy rather indistinguishable from the rest of the nation. We have a large construction industry, durable goods manufacturing and a fair amount of government institutions and organizations, including Davis Monthan Air Force Base and the University of Arizona (the city's largest employer), who account for a large number of jobs. Hughes Aircraft and IBM are main employers, and the collection of astronomical telescopes surrounding Tucson have further broadened the economy. And that only "C," left—Climate—has caused an outstanding boom in tourism, accounting a great deal for the 20 percent of service jobs provided.

WEATHER

Put on your sunglasses, as Tucson has the most sunshine of any city in the U.S. The sun shines some part of 360 days of the year and our clear, invigorating climate, with warm temperatures and low humidity, makes us one of the most healthful spots in the U.S.

You'll also want your golf clubs, tennis racquets, swimsuits and skis. That's right, in Tucson during the winter months, its possible to "ski the Lemmon" in the morning and swim in your heated pool that afternoon.

Late May or early June will see the ice break up on the Santa Cruz River, when Tucson's first 100°F day arrives. We average 139 days a year over 90°F, and June, July and August are our hottest months, with an average high temperature in July of 98.3°F and an average low of 74.2°F.

Our coolest months are December, January and February, with January's average high at 63.5°F, and the average low for those three months at 37.6°F. It does freeze infrequently and we also have snow once-in-awhile. In fact, 1987 delivered us the wonderful surprise of awakening to a sparkling White Christmas. Generally, the snow melts in the early morning, seldom allowing time to build a snowperson.

We average 11" of rain a year, mostly July—September and December—March. Although if visiting during our July/August monsoons, you may insist the entire 11" fell in one brief hour's time. Tucsonans gleefully anticipate the build-up of thunderheads over the Catalinas which ultimately means the end of a long, hot, dry spell and the beginning of some cooling, welcome moisture in the Old Pueblo. As the storms are frequently preceeded by quite strong winds it's wise to wait until the wind and rain abate before venturing forth. Some of Tucson's streets frequently resemble Venetian canals and until the waters recede, driving can be dangerous.

During these storms the humidity has been known to rise considerably, however our usual low relative humidity averages 29% (and sometimes sinks to 5% or lower), making even a summer day of 100° tolerable.

Flash Floods

We do have flooding during our heavy rains, creating more driving problems than anything else. For further information, see RULES OF THE ROAD.

Summer lightning, although awesome and exciting, can also be dangerous. Stay indoors, when possible, and don't handle electrical appliances, bathe, wash dishes or use the phone. Lightning bolts can follow plumbing and wiring into your home. If in a car, roll the windows up and keep your hands off metallic parts. Don't ride a bike or motorcycle. If on a golf course, don't seek shelter under a tree, but head for low land and/or the clubhouse.

CLOTHING

Light woolens, suits, sweaters and leather-wear are ideal for wintertime. Blue jeans were a part of our lives long before they became stylish on the Eastern seaboard and they are still accepted most anywhere in town, if not at times *de rigueur*.

Summer is casual; it's just too darned hot for anything else! In fact, there's a tale told by an old pioneer that Tucsonans aren't too concerned about either heaven or hell. They know what heaven is from living in Tucson in the winter and they've already suffered through hell by living in Tucson during the summer!

Dress comfortably and wisely and wear a hat if you're going to be out in the summer sun. Men frequently enjoy Mexican Guayaberra shirts and many wear bola ties (a leather braid held in place by a decorated slide) year-round. Overcompensation in air conditioning in restaurants, theatres and stores frequently leaves a person shivering. Best to grab a wrap or sweater before venturing out in that bareback dress in the summer.

Not too many Tucsonans have raincoats or umbrellas as most rains are block-busters and not too long-lived. If you're caught in one, head for the nearest shelter until it passes, which it will, rather quickly.

Large public events, such as concerts, the Tucson Symphony, theatre presentations, and museum openings will find dress from blue jeans and street clothes, to cocktail and ethnic dresses. Although the influx of residents from back east has determined a slightly more sophisticated mode, "southwest casual" still describes both Tucson's dress and lifestyle.

A few exceptions, such as the Silver and Turquoise Ball, *the* event of the Tucson Festival season, and the Angel Ball, a glittering, successful annual fund raiser begun in 1984, change the rules. These events find women in elegant, formal dresses and men in either tuxes or dark business suits. Tucsonans also get fancied up for weddings and such, but the event must be quite special.

SUMMERTIME—AND ITS PROBLEMS

Ol' sol raises havoc with any plastic items in a closed-up auto, including tapes, camera film, compasses, and sunglass holders. Don't leave anything you value in a closed-up vehicle.

If traveling on the highway, or in undeveloped areas, take drinking water. If your car breaks down, DO NOT leave it and wander off for help. If you stay with your car, you will be spotted more easily.

Old desert buffs used to carry a towel to throw over the steering wheel in the summer, but now we use those great cardboard windshield covers, which I highly recommend. Otherwise, the steering wheel and ignition switch become hot as molten metal. Crack a window slightly when you leave your car, to allow for circulation.

Children and Pets

NEVER leave a child or pet in your vehicle in the summer for even a "minute;" not only because its unsafe, but it is against the law. The interior of an auto sitting in the sun rapidly becomes an oven, with temperatures reaching over 130°F in less than ten minutes and ultimately reaching 160°F. An animal receives brain damage within a few minutes at that temperature. It isn't safe to leave a child alone in an auto at any time, but particularly in such temperatures.

Sadly, deaths are recorded of both children and pets who have been left in locked automobiles.

Dehydration

Dehydration is a very real problem during the summer. Your body's adjustment to extreme heat is quite limited, and inadequate water intake in relation to the heat load can cause extreme dehydration, resulting in your body weakening rapidly and collapsing. Your sweat glands may increase their output to a quart of water per hour in an effort to cool you off, even though, due to the dryness, you may not realize you're losing water so rapidly. A loss of 5% or more of your body water is very dangerous.

This is not to frighten you; several hundred thousand of us live here year-round and we don't collapse every summer. But we have learned how to live with our heat. Be cautious and consume at least three quarts of water a day, particularly if you are exercising or doing a lot of work in the sun, or just touring the Arizona-Sonora Desert Museum.

Sun Awareness

Not to belabor the matter, but one more bit of respect must be accorded the sun. As a mixed blessing, we receive warm, bright, sunny days, but we also have the highest skin cancer rate in the U.S.

Due to the high sun intensity, latitude, altitude and clear skies, everyone in Tucson is at high risk for developing skin cancer. Those who have light skin or eyes, sunburn or freckle easily, or work outdoors are also susceptible. Tanning has been found to be very damaging to the skin, causing sunburn, premature aging, leathery and rough skin and ultimately the possibility of skin cancer. A tan is not a sign of health, but instead is a sign your body is trying to defend itself from the sun's burning rays. A tan may protect you from sunburn, but it does not protect you from premature aging, wrinkling or skin cancer. And worse of all, the effects are cumulative over a number of years.

The leading cause of skin cancer is the ultraviolet (UV) portion of sunlight. UV light is invisible and cannot be felt, but can penetrate cloud cover and water. It also reflects off surrounding surfaces, burning you under a hat, umbrella or shade tree.

To prevent wrinkling, aging and ultimately, cancer:

1. Use a sunscreen with a high SPF (Sun Protection Factor). SPF 15 gives maximum protection. Use year-round and apply 30 minutes before going out in the sun to every part of your body that is exposed. Reapply every couple of hours or after you have been swimming.

2. Avoid the sun between 10am and 3pm when the rays are the strongest.

3. In addition to the sunscreen, cover up with a hat, long sleeves and slacks (cottons are best), and wear sunglasses that screen out ultraviolet light.

4. Pay attention to any changes in a mole or blemish appearing on your body.

For further information, contact the Arizona Sun Awareness Project, Tucson AZ 85724, 626-7935.

278

RULES OF THE ROAD

Although traffic laws are basically similar, we may have a few different regulations than you are used to.

Speed Limits

School zones: posted signs do mean SLOW—at 15mph; the law is strictly enforced. "No passing" means: do not edge the front of your auto past an auto beside you, until you are through the zone. **Business** and **residential:** 25mph limit. Local authorities may change these speeds.

    Freeway driving: 55mph on state highways; 65mph on interstates. Use caution and wait for traffic to clear when approaching on-ramp. Use turn signals before changing lanes. Do not make U turns or back up if you miss an exit. Drive to next off-ramp and re-enter freeway through the proper road exchange.

Safety Zones—Pedestrian Crosswalks

Pedestrians DO have the right-of-way over motor vehicles in ALL crosswalks, whether marked or not. You must come to a full stop until the pedestrian has reached the other side of the street.

School Buses

Arizona law requires all vehicles approaching a stopped school bus displaying red flashing lights and stop arm to stop from either direction until the bus resumes motion or the stop arm and flashing lights are no longer displayed. A first offense carries a maximum fine of $500 and thirty days in jail! The only exception is a multiple roadway with a curbed median; if you are on the opposite side of the median from the bus, you may proceed with caution.

Buckling up Baby

We don't have a seat belt law for adults, but we do have one children. It is mandatory that a child under four years of age or a child weighing under forty pounds be restrained in a car seat. It is possible to rent kiddie seats from Tucson Medical Center; phone 327-5461.

Drinking and Driving

Arizona's drunk-driving law is tough. Anyone convicted of driving while intoxicated must spend 24 continuous hours in jail, *will* be fined $250 and can lose his or her license for up to ninety days. A police officer may take away the license of anyone who refuses to take or fails blood, breath or urine tests for drugs or alchohol. A second offense within five years means sixty days in jail and a one-year suspension of driving privileges. A third offense means six months in jail, a loss of license for three years and a fine of up to $150,000.

279

Traffic Signals

A right turn may be made on a red light (after coming to a full stop), if no sign prohibits it. (In fact, if you don't make that turn a chorus of horns will remind you to do so.)

Tucson has "lagging left turns" at most intersections: that is, the left-turn arrow comes after, not before, the green light. Unless posted otherwise, a left turn may be made on a green light if oncoming traffic allows. CAUTION: a momentary pause occurs after the light turns red and before the left turn signal appears and if your auto has not triggered the light mechanism, you must wait for the next green light. It is illegal to enter an intersection on a yellow light.

The Turning Lane

Speedway, Broadway and Grant provide a continuous center turning lane, where left turns may be executed when traffic permits. This lane is for left turns only, not for passing or for continual driving.

Conflict regarding previous sentence. On these same streets this lane, aptly called the "suicide lane," becomes one way during rush hours: one way going west from 7am—9am and one way going east from 4pm—6pm and **no left turns allowed**. As even we residents become confused, be cautious during rush hours. The streets utilizing this type of traffic control are Speedway, Broadway, Grant and 5th Street.

Flash Floods

Tucson's summer rains are known as the **monsoons** and when they arrive, the super-charged air livens up the atmosphere with drenching downpoors and flooded streets. (Such storms can also occur other times of the year, as in our October 1983 floods.) If possible, postpone your trip for 30—45 minutes; most water problems disappear by then! If you are already out or that dinner reservation is waiting, use caution.

Low lying areas are posted "flash flood." Underpasses have footage markings on their walls. The average auto will have water to the bottom of its doors at 12″, the hood will be covered at 32″ and at 54″, you'll need scuba gear! I'm sure you don't want to be in one of the numerous autos pulled out of Lake Elmira (or as it is listed on maps, the Stone Avenue Underpass). If you find barriers or safety lights on any highway, find another route.

Although it may be dry in your vicinity, that doesn't mean we won't have flooding. Our normally dry rivers are major runoff channels for the surrounding mountains. Mount Lemmon or Santa Rita rain eventually arrives in Tucson. **Do heed this information.** Flooding causes more deaths in Arizona than any other weather-related cause.

Dust Storms

Dust storms blow in also and frequently the two go hand in hand, with rain immediately following a big wind. Arizona's dust storms vary in intensity, however a severe one can reduce visibility to zero. If involved in a dust storm, reduce your vehicle speed and drive off the pavement as far as possible. Turn your lights OFF (lights left on can attract other drivers, creating rear-end collisions). UNDER NO CONDITION SHOULD YOU STOP ON THE PAVEMENT. Most dust storms clear up shortly. If on the interstate between Tucson and Phoenix, note the posted signs and a call number on your radio for further safety instructions.

Icy streets

You don't have to drive up Mount Lemmon to slip and slide on the ice. It can happen right in town. Tucson's ice tends to be invisible and is referred to as "black ice," found usually on bridges and overpasses. These sites will be posted when necessary. If you find yourself in a skid, steer in the direction of the skid and don't jam on the brakes.

Mountain Roads

If not a seasoned mountain driver you may find mountain travelling a bit unnerving; particularly with our narrow roads. Stay to the right at all times and be sure you can see a good distance ahead before passing. If you are detaining other autos, be courteous enough to pull over in provided pull-off areas and let them pass.

Both the Catalinas and the Santa Ritas receive a good deal of snow. Check road conditions before driving up either range. Chains may be required or the roads may be closed. Be cautious on shady areas; ice, or melting snow becoming ice during late afternoon and evening hours creates treacherous stretches. For road conditions, call the Pima County Sheriff's office at 882-2800. (*See also* MOUNTAINS.)

Off—road Traffic

Please don't leave established roadways and head across the desert. It is a dangerous practice for you, your vehicle and our desert. Desert temperatures soar, and being stuck in sand at noon of a 115 degree day can mean your life. Although our desert seems tough and unbreakable, it is a fragile and easily-damaged environment; desert flora require many years to seed and grow and vehicle damage is unrepairable in a lifetime.

MASS TRANSPORTATION

Local

Sun Tran provides public transportation throughout Tucson. A variety of passes are available with students and senior citizens discounts. Park and Ride lots are located along express routes. Schedules are available at Sun Tran kiosk information centers near the main entrances of El Con, Park Mall and Foothills Mall, and at City Hall, the UA, Pima College and most banks.

Sun Tran frequently provides shuttle service to UA games, the symphony, etc. For schedules, special events shuttle information and a free Sun Tran transit map, call 792-9222.

Transportation for the Disabled

Sun Tran provides buses with wheelchair lifts on Route 8—Broadway/South 6th. For further information, call 628-1565.

The City of Tucson provides transportation service for those unable to use Sun Tran. Ride requests must be made in advance for either Handi-Car or Special Needs services and passengers must have valid I.D. cards and trip passes which may be purchased through the mail. For further information, call Handi-car 881-4333 or Special Needs 791-3211.

Most state and interstate bus companies are located downtown. Several offer charter service and tours. Citizen Auto Stage has trips to Nogales every two hours. For further information, check in the yellow pages under Bus Lines.

Amtrack serves Tucson for inter-city rail passenger service. The depot is located downtown at 400 East Toole. For information and reservations, call 1-800-872-7245.

Tucson International Airport is served by numerous airlines. For information, call the airlines directly. The airport itself is located south of Valencia Road between the Nogales Highway and Country Club Road.

THE MEDIA

Television

Tucson is served by several cable systems and has five VHF channels and two UHF channels.

KVOA	Channel 4	NBC affiliate
KUAT-TV	Channel 6	Public Broadcasting Service
KGUN	Channel 9	ABC affiliate
KMSB	Channel 11	Independent station
KOLD	Channel 13	CBS affiliate
KDTU (UHF)	Channel 18	Independent station
KPOL (UHF)	Channel 40	Independent station

Radio

Adult Contemporary:
  KTKT (990—AM), KWFM (92.9—FM),
  KRQQ (93.7—FM),

Airport Advisory
  KNDL (530—AM)

Big Bands:
  KGVY (1080-AM)

Classical:
  KUAT (90.5—FM; 103.1—FM, on northwest side)

Community radio:
  KXCI (91.7—FM)

Contemporary:
  KRQQ (93.7—FM)

Country music:
  KCUB (1290—AM), KOPO (98.3—FM), KIIM (99.5—FM), KCKY (1150—AM)

Easy listening:
  KJYK (94.9—FM), KEZG (92.1—FM), KTKT (990—AM)

Jazz, mixed with public affairs programming from
  National Public Radio:
  KUAT (1550—AM)

Mexican Country:
  KXEW (1600—AM)

New Age, Jazz:
  KAWV (101.7—FM)

News, Sports, etc.:
  KNST (940—AM) and KTUC (1400—AM)

Christian:
  KFLT (830—AM) and KVOI (690—AM)

Rock:
  KLPX (96.1—FM), KHYT (1330—AM)

Rock, adult:
  KFXX (92.1—FM)

Rock, hard:
  KTZR (1450—AM)

Rock, light:
  KWFM (92.9—FM)

Rock oldies:
  KCEE (790—AM), KAIR (1490—AM)

Spanish-language:
  KXEW (1600—AM), KQTL (1210—AM), KXMG (98-3—FM)

Swing:
  KMRR (1330—AM)

Newspapers

The *Arizona Daily Star,* Tucson's a.m. paper prints seven days a week. Daily, in the ACCENT section, you will find movie listings, television and radio programs, and "Tucson Today," a directory of special happenings and hours and times of local sightseeing attractions. Friday's ACCENT includes an Art Calendar, openings, movies and an "After Dark" section. Sunday's ACCENT includes movies and art, and Wednesday's ROUNDUP includes short trips around the Old Pueblo.

The *Tucson Citizen,* the evening paper, is delivered six days a week (no Sunday edition). The LIVING section covers local and national entertainment, fashion, trends and the arts.

Thursday's TUCSON CALENDAR is an excellent guide to all entertainment and activities in Tucson for the up-coming week. Movies, nightclubs, what's to do, kid stuff and restaurant reviews will help you plan your week.

The *Daily Territorial,* located in the northwest part of town, publishes Monday through Friday with extensive local news coverage. Supreme Court decisions are boldly noted, along with good business coverage. Thursday's special edition has comprehensive coverage of the community along with regional and state news. As the official newspaper of the City of Tucson and Pima County, the *Territorial* includes all public notices.

Several newspapers publish on a weekly, bi-weekly, monthly or bi-monthly basis: *Dateline: Downtown,* official publication of the Downtown Business Association, the *Arizona Cracker Barrel* for senior citizens, and the very popular *Tucson Weekly,* with its extensive coverage of the arts and entertainment in Tucson. These newspapers are free and can be found in various locations about town.

In its short 18-month history, *City Magazine,* has become the biggest selling local monthly publication. Letters to the editor, although sometimes damning, are more frequently praising and Mayor Tom Volgy said it best with: "There is a sense of life conveyed to your readers about the community that clearly doesn't exist anywhere else in Tucson. Thank you! You underline the best and worst in us, highlight our weaknesses and strengths, and show, despite warts and all, why we love living in this city so much." I recommend it highly if you wish to understand and learn the nuances of our Old Pueblo.

EMERGENCY CENTERS AND HOSPITALS

Tucson's health care scene is one of the best in the nation with thirteen hospitals to meet the city's health needs.

Several **Urgent Care Centers** provide an alternative to hospital emergency rooms for non life-threatening medical needs. These centers provide excellent health service at much less cost than regular emergency rooms.

University

The Tucson Clinic   Daily 10am—10pm
116 North Tucson Blvd.
327-5531

El Con

Thomas Davis Medical Center
East 5th Street and Alvernon
881-7100

Daily 8am—10pm

Pantano

Thomas Davis Medical Center
9302 East 22nd Street
298-0147

Daily 8am—8pm

Foothills

Thomas Davis Medical Center
4720 North Oracle Road
293-6945

Daily 8am—8pm

Tucson General Hospital
1601 West Ina Road
742-1101

Open 24 hours

Tucson's Public Hospitals:

Life-threatening emergencies should be taken to a regular hospital-based emergency room. By law, emergency rooms must accept any patient who comes to their doors.

Santa Cruz

St. Mary's Hospital and Health Center, 1601 West St. Mary's Road, **622-5833**

University

University Medical Center, 1501 North Campbell Avenue, **626-0111** Emergencies **626-6093**

Rillito

Tucson General Hospital (Osteopathic), 3838 North Campbell Avenue, **327-5431**

Pantano

Tucson Medical Center, 5301 East Grant Road (at Beverly Blvd.), **327-5461**

El Dorado Medical Center, 1400 North Wilmot Road, **886-6361**

St. Joseph's Hospital, 350 North Wilmot Road, **296-3211**

Airport

Kino Community Hospital, 2800 East Ajo Way, **294-4471**

PHONE NUMBERS

The following phone numbers will assist you in emergencies and provide specific information. A disclaimer at this point: all phone numbers (and addresses) in *This is Tucson* are accurate as of July, 1988. By the time you purchase the guide, some numbers may have been changed. Update of *This is Tucson* is made as frequently as feasible to keep it current.

EMERGENCY	**911**

In any incident that involves immediate threat
to human life or property
(this number will connect you with
police, fire and ambulances)

CHILD ABUSE/PROTECTION SERVICES	**628-5946**
CITY HALL INFORMATION	**791-4911**
COUNSELINE/PARENT TALK	**745-4655**
CRIME PREVENTION	**88-CRIME**
CRISIS COUNSELING/ SUICIDE PREVENTION	**323-9373**
DISABLED SERVICES (EASTER SEAL SOCIETY)	**745-5222**
HELP ON CALL	**323-9373**
HOSPITALS (See EMERGENCY CENTERS & HOSPITALS)	
HUMANE SOCIETY	**327-6088**
INFO-LINE (TUCSON PUBLIC LIBRARY)	**791-4010**
INFORMATION AND REFERRAL (A central source of information)	**881-1794**
KIDLINE	**795-8855**
METROPOLITAN TUCSON CONVENTION and BUSINESS BUREAU	**624-1889** **1-800-99TUCSON**

MISSING CHILD NETWORK (To report a missing child or give information about a missing child)	**1-800-235-3535**
PARKS AND RECREATION (City) (County)	**791-4873** **882-2690**
PHYSICIANS REFERRAL	**323-7800**
PIMA ANIMAL CONTROL	**743-7550**
POISON AND DRUG INFORMATION	**626-6016**
RAPE CRISIS CENTER CRISIS LINE INFORMATION	**623-7273** **624-7273**
SHERIFF'S DEPARTMENT EMERGENCY NON EMERGENCY ROAD CONDITIONS	**911** **622-3366** **882-2800**
TIME AND TEMPERATURE	**1-676-1676**
TRANSPORTATION—SUN TRAN TRANSPORTATION—DISABLED	**792-9222** **791-4100**
TUCSON CONVENTION CENTER BOX OFFICE VISA OR MASTERCHARGE	**791-4266** **791-4836**
TUCSON METROPOLITAN CHAMBER OF COMMERCE	**792-1212**
TUCSON POLICE DEPARTMENT EMERGENCY INFORMATION	**911** **791-4552**
SUN TRAN	**792-9222**
UNIVERSITY OF ARIZONA—TICKET OFFICES ASUA CONCERT HOTLINE ATHLETICS CONCERTS & PUBLIC AFFAIRS CULTURAL AFFAIRS DRAMA/MUSIC	**621-1111** **621-2411** **621-3341** **621-3341** **621-1162**

VOTER REGISTRATION	**792-8101**
WEATHERLINE	**623-4000**
WOMEN'S & CHILDREN'S SERVICES	**792-1929**
YOUTH—NATIONAL RUNAWAY SWITCHBOARD	**1-800-621-4000**

SE HABLA ESPANOL

Yes, Spanish is spoken here. We are a bi-lingual city and our second language is Spanish. Our streets, our restaurants, our businesses and a great deal of our language reflects our Spanish/Mexican heritage.

Spanish is an easy language to pronounce, when you follow the rule of uttering every syllable of every word clearly and distinctly. Vowel sounds are always pure and full-rounded and consonants are always plainly audible, never dropped.

The following are some very brief rules.

The vowel sounds remain fairly constant, with one particular sound:

a	as in father		i	as in police
e	as ay in day or		o	as in go
	sometimes as in ten		u	as in food

The h is always silent.

The j is pronounced like an h as in hoe.

The double ll as in tortilla or rillito is pronounced like the y in yes.

The ch is pronounced like the ch in church.

The n with a tilde over it—ñ—has the sound of *ny* as in canyon.

The x is soft like the j's. San Xavier is pronounced Sahn HahVear.

The g in saguaro sounds like wha; and in Gila like he.

The b and v are both pronounced as a soft b.

The above information won't get you an A in Spanish class, but it will assist you in pronouncing some of the words you might come across. The following are some frequently-used words you might wish to become familiar with.

adios	ah-dee-OSE	goodbye
agua	AH-wah	water
amigo	ah-ME-go	friend
avenida	ah-be-nee-dah	avenue
bienvenido	be-en-beh-NEE-tho	welcome
buenos dias	BWAY-nose DEE-ahs	good morning
buenos noches	BWAY-nose NO-chess	good evening/night
buenos tardes	BWAY-nose TAR-des	good afternoon
caballero	kah-bah-YARE-oh	gentleman
calle	kah-yay	street

casa	kah-sah	home
cuidad	see-oo-DAHD	city
conquistador	kone-KEES-tah-dore	conqueror
damas	DAH-mas	women
de nada	day NAH-thah	you're welcome
espanol	es-pahn-YOL	Spanish
frijoles	free-HOE-lays	beans
gracias	GRAH-see-us	thank you
hasta la vista	AHS-tah la VEES-tah	so long
hola	OH-lah	hello
hombres	OHM-brays	men
la casa	la CAH-sah	house
manana	mahn-YAH-nah	tomorrow
mujeres	moo-HAIR-ess	women
nada	NAH-thah	nothing
no hablo espanol	no AH-blow es-pahn-YOL	I do not Speak Spanish
por nada	pore NAH-thah	you're welcome
quien sabe?	kee-en SAH-bay	who knows?
rillito	ree-YEE-tow	little river
saguaro	sah—WAH-row	saguaro
si	see	yes
un poquito	oon po-KEE-tow	a very little
verde	bare-day	green

IF YOU DECIDE TO STAY

WELCOMING SERVICES

The **Metropolitan Tucson Convention and Visitors Bureau** is available to assist you in any manner with brochures, information and schedules. Their offices are at 130 South Scott Avenue, an attractive Tucson landmark built in 1928. Phone 624-1889 or for out-of-state calls: 1-800-999 TUCSON.

The **Tucson Metropolitan Chamber of Commerce** also will be able to assist you and answer questions. They are located at 465 West St. Mary's Road, phone 792-1212.

The *only* purpose of two other services in town is to welcome you and provide answers to some of your many questions (that you've not found already in *This is Tucson*). They are **Welcome Newcomers,** 630 North Craycroft Road, 745-0442; and **Welcome Wagon International,** 425 East 7th Street, 622-3492.

Hostesses will visit you, bringing coupons, product samples and magazines and newspapers, all supplied free by area merchants. They also provide information on local civic and cultural organizations and businesses.

UTILITIES

Telephone

Serviced by US West Communications, whose administrative offices are at 100 East Alameda. Call your service representative to order new service. You'll find the number listed in the Customer Guide section in the front of the White Pages Directory.

Gas

Southwest Gas Company, 5151 East Broadway, 747-3535. Outside Tucson: 1-800-223-5369.

Electricity

Tucson Electric Power, 220 West Sixth Street, 623-7711.
Trico Electric Cooperative, 5100 West Ina Road, 744-2944
(Service for rural areas).

Water

Supplied by Tucson City Government, City Hall, 250 West Alameda, 791-3242; 24-hour emergency service, 791-4133.

Garbage Service

City service is automatic on a twice a week basis, 791-3171.
For county service, see Yellow Pages under Garbage Collection.

AUTOMOBILES

Motorists are required to get Arizona plates and driver's licenses immediately upon moving to Tucson permanently, putting children in school, or taking a job.

Insurance

State law mandates automobile liability insurance. It is best to review your insurance with a local agent.

Automobile Registration

You will need your car title, current registration forms and, depending upon the state you are arriving from, possibly several other documents, such as: copy of any lien agreement with name and address of the lien holder; lien clearance if car is paid for; a security agreement if a lien is to be placed on the new title; and, if newly purchased from a private party, a title transfer document for assessment of 4% tax. For complete information, call 624-7010.

Take your automobile and title to one of three emissions testing centers: 1420 East Benson Highway, 8125 East 22nd Street or 755 West Grant Road, for a Certificate of Compliance.

After passing the emissions test, register your auto at one of three locations: 2499 East Ajo Way, 1102 South Sherwood Village Drive or 7330 North Shannon Road. (Driver's licenses may also be obtained at these locations.) First, have the identification number of the auto checked against the number on the title. You must then remove the old plates before continuing; be sure to bring a screwdriver and pliers to accomplish this. After removing the plates, join a line inside to complete registration. THIS MAY TAKE A COUPLE OF HOURS. All locations are open 8am—5pm, Mon—Fri and the Ajo Way location is open 9am—4pm Sat, for auto registration only. For additional info call 628-5311.

Be prepared to pay a license tax fee, which is computed on the year of the vehicle and its factory list price. The older a car, the less the cost of registration. You may pay either by cash or by check.

Driver's License

You must obtain an Arizona driver's license when you become a resident of the state. Licenses may be obtained at: 635 East 22nd Street, 1102 South Sherwood Village Drive or 7330 North Shannon Road. The Arizona Driver License Manual, is helpful and is available at all locations. YOU MUST pay cash for your driver's license; no checks are accepted. All locations are open 8am—5pm, Mon—Fri; the 22nd Street location is open 9am—4pm Sat. For further information, call 628-5311.

VOTER REGISTRATION

Save time and register when you obtain your driver's license. You may also register at the Pima County Recorder's Office in the County Courthouse, 115 North Church Avenue, 792-8683 or 792-8101 or at any City Council office. You can also contact the Democratic Party of Pima County, 4439 East Broadway Suite 202, 798-1001 and 326-3716 or Republican Headquarters, 2235 East Broadway, 628-9566. If you are unable to travel, either will be happy to send a deputy registrar to register you. Contact League of Women Voters at 327-7652.

EDUCATION

Public Schools

Kindergarten through High School

Children may begin kindergarten if they are five years old by Sep 1. If going into first grade, they must be six by Oct 1. Arizona law states children must attend school from the ages of eight years through sixteen or until they complete the 8th grade, whichever comes first.

Tucson Unified School District No. 1 covers the central Tucson area, with fourteen other school districts in the surrounding areas. Call the Pima County Superintendent of Schools' office at 792-8451 and personnel there will assist you in locating your correct district.

Continuing Education

The **University of Arizona's** Continuing Education Classes offer several options. You may work toward a university degree earning up to twelve credits through extension classes or you may take classes just for fun. Frequent seminars, senior citizen classes and an Opportunities for Women program are provided. Contact Continuing Education at 1717 East Speedway, 621-7724. (*See also* A CULTURED COMMUNITY.)

Pima Community College provides a full range of academic classes as well as a community service program for the less-serious students. Community Services classes are offered at more than two dozen locations around Tucson. Classes include sales techniques, microwave cooking and hypnosis. Some of the most interesting classes include educational study tours in southern Arizona and Mexico. Contact Community Services, 220 East Speedway, 884-6867. (*See also* A CULTURED COMMUNITY.)

Tucson Museum of Art School provides classes for adults and children in ceramics, photography, printmaking, stained glass and many other related art fields. Contact the TMA School at 180 North Main Avenue, 884-8673. Classes fill rapidly so call early for registration. (*See also* LA CIUDAD DE LOS MUSEOS.)

The **YMCA** branches offer varying classes. Call the individual fices for information, as classes differ at each branch.

The **Tucson Open University,** a school without a campus, offers classes from Home Security and Personal Protection, to Yoga, the Foods of Mexico and a Horse Sense Workshop. Classes meet about town and fees are minimal. If you can't afford the fees, you may be able to arrange barter of office work, maintenance, or goods or services with the instructor. Contact Tucson Open University, 1041 East 6th Street, 622-0170.

The **Arizona Theater Company,** 56 West Congress, 884-8210, presents theater classes for adults and youths. Classes include dramatic acting, scene study and workshops and a production at the end of the term. (*See also* A CULTURED COMMUNITY.)

Tucson Parks and Recreation offers over 300 classes four times a year, including crafts, recreation, dance and exercises. Brochures are available through newspapers, shopping centers and libraries, or contact Tucson Parks and Recreation, 791-4877. (*See also* BACK TO NATURE.)

RETIREMENT

Our exceptional weather (discounting 1988's 114°), beautiful environment and cultural amenities have long made Tucson ideal for retirement. Special newspapers and social clubs, and many discounted activities are available.

Two monthly newspapers especially for senior citizens, are the *Arizona Cracker Barrel* and *Arizona Senior World,* both of which can be found at libraries, park recreation centers, senior citizen centers, savings and loan associations and banks.

The **Pima Council on Aging,** 100 East Alameda, 624-4419, provides information for senior citizens. *Never Too Late,* a newspaper published monthly by the council, lists additional clubs and special events of interest to senior citizens. (*See also* SENIOR OLYMPIC FESTIVAL IN SEASONAL EVENTS.)

Persons with a Medicare card can ride the Sun Tran bus for 25 cents per trip (regular fare is 60 cents); discounted monthly pass is $8.50. If you are 65 and do not have a Medicare card, you may obtain a bus pass for the same reduced rate at the City Hall Annex, 110 East Penningston St. A birth certificate or driver's license is required and there is a $1.50 charge. Call 791-4100.

Senior discounts are offered at movie theaters in town and at the Invisible Theatre and Arizona Theatre Company (*see also* A CULTURED COMMUNITY).

Social clubs include: the A.C.E.S. (Amphitheater Community Education Seniors) sponosred by Pima County Parks & Recreation and Amphitheater School district. You must be over 55 and attend three business meetings a year. For info, call 742-8064. Golden Age Clubs, also sponsored by Pima County Parks & Recreation have the same membership requirements. Call 742-8044.

Tucson Parks and Recreation offers a $5 Senior Citizen's Golf Pass to those 62 and over toward lower greens fees (weekdays only) at all city courses. Submit AZ driver's license (with Tucson address) or proof of residency to Parks and Recreation at 900 South Randolph Way.

Arthur Pack Desert Golf Course, the only county course, also has a $5 discount card, which can be purchased at 1204 West Silverlake Road.

Pima Community College offers special non-credit classes at their Senior Citizens Education Center, 884-6866.

Additional information can be obtained from **Information and Referral** at 881-1794, or from the Chamber of Commerce at 792-1212. Service groups are listed in the yellow pages under Senior Citizens Services.

Retirement communities in Tucson include La Cholla Hills at 8770 North La Cholla Blvd., Santa Catalina Villas at 7500 North Calle Sin Envidia, The Fountains at La Cholla at North La Cholla Blvd. and West Rudasill Road and Campana del Rio at 1550 East River Road. About 8 miles north of town on Highway 89 are Sun City Vistoso and further north on Highway 89 is SaddleBrooke, just across the Pinal County line, north of the city of Catalina. Highway 89.

A number of retired persons live in **Green Valley,** thirty miles south of Tucson. The community opened in June of 1964 and has a winter population of about 14,000 and a summer population of about half that. They have an annual Tour of Homes every March. A number of retirees also live in Tubac a little further south.

Most of these neighborhoods include shopping and recreational centers and provisions for shuffleboard, square dancing, music, cards and clubs.

The **American Association of Retired Personnel,** with fourteen million members nationwide, has three chapters in Tucson and one in Green Valley, all of which are dedicated to making life pleasant for senior citizens. Among their numerous goals are keeping you abreast of what's happening throughout the nation and assisting you in speaking up to your federal, state and local lawmakers. Countless activities are available for those who wish to participate in much-needed volunteer work.

Their national membership address is 215 Long Beach Blvd., Long Beach, CA 90801. Locally, you can contact E. F. (Ed) Karn, Assistant State Director, at 225 North Camino Del Varonil, Green Valley, AZ 85614 (phone 1-625-4473). He will be more than happy to provide further information.

SOME OTHER GOOD BOOKS

ART AND ARCHITECTURE

Burba, Nora, and Panish, Paula. *The Desert Southwest*. New York: Bantam Books Inc., 1987. Fifteen homes located in New Mexico, Texas, California and Arizona are presented in this magnificent collection of styles including Victorian, Pueblo, Colonial, Mediterranean, Santa Fe and Contemporary. Three of these homes are in Tucson. Outstanding color photography by Tucson resident Terrence Moore.

College of Architecture. *Look Around Arizona!* Tucson: College of Architecture University of Arizona, 1987. An architectural guide to the University of Arizona Campus Historic District, listed in the National Register of Historic Places in June 1986. Includes a walking tour of the historical portions of the campus. Compiled by Robert C. Giebner, Allan C. Lamper and Douglas Hawkins.

Quinn, Robert, ed. *Guide to Public Art in Tucson*. Tucson: Tucson/Pima Arts Council, 1987. With Tucson's increased efforts to provide public art, this guide is helpful for identification. It includes works of art that are accessible to the public, whether privately or publicly funded or owned. Photographs by David Burckhalter.

THE ENVIRONMENT

Bowden, Charles. *Blue Desert*. Tucson: The University of Arizona Press, 1986. A view of southwestern growth from a reporter's eyes. Laced with humor, but sad, disconcerting and depressing to those who love the desert in its native state.

———. *Frog Mountain Blues*. Photographs by Jack W. Dykinga. Tucson: The University of Arizona Press, 1987. The native Tohono O'odham call Mount Lemmon in the Santa Catalina Mountains Frog Mountain. The author questions civilization's impact on this wilderness, suggesting maybe we should lock the gate and throw away the key to save this mountain from ultimate destruction. Jack Dykinga's winning photographs provide a sense of awe at the beauty of nature and a feeling of rage at the desecration of nature's wonderment.

Cabat, Erni, and Cardon, Charlotte M. *Life on the Tanque Verde*. Tucson: Cabat Studio Publications, 1983. The Tanque Verde Ranch nestles at the foot of the Rincon Mountains, twenty miles east of Tucson. Erni's whimsical paintings immortalize this magnificent location in the Tanque Verde area, a favorite retreat of persons visiting from around the world. The text by Charlotte M. Cardon gives past history of the area.

Cabat, Erni, and Engard, Rodney G. *Arizona Cacti and Succulents Book I and Book II*. Tucson: Cabat Studio Publications, 1984. Kaleidoscopic paintings by Erni of some of Arizona's most outstanding flora, with text by the director of the Tucson Botanical Gardens. An excellent, colorful way to learn about Tucson's exotic desert plants.

———. *Arizona Wildflowers Book I and Book II*. Cabat Studio Publications, 1984. Erni's portrayal of Life on the Desert continues with this wonderful collection of paintings of some of our more exclusive desert plants. Text by the director of the Tucson Botanical Gardens.

Helms, Christopher L. *The Sonoran Desert*. Las Vegas: KC Publications, 1980. Chris's stories of the origination of the Sonoran Desert, its magnificent contrasts, its beauty and its flora and fauna present an excellent opportunity to learn more about one of the most unique areas of the world. Color photographs include several by David Muench.

Krutch, Joseph Wood. *The Desert Year.* New York: William Sloan, Assoc., 1951. A unique collection of essays about the desert. Krutch lived the last decades of his life in Tucson and his writings are the predecessors of naturalist essayists like Lewis Thomas and Stephen Jay Gould.

Wooden, Ann. *Home is the Desert.* 1964. Reprint. Tucson: University of Arizona Press, 1984. Originally released in 1964, Ann's story of her and her family's life as newcomers to the desert has become a classic to all who love our life and lifestyle. The story tells of their involvement with the desert flora and fauna, not only because of her wondrous discovery and love of same, but because her first husband was director of the Arizona-Sonora Desert Museum, resulting in the more than normal association with the numerous desert animals in the Wooden home.

GHOST TOWNS AND TOURING

Cowgill, Pete, and Glendening, Eber. *Trail Guide to the Santa Catalina Mountains.* 2nd ed. Tucson: Rainbow Expeditions, 1977. An excellent pocket-size guide, including maps and photographs, to be carried on any hikes through the Catalinas. Characteristics, history and development of the mountain, along with conditions and precautions for hikers. Mileage and altitude is given for each hike, along with specifics about difficulties or ease of the trails, the best spot to settle for the night and location of water.

Heylmun, Edgar B., PhD. *Guide to the Santa Catalina Mountains of Arizona.* Tucson: Treasure Chest Publications, Inc., 1979. A guide containing history, hiking maps, information on camping and picnic grounds, and sketches of both plant and animal life to be found on the mountain.

Sherman, James E. and Barbara H. *Ghost Towns of Arizona.* Norman: University of Oklahoma Press, 1969. Old-time photographs, specific locations, and brief histories will assist the lover of ghost towns in her search about Arizona. Included for the southern part of the state are: Mowry, Washington Camp, Duquesne, Harshaw and Lochiel.

Stiles, Ed, and Solot, Mort. *Bike Tours in Southern Arizona.* Tucson: Breakaway Press, 1980. A pocket-size guide with capsule history, local attractions, restaurants, motels, and museums, along with photographs, maps, mileages and humor. This little book is a "must" for any serious biker.

Thollander, Earl. *Back Roads of Arizona.* rev. ed. Flagstaff: Northland Press, 1979. An interesting book to peruse, even if you don't intend on taking some of the backroads Mr. Thollander has sketched out. He travels throughout the state and has included charming and accurate drawings of the views and items he found along the byways of his travels.

Varney, Philip. *Arizona's Best Ghost Towns: A Practical Guide.* Flagstaff: Northland Press, 1980. An excellent all-round guide with accompanying maps, road directions and photographs, some in color. Mr. Varney includes tidbits of history and suggestions of items to search for. He particularly suggests traveling in the area south of Sonoita and Patagonia. Photographic suggestions and driving and walking survival tips are included.

HISTORY

Bret Harte, John, Tucson: *A Portrait of a Desert Pueblo.* Woodland Hills: Windsor Publications, Inc., 1980. Bret Harte has put together a fascinating history of Tucson from its beginnings to its present day problems and future anticipations. Numerous old photographs, some of which have never before been published, show Tucson as it used to be.

College of Architecture. *Armory Park: 74ff.* Tucson: College of Architecture, University of Arizona, 1974. This report discusses the history of the town and the importance of the railroad in shaping the Armory Park Neighborhood and the transition of Tucson to a 20th century cosmopolitan center.

College of Architecture. *Barrio Historico: Tucson.* Tucson: College of Architecture, University of Arizona, 1972. An in-depth view of the city's historic neighborhoods. An analyzation of the Barrio from its visual and historical qualities to its present social and economic status.

Dreyfuss, John J., ed. *A History of Arizona's Counties and Courthouses.* Tucson: The Arizona Historical Society, 1972. This short, general history of the fourteen counties of Arizona and the courthouse built therein was published under the auspices of the National Society of the Colonial Dames of America in the State of Arizona.

Martin, Patricia Preciado. *Images and Conversations: Mexican Americans Recall a Southwestern Past.* Photographs by Louis Carlos Bernal. Tucson: University of Arizona Press, 1983. Memories of barrio and ranch life in Southern Arizona, when times were simpler, recorded through oral histories of thirteen individuals.

Schellie, Don. *The Tucson Citizen: A Century of Arizona Journalism.* Tucson: The Citizen Publishing Company, 1970. With excerpts and photographs from the Tucson Daily Citizen, the oldest continually published newspaper in Arizona, Mr. Schellie compiled a historically interesting and accurate chronicle of the newspaper.

Sonnichsen, C. L. *TUCSON, The Life and Times of an American City.* Norman: University of Oklahoma press, 1982. This very comprehensive history of our unique southwestern city was written by the dean of southwestern historians, a Tucsonan by adoption. Lots of humor and affection about two centuries of growth of one of the region's most colorful communities.

Walker, Henry P., and Bufkin, Don. *Historical Atlas of Arizona.* Norman: University of Oklahoma Press, 1979. A wealth of statistical information regarding the State of Arizona, including sixty-five detailed maps with descriptions setting each map in historical perspective.

Williams, Judith, ed. *Plaza of the Pioneers.* Tucson: Tucson Museum of Art, 1982. A historic document with photographs, dates, legends, and stories about the early pioneers of Tucson. The book was prepared as a complement to the dedication of the Plaza of the Pioneers at the Tucson Museum of Art on Saturday, November 6, 1982.

SAN XAVIER DEL BAC AND FATHER KINO

Ahlborn, Richard E. *Saints of San Xavier.* Tucson: Southwestern Mission Research Center, Inc., 1974. A detailed description of the saints and statuary located in San Xavier. Descriptions and photos showing construction of statuary and placement in the mission. Also notes on the statues at Tumacacori.

Cabat, Erni, and Polzer, Charles W., S.J. *Father Eusebio Francisco Kino and His Missions of the Pimeria Alta.* Book 1: The Side Altars. Tucson: Southwestern Mission Research Center, 1982. This trilogy, containing reproductions of paintings by Erni Cabat, is an animated, colorful documentary of the numerous missions located in southern Arizona and the northern Sonora regions of Mexico. The paintings are Erni's fascinating and joyful interpretations of the life, color and love explicit in these outstanding missions. Included with the paintings are historical notes and chronicles from the excellent knowledge and memory of Charles W. Polzer, S.J., all of which is translated into spanish by Carmen villa Prezelski. For preservation, the books are printed on acid-free paper.

Fontana Bernard. "Biography of a Desert Church: THE STORY OF MISSION SAN XAVIER DEL BAC." *The Smoke Signal,* The Tucson Corral of the Westerners. 1961 (Reprinted 1971). An extensive research on Father Kino, the mission, its builders and its growth through the years. Dr. Fontana and his wife have made their home within a mile of the church since the 1950s.

Frontain, Dick. *San Xavier del Bac: A Living Mission.* Tucson: Los Amigos, 1968. A short history of San Xavier including festivals celebrated there. Many black and white photographs of the mission and festival celebrants.

Polzer, Charles, S.J. *A Kino Guide: A Life of Eusebio Francisco Kino, Arizona's First Pioneer and A Guide to His Missions and His Monuments.* Tucson: Southwestern Mission Research Center, 1968. A history of the life of Father Kino, with accompanying maps, photographs and descriptions of eleven of the Kino missions.

NATIVE AMERICANS

Baylor, Byrd. *Yes is Better Than No.* New York: Charles Scribner's Sons, 1977. After leaving their reservation for the civilized comforts of Tucson the Papago (Tohono O'odham) find their values and ideals at odds with an Anglo society that does not understand them and doesn't really try. This delightful romp through Tucson's Indian ghetto portrays their methods of dealing with the Anglo bureaucracy.

Nabhan, Gary Paul. *The Desert Smells Like Rain: A Naturalist in Papago Indian Country.* San Francisco: North Point Press, 1982. A heartwarming visit with the contemporary Papago (Tohono O'odham) in their lands. You'll read of their feelings and knowledge of the desert and how their way of life has persisted despite the encroachments of modern civilization.

Bahti, Mark. *Pueblo Stories and Storytellers.* Tucson: Treasure Chest Publications, Ind. 1988. Mark's interest in Indian art began as a child with the opening of an Indian art shop by his father in the 1960s, which Mark now operates. He includes brief resumés of the pueblos and the stories relating to the storyteller folk arts.

SPORTS

McDannel, Wally. *A Guide to Arizona's Waterways.* Tucson: Arizona Waterways, 1977. An excellent guide to the waterways of Arizona, of which there are many. Invaluable information regarding camping facilities, fishing, waterskiing, boating, picnic areas and available fuel and supplies. Lots of maps and photographs and excerpts from Arizona boating and fishing regulations. Also a section on the coastal waterways of Sonora, Mexico, going as far south as Guaymas, and including Mexican sport fishing regulations.

INDEX